LEADERSHIP
AND STATECRAFT

LEADERSHIP
AND STATECRAFT
Studies in Power

EDITED BY

KURT ALMQVIST, ALASTAIR BENN
AND MATTIAS HESSÉRUS

BOKFÖRLAGET STOLPE

CONTENTS

INTRODUCTION

'All courses of action are risky, so prudence is not in avoiding danger – it is impossible – but in calculating risk and acting decisively.'

Machiavelli's observation on the fine margins of leadership remains as true in our perilous age of renewed military, economic, and cultural conflict as it did in sixteenth-century Florence. Half a millennium on, this anthology, derived from the Engelsberg seminar held in 2023, will explore the complexities of 'leadership and statecraft' and seek to offer historically informed answers to questions old and new.

The rise of China, Russia's attack on Ukraine, and the growing political and economic emergence of the Global South, all present novel and complex challenges to the West, ones that put a premium on political leaders capable of guiding us safely through this already troubled century. How do we create a culture that generates such figures?

This anthology explores how leaders have used founding myths to shape and expand policies throughout history. It delves into the evolution of leadership, including Machiavelli's statecraft, empire management like Persia's, and inspiring leadership examples from Russia and Finland.

The authors also discuss the successes and failures of statecraft, particularly in the face of 21st-century challenges like AI. They examine leaders such as De Gaulle, Adenauer, Kennedy and Thatcher in their navigation of the Cold War era, before addressing the more contemporary challenges posed by Russia and China. These are faced, in the concluding chapters, with a look at potential flashpoints, particularly in the Pacific, and at the wider, heightened fear of nuclear conflict.

Can we create the political elites capable of guiding the West effectively through the many, sometimes lethal challenges which confront us now or are on the near horizon? If the West and its allies cannot navigate the future successfully, someone else surely will.

Stockholm, January 2024

Kurt Almqvist
President
Axel and Margaret Ax:son Johnson Foundation for Public Benefit

David Garrick as Richard III, oil on canvas,
by William Hogarth, 1745.

MACHIAVELLI AND THE
PUZZLE OF THE PRINCE

Alexander Lee

I can add colours to the chameleon,
Change shapes with Proteus for advantages,
And set the murderous Machiavel to school.
Can I do this, and cannot get a crown?
SHAKESPEARE, *Henry VI, Part 3*, 3.2.191–94

Few texts loom so large over concepts of leadership as Niccolò Machiavelli's *The Prince*. Though characterised by its author as nothing more than an *opusculo* (a 'little book'), it established a completely new way of thinking about power; and – as the adjective 'Machiavellian' testifies – continues to dominate our political imagination 500 years after its completion.

At its heart is a deceptively simple question: how can a prince who has gained a state with the help of fortune and another's arms maintain his power? Machiavelli was not the first person to tackle this. Since the beginning of recorded history, learned men had been advising princes about the qualities they needed to cultivate; and these *ad hoc* works later evolved into a distinct literary genre, the so-called *specula principum* ('mirrors of princes'). This had acquired particular significance during the Renaissance. From the fourteenth century onwards, a growing number of treatises began to be produced, the most striking examples of which were Bartolomeo Platina's *De vero principe* (*c.* 1478) and Francesco Patrizi's *De regno et regis institutione* (*c.* 1481–84). But where Machiavelli differed was in his approach. Whereas earlier Renaissance writers had generally argued that a prince could safeguard his rule by cultivating Christian virtue, Machiavelli rejected such an idea as dangerously – even wantonly – unrealistic. The problem, as he saw it, was Fortune. Just like a coquettish girl, she gives or withholds her favour without regard for human merit. If you stuck blindly to a particular moral code, or were too weak-willed to stand up to her, she would invariably treat you badly. Only a circumspect man, who could 'beat and coerce' her would receive her favour, Machiavelli argued. What a ruler needed, therefore, was not virtue but *virtù* – the quality of being a man (*vir*). He needed to be daring and courageous; he needed to forsake the base pursuit of wealth; and – most importantly of all – he needed to govern in such a way that he would earn glory and honour. In practice, this meant relying on his own soldiers rather than treacherous mercenaries; being parsimonious rather than generous; cruel rather than kind; and dishonest rather than honest. Most of all, it meant avoiding hatred at all costs.

It is a bold and original argument, so much so that it still retains its ability to shock. Yet, nevertheless, *The Prince* presents something of a puzzle. Precisely because Machiavelli's book is so surprising, so different from most previous political writings, it is sometimes difficult to know how it should be interpreted – even in the context of his own oeuvre. Many of his other works – such as the *Discorsi sopra la prima deca di Tito Livio* and the *Istorie Fiorentine* – appear oriented more towards republicanism than princely rule, making *The Prince* even more of an enigma. Since the text first appeared in *c.* 1513, it has evoked strong, but contrasting opinions. Some early readers saw it as a handbook for tyrants. In his *Discours sur les moyens de bien gouverner* (1576), for example, Innocent Gentillet (1532/3–88) claimed that *The Prince* proposed 'a tyrannical, rather than political science'; while Cardinal Reginald Pole (1500–58) painted Machiavelli himself as 'an amoral teacher of force, fraud, cunning, and deception'. It was also this view which later influenced Richard III's famous monologue in Shakespeare's play. Others thought that *The Prince* was merely a satire, and that Machiavelli was really a *critic* of tyranny. It was for this reason that the French historian Abraham-Nicolas Amelot de la Houssaye (1634–1706) cast Machiavelli as a latter-day Tacitus, and that Maximilien de Robespierre (1758–94) later claimed him as the architect of the French Revolution. Others still believed that Machiavelli was merely describing the world of politics, rather than recommending a particular course of action. In *The Advancement of Learning* (1605), Sir Francis Bacon (1561–1626) praised Machiavelli for writing 'what men do and not what they ought to do' – and *The Prince* as a work of empirical science *avant la lettre*. And a final group felt that Machiavelli was really just proposing a *technique* of politics, which could be used either badly or well.

Yet if we want to understand the 'meaning' of *The Prince*, we should start with Machiavelli himself. Regardless of what one thinks of Machiavelli's hopes for posterity, it is impossible to deny that *The Prince* was written in a specific context, for a specific readership, with a specific aim in mind. As such, it is only by taking account of the political circumstances in which he wrote his treatise, his intellectual background, his private motivations and his hopes and fears that we hope to establish what – if anything – he was trying to 'do' with *The Prince*, how it related to his other works and how he wanted it to be read.

Until a few months before writing *The Prince*, Machiavelli's life had been framed by republican – rather than princely – government. When he was born, in 1469, Florence had been dominated by the Medici family, who exercised *de facto* authority through a network of clients and allies. In 1494, however, the French King Charles VIII marched into Italy, intent on conquering the Kingdom of Naples. In the ensuing chaos, the Medici were driven out, and a 'popular' republic was established. At first, this was overshadowed by the Dominican friar Girolamo Savonarola, whose attempts to turn the city into a 'new Jerusalem' nearly brought it to perdition; but after his execution in 1498, broad-based governments necessarily became the norm. The Great Council – with over 3,000 members – had the final say on legislation; the Council of Eighty appointed ambassadors and military commanders; and the Signoria – headed, in time, by the *gonfaloniere a vita* ('standard-bearer for life'), Piero Soderini – acted as the executive.

From the outset, the Florentine Republic was perilously unstable, however. For all its 'popular' pretensions, civil society was bitterly divided. While the wealthiest families, known as the *ottimati*, wanted a greater share of public office, the rest of the political class, known as the *popolo*, were determined to restrict their influence as much as possible. Subject towns were in rebellion. Pisa – Florence's main port – had been lost. On all sides, Florence was surrounded by enemies. Cesare Borgia was threatening from the Romagna; Venice was conspiring with the Pisans; and from abroad, the Medici were constantly looking for a way to return. Worst of all, Florence had few means of defending itself. Its only ally was France; and – in the absence of a standing army – it was reliant on mercenaries, who were not only exorbitantly costly but also as likely to flee as they were to fight.

Machiavelli was thrust into the heart of this danger while he was still a young man. On 19 June 1499, he was elected second chancellor of the Florentine Republic. This was a bureaucratic post, much like that of a civil servant today, and came with responsibility for handling Florence's relations with its subject towns. The following month, he was also appointed secretary of the *Dieci di balìa*, a committee tasked with overseeing military operations during times of war; a few years later, he was given the task of re-establishing a citizen militia, as well. That wasn't all. Throughout his public career, he was often sent on diplomatic missions abroad – and was widely admired for the perspicacity of his despatches.

During this period, Machiavelli penned several political works – generally in the form of reports, letters and poems. Unsurprisingly, most are devoted to exploring how the Florentine Republic could defend itself against its enemies, recover its territories and organise its military forces. Yet we can already see him experimenting with many of the ideas that he would later develop in *The Prince*. He was fascinated by Fortune. In the *Ghiribizzi*, written after watching Pope Julius II take Perugia 'almost unarmed' in 1506, he marvelled at her fickleness and argued that a good leader should know how to adapt himself to her wiles. He disparaged 'foreign and hired arms', while praising citizen soldiers for their loyalty. He was also convinced that cruelty could be a legitimate tool of government. The seeds of this were most likely sown in 1499, when the Florentine government voted to execute the mercenary commander Paolo Vitelli, on suspicion of treachery, but without any firm proof, simply *pour encourager les autres*. But it appears most vividly in *Del modo di trattare i popoli della Valdichiana ribellati* ('On the manner of dealing with the rebellious people of the Valdichiana'). Written in the summer of 1503, this argues that, if Florence wanted to stop Arezzo from rebelling again, it needed to imitate Cesare Borgia, and be severe rather than kind. Even at this early stage, however, Machiavelli recognised that cruelty had its limits. In the *Ghiribizzi*, he noted that, if the rebel cities of the Valdichiana were treated *too* harshly, their hatred of the Florentines would soon outweigh their fear – with potentially disastrous results.

In 1512, however, everything fell apart. A papal-Spanish army advanced into Tuscany, sacked the nearby city of Prato and forced Piero Soderini from office – leaving the way clear for the Medici to return. At first, they had to tread carefully. Their position was far from secure. The *popolo* was hostile; their supporters were divided; and they were reliant on a foreign army, which aroused more hatred with every passing day. Aside from doing away with a few offices, they therefore avoided any wholesale reforms and showed themselves willing to work with former members of Soderini's government. This gave Machiavelli cause for hope. He appears to have reasoned that, if he could show his worth to the Medici as a counsellor, they might allow him to keep his job. Indeed, given that he had known Giuliano de' Medici in his youth, he may have been reasonably confident. He therefore penned a letter to the current head of the family, Cardinal Giovanni de' Medici, outlining some of the ways they could avoid arousing further resentment. But, by then, the Medici's policy had already begun to harden. Fearing that their caution would encourage rebellion, they began dismantling the old system of government. The Great Council was abolished, along with the militia; and the Council chamber itself was turned into a barracks. Machiavelli was alarmed. Realising that he was now in danger, he dashed off another letter in a desperate bid to prove his use. Known as the *Ai Palleschi* ('To the Mediceans'), this clumsily written piece urged the Medici to purge the government of Soderini's supporters, destroy what was left of the republic and govern Florence with an iron fist. It was an extraordinary position to argue, even if it did evoke some of his earlier ideas about severity. But it was all for nothing. He was too tainted by his association with the old republic to have a place in the Medici's new order. On 7 November 1512, he was sacked from all his posts.

Machiavelli was understandably resentful. Over the Christmas period, he began criticising the Medici openly. Such dangerous talk unsettled his friends. Even those who hated the Medici began keeping their distance. Machiavelli couldn't see anything wrong in speaking his mind, though. He was convinced that the Medici were still too weak to clamp down on dissent. In this, he was catastrophically wrong. In mid-February 1513, a plot to assassinate Giuliano de' Medici was uncovered. It was an amateurish affair. As Giuliano noted, the plotters knew more about books than weapons. But the Medici could not afford to take any risks. The ringleaders were executed – and warrants were issued for the arrest of anyone who was even tangentially involved. Including Machiavelli. He was thrown in jail and tortured using a technique known as *strappado*. His hands were first tied behind his back. He was then lifted into the air by his wrists until his shoulders popped out of their sockets and he screamed in pain.

A few weeks later, Machiavelli was released in an amnesty granted to mark Giovanni de' Medici's election as Pope Leo X. After a brief period spent moping in Florence, he retreated, a broken man, to his farmhouse in Sant' Andrea in Percussina, a few kilometres to the south. There, he became a *gaglioffo* – a good-for-nothing. As he told his friend Francesco Vettori, he spent most mornings in the woods, chatting with neighbours, or reading a book of poems by the stream. At lunchtime, he returned home to eat with his family, before heading to the tavern. The rest of his day was spent 'slumming around' with the locals, drinking and playing cards or backgammon. When in their cups, they'd often argue – generally over nothing more than a penny – and every so often, a fight would break out. It suited Machiavelli, though. It helped him to 'get the mould out of [his] brain and let out the malice of [his] fate'.

But he had not entirely given up hope of one day returning to his former life. Every evening, he would go into his study, take off his rough, country clothes and 'put on the garments of court and palace'. Then, seated at his desk, he began to write *The Prince*.

As he explained in the preface, he intended to offer the Medici 'some token of my devotion', in the hope that it might prove his value as a counsellor and win their favour. So as not to appear *too* obvious, it was couched in deliberately abstract terms. He began by discussing the different varieties of principalities, before gradually working his way around to that which most closely resembled the Medici's own position.

Dedicated first to Giuliano, then, after his death, to Giuliano's nephew Lorenzo, it systematically – if discreetly – addressed each of the challenges which threatened the stability of the Medici regime: social divisions, a dependence on foreign or hired soldiers, lingering unrest and persistent financial problems. Since many of these had been familiar to previous Florentine governments, it was only natural for Machiavelli to draw not only on his reading of classical history but also his own experience – including many of the ideas which he had begun to develop while second chancellor. And, in the circumstances, his advice was perfectly reasonable. However shocking it seemed to some of his early readers, it was certainly intended to be taken seriously. Unless we assume that he emphasised his experience, only to mock everything he had ever learned, or dismiss the disappointment he reportedly felt when Lorenzo de' Medici showed no interest in his book, there are no grounds for assuming that it was satirical. Nor, indeed, did he believe he was defending tyranny

– least of all in the Aristotelian sense of a perverted form of monarchy. He never sought to defend arbitrary rule. He was careful to stress, as he had before, that cruelty must be tempered by circumstance; that social classes should be balanced; and that dishonesty should be used only according to necessity. It is just that his originality – his desire to show off the 'novelty' of his thought – sometimes occludes the practical, almost sympathetic, purpose of his work.

Books, however, are never *quite* what their authors intended them to be – any more than authors are *just* the sum of their books. Whatever Machiavelli may have wanted to do with *The Prince*, his readers are not constrained to respect his wishes – and never have been. There is no reason why *The Prince* cannot be read differently. Indeed, like all texts, it is 'open'. Taken on its own terms – away from the context of Machiavelli's own life – it can sustain any number of readings. Like Shakespeare's Richard III, it can 'add colours to the chameleon, / Change shapes with Proteus for advantages'. Such is the brilliance of Machiavelli's writing, such the novelty of his argument, that we can find in its pages whatever model of leadership we want. And in the end, perhaps that is what makes it so compellingly, dangerously Machiavellian.

Cyrus, King of Persia, from
'Four Illustrious Rulers of Antiquity',
by Adriaen Collaert, 1590s.

THE ENDURING SECRET TO
CYRUS THE GREAT'S SUCCESS

Ali Ansari

It is a peculiarity of current scholarship that given the longevity of the Persian imperium (in its various manifestations) – over a thousand years, from the sixth century BC to the seventh century AD – and the impact of Persian ideas of government in the wider Islamic world, greater attention is not expended on Persian statecraft and ideas of leadership. It was not always thus. When British administrators from the East India Company sought to govern the legacies of the Mughal Empire, it was Persian they learnt and Persian ideas of government that they absorbed. Earlier Muslim dynasties, not least the Abbasid Caliphate, were also enthusiastic students of Persian ideas of kingship, defined as it had been by a moral code and an intimate relationship with religion. They were enabled in their appropriation by the Persian bureaucrats who came to staff their burgeoning bureaucracies.

But perhaps most striking was the admiration of the Greeks: the very people whose confrontation with the Persians has come to define our understanding of the 'West' and its tensions with the 'barbarian' East. Yet for all the popularity of the Persian Wars as the foundational moment in the narrative of the ascent of the West, the attitude of the Greeks towards their Persian rivals was a good deal more respectful than modern perceptions allow. We tend to focus on Alexander the Great as the epitome of leadership and empire building, despite the fact that the empire he 'built' was inherited and the man he admired was Cyrus the Great.

Cyrus loomed large in the Greek imagination as someone who had achieved what their own political experience had suggested was impossible. As Xenophon explained in his largely fictive account of the education of Cyrus (*The Cyropaedia*) – though some historians now argue that Xenophon was merely recounting the Persian account of Cyrus (distinct from that provided by Herodotus) which had over time become more mythic and heroic – the Greeks could not but conclude 'that man is by nature fitted to govern all creatures, except his fellow man.'

Yet, Xenophon continued, 'when we came to realise the character of Cyrus the Persian, we were led to a change of mind...Cyrus, we know, found the readiest obedience in his subjects, though some of them dwelt at a distance which it would take days and months to traverse, and among them were men who had never set eye on him, and for the matter of that could never hope to do so, and yet they were willing to obey him'.

Just how Cyrus managed to bring together peoples from as far afield as the Oxus to the Aegean and to command their allegiance was an achievement which both awed the Greeks and demanded an explanation. Xenophon's explanation, meanwhile, was to prove one of the most influential manuals for government beloved by aspiring statesmen down to the period of the Enlightenment. But it was another book that served to popularise Cyrus in the Western imagination and to hint at the secret of his success.

This was of course the Bible, where Cyrus was one of only two leaders to be accorded the title Messiah in the Old Testament (the other being King David), on account of his liberation of the Jews from the Babylonian captivity in 539 BC, one of the central myths of emancipation within the Judeo-Christian world, which retained its potency in our more secular environment on account of its apparent religious tolerance. Historians have since criticised such idealised accounts of Cyrus and the attempts to ascribe liberal motives to his empire building, but as Greek writers testify, his dominion clearly represented something different – and this distinction is exemplified in the biblical account, which suggests that Cyrus was not only unusually political in his empire building but also aspired in some way or form to a moral code and purpose.

We may rightly question what that was, but there is little doubt that Cyrus approached his task with a degree of political subtlety which escaped his Babylonian and Assyrian predecessors. A brief look at Assyrian bas reliefs will show scenes of war and bloodshed, extolling the military virtues of the conqueror and serving as a terrible warning to those who might oppose him. Go to Persepolis, the ceremonial capital of the Persians, and the reliefs are quite different. There are bas reliefs of guards, but instead of scenes of war we have subject peoples lining up to pay tribute, not in bondage, but in apparent harmony. Some are even shown holding hands.

This of course also goes to the heart of what Xenophon seeks to explain: how Cyrus and his immediate successors, at least, were able to convince a diverse and dispersed collection of peoples that the dominion of Persia was not only something desirable, but reflected the right and natural order of things. What we see here, in essence, is the construction of authority as the basis of power, as the basis of a political rather than a military imperium. This is not to say that the Persians did not exercise military force, but it was selective rather than routine and did not serve as a central pillar of their dominion.

Of the three Persian empires (Achaemenid, 559–330 BC, Parthian 240 BC–AD 224, and Sasanian AD 224–642) that held sway in the ancient world, the Achaemenid was the most extensive and arguably the least militarised. It could, as Xerxes' invasion of Greece in 480 BC indicated, mobilise forces on a tremendous scale, but as a rule it did not maintain a large standing army and, as Xenophon experienced (and recounted in his *Anabasis*), it was possible for an armed force of rebels to exit the heart of the empire effectively unopposed.

The Persians justified their dominion on the basis of good governance, law and access to justice, underpinned by a moral purpose. This provided for a harmonious existence as explained and provided for by a Zoroastrian worldview. In the Achaemenid period this worldview enjoyed more flexibility and fluidity than it was to have later, but some basic themes already existed. The duality of creation and man's function, as a key aspect of the Wise Lord's (Ahura Mazda) good creation to partake in the battle against evil, and the wicked creation of Ahriman. Mankind was an agent in this struggle, in which the king was the best among men and the link between the material and the spiritual worlds.

This moral universe was perhaps best encapsulated by a prayer of Darius the Great, in which he beseeched Ahura Mazda to protect his people from the Lie and keep them in the service of the Truth – this is reflected in Herodotus's claim that Persian youths were all taught to ride, shoot the bow and tell the truth. The Truth represented the good order, which was in turn reflected in the king as the chief representative of Ahura Mazda. To rebel against the king therefore was to rebel against the Truth and the right order, and deserved the swiftest and most violent of punishments. This moral universe was not a matter of debate. It justified and supported the political order and reinforced the authority of the king. It provided a political clarity that proved attractive in an otherwise chaotic world. The biblical statement that 'the laws of the Medes and the Persians which altereth not' can be seen as both boast and warning, but it is above all clear, and people knew where they stood. The Greeks, on the other hand, revel in a 'disorder' that Herodotus has Cyrus decry as bewildering: 'I have never yet been afraid of men who have a special meeting place in the centre of their city where they swear this and that and cheat each other.' For the Greeks, this Persian order represented bondage. For the Persians it represented common sense as long as governance was good, administered with moderation and above all just.

The centrality of justice, which also relates to balance and harmony, was key to Persian statecraft and offered them an explanation for failure. As long as the Achaemenids survived there was no need to explain why the good order might fail, but Alexander's conquest was not simply a military failure, it was also a moral one. Indeed, Persian failure has rarely relied on military explanations alone, preferring to see this as an aspect of deeper moral collapse, or to use a Western expression, decadence.

This leads us to another important aspect of statecraft and leadership that came into focus in the post-Achaemenid period and was acutely defined under the Sasanians – the contingency of Divine Grace (*Farr-e Izadi*). The king represented the great agent of the Divine will on earth and was Ahura Mazda's chief lieutenant in the struggle against the Lie. All mankind of course had a role to play but the king's was the most important. If, however, the king strayed off the true path into the Lie, suffered from hubris and failed to dispense justice, then he too might lose the Divine Grace. Moral turpitude would inevitably lead to decline and fall. Good behaviour would enhance one's moral capital and reinforce the protective grace. Bad behaviour would see that protection withdrawn. It was incumbent on the monarch, therefore, to behave well and, unlike other theories of Divine Right or indeed straight divinity, there was no such concept of absolute loyalty to the king. Bad, unjust kings deserved not only to fall but to be opposed and overthrown.

Many of these ideas were refined and redacted during the late Sasanian period, most notably during the reign of Khusrau I Anoushiravan (531–79). Khusrau became emblematic of the just king, such that long after the Achaemenids (and Cyrus) had receded from Persian memory, he was credited with every achievement of the ancient period, barring those assigned to mythical times. It was Khusrau's rule that became emblematic of 'just' rule during the Caliphate – and a manuscript recounted by the British soldier-diplomat Sir John Malcolm in the early nineteenth century relates how the Abbasid Caliph Harun al

Rashid discovered Khusrau's tomb, where he acquired the secrets of good governance. Naturally the caliph then decided to destroy the entrance to the tomb so that no others could discover it.

Whatever the veracity of this tale, and there are many reasons to doubt it, it testified to the attractions of Persian ideas of government in the Islamic world, and it is quite clear that Sasanian ideas of statecraft and leadership cast a long shadow. This reflected the moral core in these Persian ideas, and the centrality of religious belief, all of which meant that these ideas would translate and adapt quite easily to the new Islamic rubric. Indeed, a favourite among Muslim rulers were the words ascribed to Ardashir I, the founder of the Sasanian dynasty on the close relationship between religion and kingship:

> Know that Kingship and religion are twin brothers; there is no strength for one of them except through its companion, because religion is the foundation of kingship, and kingship the protector of religion. Kingship needs its foundation and religion its protector, as whatever lacks a protector perishes and whatever lacks a foundation is destroyed.

These ideas were burnished and disseminated by the large cohort of Persian bureaucrats who staffed the administration of the Caliphate as well as successive dynasties. The Sasanian Empire had of course been completely absorbed into the new Caliphate, unlike the Byzantine Empire, and as such its administration was effectively swallowed whole. Persian administrators populated the entire establishment, from chief vizier down to the local bureaucrat; few converted, and many championed the old ways of doing things as recounted by the Arab satirist Al Jahiz in the 850s, who noted how the Persian bureaucrat never tired of boasting about the 'admirable way the country was run under the Sasanians'.

Among the more popular sayings ascribed to the Sasanians was the 'Circle of Justice', which decreed that authority and order depended on money, which required cultivation (trade), which in turn required justice and good governance, which required authority and so on. There were many variations on this theme, with some longer and more detailed than others, but all noted the imperative to maintain justice such that, in time, the primacy of justice over all other attributes became established. One might tolerate a heathen king but never an unjust one.

The most famous of these bureaucrats was Nizam al-Mulk, the chief vizier to the Saljuq Sultan in the eleventh century, whose manual of government remains required reading for many in Iran and the wider Muslim world to this day. Nizam al-Mulk drew on a range of sources for his manual, including the history (as he understood it) of pre-Islamic Persia. He was assisted in this task by the fact that a near contemporary of his, the poet Ferdowsi, had compiled the histories of pre-Islamic Persia in a single epic poem – for the ease of recitation – charting the ascent of man through to the fall of the Sasanians.

This epic, known as 'The Book of Kings' (*Shahnameh*) was probably the single most important means of transmission of Persian ideas of government and ethics, and was wildly popular in the Persianate world and beyond, including notably among both Mongols and Turks. The consequence of this was that Persian ideas of statecraft and leadership were absorbed among both the Mughal and Ottoman administrations (along with the Safavids in Iran itself), where they were inherited by successor states, not least the East India Company and its Indian Civil Service. Meanwhile, the biblical Cyrus remains popular in Israel and among Christian communities in the United States.

Many of these ideas have naturally been superseded by ideas of political thought and governance more suited to the complex dynamics of our own age. Attempts to ascribe modern sensibilities to ancient forebears rarely work, despite the best efforts of modern leaders, and certainly few ancient monarchs have enjoyed such a consistent positive reputation as Cyrus the Great, even if his own kinsmen had forgotten about him over time.

Yet for all the simplicity of the ideas, they retain a force and value of use to this day: the moral purpose, centrality of authority and necessity of justice. Good governance must enjoin harmony, balance and a measure of moderation; a government will only survive – and indeed thrive – if it is consistently in pursuit of its moral goals. An unjust government cannot survive and will deservedly fall, losing the Divine Grace (and moral purpose) that sustains it. It is not without reason that Cyrus and *The Cyropaedia* were so popular among Renaissance princes and their Enlightenment successors. Perhaps it's time to become reacquainted.

German Chancellor Konrad Adenauer (1876–1967)
arriving at Paris Airport on 11 April 1951.

AGAINST ALL ODDS: KONRAD ADENAUER AND THE GERMAN REALIGNMENT

Andreas Rödder

Never talk about a political leader's age before considering Konrad Adenauer. The German statesman was 57 in 1933, when he was sacked as mayor of Cologne by the Nazis. At the age of 69 he abandoned his enforced early retirement and started a comeback. He was once again appointed Cologne's mayor by the Americans, but dismissed five months later by British occupation authorities. This did not stop him either. Four years later, in 1949, he became West Germany's founding Chancellor – aged 73, he was slightly younger than Klemens von Metternich and Otto von Bismarck had been when they left their chancelleries, at ages 75 and 65 respectively. And when Adenauer was finally forced to retire in 1963, he was 87.

Adenauer's chancellorship lasted 14 years and was one of the longest democratic governments ever: longer than Franklin D Roosevelt's presidency; longer than any British prime ministership since Robert Salisbury or any French president's time in office since Napoleon III, and only more recently surpassed by Helmut Kohl and Angela Merkel.

Konrad Adenauer was the second of two politicians who dominated German politics in the middle third of the twentieth century. The first was 13 years younger than Adenauer: Adolf Hitler. While Hitler's regime ended in conflagration, when Adenauer left office in 1963, West Germany had become a respected player in the Western world on a scale nobody would have expected when Germany unconditionally surrendered to the Allies in 1945.

This was due to three revolutionary developments: domestic stability through a new catch-all political party; economic prosperity and social stability through a social market economy model; and a revolutionary change of Germany's position in the world through integration with the West.

Since the nineteenth century, the German political landscape had been highly fragmented, and one of its major cleavages was religious denomination. This fragmentation was one of the reasons the unstable Weimar Republic gave way to the Nazi Party.

Forging the Christian Democratic Union (CDU) as a new catch-all party was a revolutionary innovation within German political history. How groundbreaking this was is easily underestimated in today's times of advanced secularisation, but it was fundamental in 1949 when 96% of the German population were members of a Christian church. And still: that the CDU served as the crucial institution for integrating the centre-right into the political system of the Federal Republic hints at the continuing relevance of the party for German democracy and liberty in times of growing right-wing anti-constitutional populism.

The question of political integration points to another challenge for the new democracy: dealing with its Nazi past. Adenauer governed a country full of former perpetrators, followers and opportunists. As a realist he was well aware of the unreliability of his compatriots, but he was loyal to his people. He refrained from moral purism and expected opportunism from former opportunists. Engaging a former civil servant of the Ministry of Domestic Affairs who had provided a commentary on the racist Nuremberg laws ostracising Jews in the Third Reich as head of his Chancellery displayed his priorities. He dealt with compatriots burdened with their past by integrating and adapting them to the newly established democracy and its institutions.

Adenauer's personal integrity was beyond doubt. He was always an opponent of the Nazi regime, and did a great deal to build up relations with the state of Israel – the 1952 Reparations Agreement is just one example. Domestically, he prioritised stability, the integration of German democracy, and banked on pragmatism. Moreover, he displayed a willingness to compromise and to set priorities.

The second fundamental development after 30 years of destruction and hardship lies in the German model of the social market economy. This is what the Danish academic Gøsta Esping-Andersen has described as the conservative-corporatist Continental European model, which he distinguished from an egalitarian Scandinavian model, and a competitive Anglo-American one.

The model, however, had to be established, and this was not straightforward. After the war, within the CDU, ideas of Christian socialism were widely popular. Himself, Adenauer, rather a pro-market liberal, helped Ludwig Erhard, the political figurehead of German Ordoliberalism

– which advocates for a free market but not a welfare state – to prevail. Adenauer was also prepared, however, to make concessions, as with pension reform, for the sake of election victory in 1957.

After more than three decades of war and depression, inflation and hardship, West Germany experienced what was called the 'economic miracle': more than two decades of extraordinarily high growth rates; a transition into a consumer society; and evidence of what Erhard called 'prosperity for all'. Even if much of this success was due to financial catch-up and advantageous global economic conditions, the German model had a fundamental role to play.

It has always faced the challenge of balancing economic competitiveness and social welfare, and in its best times it has managed to square the circle, but it developed its own circularity. When the model was adored, it was seen as 'just missing necessary reforms'. And when it was considered to be in crisis, reforms were always on their way. Thus, current complaints about German decline might be a harbinger of another round of reforms. Unfortunately, history is not automated, and historical experience never provides reliable forecasts. What the history of Adenauer and the social market economy do provide is a balance of principles and pragmatism, as opposed to absoluteness and dogmatism.

Becoming a liberal democracy and a successful social market economy was not only a result of domestic decisions; it was part of a third revolutionary change: German integration with the West. No later than October 1945, Adenauer was convinced that the division of Europe between a Russian-occupied Eastern Europe and Western Europe was a hard fact, saying: 'Only an economically and culturally sound Western Europe led by England and France can prevent further Asian encroachment.' He drew the conclusion that it was necessary for the West to include and to fix the non-Russian occupied part of Germany, and that it required support from the US. One could argue that Adenauer's insights preceded those contained in US ambassador George Kennan's 'long telegram', which warned against Stalin, and contributed towards the US policy of containment. This was a strategic godsend for West Germany, and no one realised it earlier than Adenauer.

When West Germany's interests resided in security, liberty, prosperity, reunification, sovereignty, and resurgence as an equal European power, this circle was not to be squared. The newly founded West German state, still under an occupation regime, might not have had a wide variety of options at hand. But Adenauer made two decisions.

First, he set priorities, with geopolitical security as the foundation for liberty, prosperity, sovereignty and resurgence. Thus, he opted for an insoluble integration with the West – not out of '*vassalage*', as Emmanuel Macron called transatlantic relations in 2023, but as a deliberate strategy.

For much of history, modern Germany had been the 'Middle Kingdom' in Europe. It was a geographical buffer zone up to the nineteenth century, a 'half-hegemonic' empire and 'nervous great power' after 1871, a humiliated and revisionist power after 1919 and, finally, the desolator of Europe. When Adenauer aspired to turn the country into a reliable part of the West, he combined German Realpolitik and interests with a tectonic shift of European politics.

Having set his priorities, Adenauer resolutely executed them, particularly through NATO membership and rearmament – and against heavy opposition from different quarters. My own grandfather, a convinced Christian Democrat who had been a soldier in the Second World War and had come home with the conviction 'never again', left the party when Adenauer embarked on rearmament. Admirable as my grandfather's decision may have been, Adenauer had internalised the principle *si vis pacem, para bellum* ('if you want peace prepare for war') – and was prepared to bear ambiguity and dilemma.

Three years earlier, Stalin had offered German reunification in return for its neutrality. What many welcomed, Adenauer saw as a threat to West German security. He always and primarily regarded Russia, and then the Soviet Union, as the menace of world revolutionary communism and autocratic expansionism. His assessment of the country as 'Asian' or 'anti-Christian' seemed somewhat obsessive, manipulative (since it diverted attention from Germany's Nazi past) and not very imaginative. In 2023, this estimation seems more reasonable than at a time when Germany believed in 'change through trade'.

Nevertheless, turning down Stalin's offer earned Adenauer the accusation of having missed an opportunity and squandered a chance for reunification. Whatever Stalin's motives might have been, Adenauer deliberately subordinated reunification – the revisionist West German *raison d'état* with constitutional status – to his strategic priority of Western integration. He maintained the claim for reunification – and simply postponed it.

He built on the magnet theory: the expectation that one day the GDR would collapse, and, attracted by a strong West, accede to the Federal Republic. This forecast increasingly became out of touch with political realities in the 1960s, and by the end of Adenauer's chancellorship reunification had receded into the distance – to be followed by the historical irony that the magnet theory actually provided the blueprint for German reunification in 1989–90.

Looking at the bigger picture of Adenauer's leadership, it is clear he prioritised principles over popularity and sought to combine Realpolitik and German values and interests with international cooperation. The multilaterally integrated, co-operative nation state marked a fundamental innovation in a European history that for centuries had been beset with antagonistic states. The German model turned out to be the historic game-changer of European politics after 1945.

This was particularly true for the experiment of Western European integration, and a real European revolution started in the 1950s with Adenauer's vigorous support. Again, he was no naive idealist and no representative of unambiguity. He took into account the German situation of powerlessness, and realised that integration could serve as a tool for combining West German resurgence to an equal power in Europe with the French interest in security against Germany. The willingness to ensure the others perspective has always been at the core of real rapprochement. And even if it might not have always been explicit, Adenauer's committment was based on a moral conviction to overcome centuries of violent Great Power antagonism in Europe.

This was no less true for Chancellor Helmut Kohl when he pushed the transition into the European Union four decades after the beginning of the European integration process. So let us finally compare Konrad Adenauer to those who came after him: Helmut Kohl and Angela Merkel.

Kohl followed a set of a few core convictions: family politics, transatlantic relations, European integration and reconciliation with France. In 1983 he implemented the NATO dual-track decision against fierce domestic opposition – as Adenauer had done with rearmament. And regarding reunification, he always kept it in mind and acted vigorously when the unexpected opportunity emerged.

He understood European integration as a lesson learned from the history of wars, particularly between French and German territories. Kohl himself came from one of those historical battlegrounds – his uncle

Walter had died in the First World War, his brother Walter in the Second, and he named his own son after them. Even if Kohl may have had a somewhat naive idea of a 'United States of Europe', he moderated the transition from Cold War to post-Cold War Europe due to an underlying and indispensable idea of history.

Angela Merkel worked hard to hold things together and keep Europe running. During the euro debt crisis she was very good at identifying what was unrealistic and unrealisable. But she was very bad at considering what might have been possible, and thinking strategically in different scenarios. Pragmatism without strategy leads to a series of incoherent decisions, from energy to migration to Russian politics. The German need for *Zeitenwende* – a historical turning point of eras – which her successor Olaf Scholz announced after Russia invaded Ukraine in 2022, was a result of this lack of historical imagination and of political priorities.

Ultimately, Konrad Adenauer teaches us several leadership lessons. First, 'be ready to bear ambivalence and ambiguities. Balance and reconcile antagonisms, such as national interests and universal values, Realpolitik and strategy, and pragmatism and principles.'

Second, think strategically, and let history open your mind. The future is open, and it is shapeable. Allow for the improbable. And imagine what might be possible.

And last, the essence of the exceptional leadership he displayed was to identify indispensable priorities. There won't be many, but stick to them, against all odds. Put substance before popularity. Leaders do not follow. They lead.

Russian President Vladimir Putin
and President Xi Jinping, 5 June 2019.

US SECURITY STRATEGY MEETS NATO:
A COMPARISON

Anna Wieslander

The US is still the leading power in the world, but it is increasingly under pressure from rivals such as China and Russia. Its alliances are a main asset in the global arena – and NATO is the most important alliance of them all. In 2022, the US presented both a National Security Strategy (NSS) and a National Defense Strategy (NDS), while NATO launched its new Strategic Concept (SC). How well do these strategic documents compare in terms of assessing rivals and adversaries? What do they tell us about how the US and NATO are adapting to a more dangerous and competitive world? And is the transatlantic community holding together or drifting apart?

In this essay, I argue that the changing nature of the international system, in transition from the unipolarity of the post-Cold War era, fundamentally affects the relationship between the US and its allies. It raises expectations for NATO to support the global ambitions of the US to continue to lead, if not the whole world, then at least the democratic world in the fight against autocracies. While Russia's full-scale invasion of Ukraine has led to a convergence of threat perception between the US and NATO on Russia, differences remain with regard to China, as well as the prospects of a China-Russia partnership. As the China challenge is of supreme importance to the US, the divergence poses a potential threat to transatlantic unity in the future. In addition, there are different perspectives on the threat of terrorism, where the US no longer has an appetite to lead international efforts.

A world in transition

After the Soviet Union collapsed in 1991, the international system transformed from bipolarity, dominated by the Soviet Union and the US, to unipolarity, with the US the only remaining superpower, dominating the international system. It went so far that Russian president Vladimir

Putin, while complaining about American dominance at the Munich Security Conference in 2007, had to admit that after the fall of the Berlin Wall, even Russians preferred 'the American way: democracy, freedom and openness'.

At the onset of this unipolar era, US president George H. W. Bush outlined a 'new world order', which stemmed from an idealistic Wilsonian tradition and leaned on the thinking of the eighteenth-century philosopher Immanuel Kant. The realistic stance, that US dominance was dependent on the defeat and weakness of its rival, was absent. According to Kant, the interests of all peoples are at a basic level one and the same. The superiority of the values of democracy, freedom and the rule of law meant that once peoples were exposed to these values, they would prevail. In addition, he presumed that states were able to act morally and rationally, hence a linear development of civilisation could, in the end, lead to 'perpetual peace'. Historian Francis Fukuyama brilliantly captured this in his 1989 essay 'The End of History?', in which he predicted that Western liberal democracy would become the final version of government for all states, paving the way for eternal peace.

As a consequence of this shift, American journalist Charles Krauthammer came up with his theory of 'The Unipolar Moment' alongside academic Christopher Layne's 'The Unipolar Illusion'. Scholars debated how long unipolarity would last, and whether it was dangerous. On the other hand, realists, including US political scientist Kenneth Waltz and academic John Mearsheimer, argued that, as systems incentives translated into behaviour, rivals would balance against the US and unipolarity would shift into a multipolar or bipolar order. Today, some scholars have concluded that this transformation has already occurred and that the international system is once again bipolar, given the distribution of power between the US and China. Others argue it is multipolar.

American strategies in a competitive era
For the past decade, the international system has been in an increasingly transformative phase, accelerated by the global Covid-19 pandemic and, more recently, Russia's full-scale invasion of Ukraine. When Russia illegally annexed Crimea and started a war in the Donbas in 2014, the world was still unipolar, although China and Russia had started to act as rivals in global affairs. However, it took time for the US to recognise this.

By 2022, almost a decade later, when the US released its NSS and NDS, great power competition was acknowledged as a main characteristic of the international system, affecting the way that America related to its NATO allies.

For the current Biden administration, a core feature of its foreign policy is to work more closely with its allies. As the US acknowledges its decreasing power relative to other rising global actors, Washington understands it can no longer single-handedly determine the conditions of world politics. In the coming decade, the US seeks to invest in its allies while setting high expectations of them in competing against adversaries in future contests between democracies and autocracies.

But what exactly does the US envision? Recognising that the unipolar era is over, policy seems to strive towards a bipolar world in which, as during the Cold War, it is the larger pole of the two – China being the other. Its main attraction rests strongly on soft power and democracy, in contrast to authoritarian China. In other words, the US wants to maintain its leadership role and expects the rest of the free world to join forces. The strategy still carries fragments of Kant's and Fukuyama's ideas, as it presumes democracies are the best proposition for citizens, and that democratic values will prevail if people are exposed to them – but with the addition and precaution that democracies also have to be safeguarded at home.

Both President Biden and his predecessor Barack Obama have often used the phrase 'iron-clad' in speeches and official documents, including in the 2015 NSS, to reassure allies of continued American engagement in Europe. Russia's invasion of Ukraine has undoubtedly reinvigorated Allied cohesion. In line with this commitment, the 2022 Madrid Summit Declaration stated that NATO was set to defend 'every inch of Allied territory'. Since its foundation in 1949, NATO has been the concrete expression of US guarantees of European security, built on the premise that American and European security are indivisible. The Alliance is seen by the US as an American instrument to pursue its leadership and maintain its supremacy with regard to the international rules-based order. Practically, NATO is the means to efficiently handle European affairs, against the backdrop of the question posed by the American secretary of state Henry Kissinger in the 1970s: 'Who do I call if I want to call Europe?'

The emphasis on working with allies brings NATO back into the core of US foreign policy but in a new manner. The NSS states that the

American agenda with its European allies is transatlantic in foundation but global in ambition. This means the US wants to engage European allies on a broad spectrum of policy areas, from trade and investment to combatting corruption and climate change. This engagement, which rests on shared democratic values, aims to take place across several multilateral formats, with NATO one of many. On security and defence, and particularly in response to Russia, the US foresees its allies taking on greater responsibility, while America is investing in a transatlantic link and its relationship with the EU. European defence investments, 'through or complementary to NATO', are seen as critical, paving the way for a stronger European pillar in NATO, if the Europeans take on the challenge. This strategic shift has been visible since Russia's full-scale invasion of Ukraine, as the US is now working with allies, rather than incorporating them into existing defence plans. They are no longer described as assisting but partnering.

NATO and the return of war to Europe – balancing threats
At the London Leaders Meeting in December 2019, NATO began a reflection process that ended at the Madrid Summit in June 2022 with the approval of the new Strategic Concept, a document second in importance only to the founding 1949 North Atlantic Treaty. The Strategic Concept guides NATO's tactical adaptation and drives its political and military development for the coming decade. It sets out a shared vision of the threats, challenges and opportunities it faces based on a collective assessment of the security environment.

Balancing Russia and China
By comparison, both the Strategic Concept and the 2022 NDS identify Russia, China and terrorism as core security threats, but they prioritise them differently. The following comparative analysis builds on work that I conducted in 2022 for the Swedish Armed forces together with Eric Adamson, which resulted in an unpublished working paper. For NATO, its regional focus implies that Russia is 'the most significant and direct threat to allies' security'. Contrastingly, the NDS states that the US is 'prioritising the [China] challenge in the Indo-Pacific, then the Russia challenge in Europe'. From an American perspective, while Russia poses an

immediate threat to the international system, only China has the means and intent to reshape the international rules-based order that has been upheld by the US and its allies since the Second World War. Both with regard to hard and soft power, as well as in the short to long term, the US views Russia as a waning power.

In a major shift for NATO, the Strategic Concept states that Russia can no longer be seen as a partner in light of its aggressive behaviour and inability to comply with international law. In the 2010 Strategic Concept, partnership with Russia was a major component. The shift is drastic. On the one hand, NATO emphasises it 'does not seek confrontation [with] and poses no threat to' Russia. On the other, the Alliance states clearly that the Euro-Atlantic area is not at peace and that an attack against an ally cannot be ruled out. This shift has fundamental consequences for the defensive measures that NATO now pursues. The Strategic Concept also describes the variety of hybrid warfare activities conducted by Russia, China, Iran and other authoritarian actors aimed at undermining Allied security and, ultimately, the rules-based international order.

Released in mid-October, the 2022 NSS labels Russia's foreign policy as 'imperialist', seeking to 'overturn key elements of the international order', which 'culminated with the war in Ukraine'. The US is striving to make the war a strategic failure, together with allies and partners. Consequently, America is fully committed to defending NATO territory and deepening partnerships with European allies. To deter and, if necessary, respond to Russian actions that threaten core US interests is part of the strategy. Russia cannot be allowed to fulfil its ambitions through the use of force and the threat of nuclear weapons. The US is equally committed to supporting Ukraine and helping it recover economically and integrate with the EU. In sum, at least in the short term, the US and NATO are aligned on Russia.

China as a strategic challenge

In contrast to Russia, China is seen by the US as having the economic, diplomatic, military and technological power to fundamentally reshape the international order. The National Defense Authorization Act, passed by Congress in December 2022, authorised $11.5 billion for the Pacific Deterrence Initiative (PDI), nearly double the amount requested by the Department of Defense. This is the first time the PDI has received dedicated funding, which suggests that US lawmakers at last are providing resources needed for a true US pivot to Asia. According to the NSS, the American strategy toward China has three dimensions. First, the US must invest in competitiveness, innovation, resilience and democracy at home. Second, the US must align efforts with allies and partners; and third, compete responsibly to defend interests and build a vision for the future. Similarly, the NATO Strategic Concept emphasises making investments at home while remaining open for constructive engagement with China.

For many years, China was of no concern to NATO. It was not until the 2019 London Declaration that the organisation officially addressed China: 'We recognise that China's growing influence and international policies present both opportunities and challenges that we need to address together as an alliance.' Gradually, its stance has become more stringent. The June 2021 summit in Brussels called China a 'destabilising force and systemic challenge, whose actions threaten the rules-based international order'. The 2022 SC highlights China's tactic to use 'economic leverage to create strategic dependencies' and enhance influence to 'subvert the rules-based international order'. As Washington has pushed NATO to consider geopolitical confrontation further, China has emerged – for both NATO and the US – as a multi-domain challenge, using a wide range of political, economic and military instruments to undermine allies' interests, security and values. China's inclusion in the NATO Strategic Concept for the first time is thus a policy victory for the US.

China also affects US nuclear policy and NATO's defence and deterrence posture through the rapid build-up of its nuclear arsenal, which demands greater American attention and resources. Beijing is constructing at least 250 missile silos and could have 1,000 nuclear warheads by 2030. In its current form, US nuclear policy is not designed to meet two nuclear adversaries, which could be the reality by 2030. To address this challenge, the US must modernise the Nuclear Triad, nuclear command, control, communications, and infrastructure. Allies will likely need to strengthen their extended deterrence commitments.

Russia-China, an alignment in the making

Both the Strategic Concept and the NSS mention the growing tactical partnership between Russia and China as running counter to Allied interests and values, and posing a threat to rules-based international order. However, the NSS notes that recent events in Ukraine have partly weakened it.

The key difference in approach to China is that NATO limits itself to addressing Chinese threats as they relate to Euro-Atlantic security. Its defence planning does not include the Indo-Pacific, nor its capabilities or operations (at least not yet). The main tools for NATO to address Indo-Pacific issues are intensified dialogue and cooperation with regional partners. Meanwhile, Europe and NATO allies will have to address the China-Russia strategic partnership in the Arctic – definitively within the Euro-Atlantic area. As Moscow and Beijing seek to reshape the international order, so, too, are they challenging Arctic governance in pursuit of new economic, and possibly military, interests.

It is noteworthy that the NATO Strategic Concept has a very limited view on the latter, mentioning the region only once in terms of Russia posing a strategic challenge in the High North. The US released an updated Arctic strategy in September 2022, after many years of neglect. Recognising changes to the geopolitical and physical environment in the Arctic, the US now seeks greater engagement and presence in a region where cooperation with Russia is 'unlikely in the foreseeable future'. To protect interests and maintain stability, the US seeks to work closely with allies and take a 'whole-of-government approach'. Increased Arctic exercises and coordination with NATO allies in the region are a part of this strategy.

Terrorism and domestic instability

On terrorism, which both the US and NATO define as a third core security threat, there is also an increasing divergence, with the US shifting focus from combatting terrorism abroad to dealing with terrorism at home. In June 2021, the Biden administration released the first-ever National Strategy for Countering Domestic Terrorism, which identifies domestic violent extremists – specifically white supremacist and anti-government militias – as posing the 'most persistent and lethal threat' to the US. For international counter-terrorism, the US signalled a shift from a

'US-led, partner-enabled' approach to a 'partner-led, US-enabled' one, according to the 2022 NSS – which also substantially downplays the importance of the Middle East.

The Strategic Concept states that terrorism is the 'most direct asymmetric threat' to citizens and that combatting terrorism is 'essential' for completing its three core tasks and 360° approach towards deterrence and defence. Terrorism remains high on the agenda for NATO allies with closer ties and geographic proximity to countries in the Middle East, North Africa and the Sahel. Domestic terrorism is not specifically referred to in the NATO Strategic Concept, but it makes mention of adversaries seeking to interfere in open democratic processes and promote authoritarian models of governance both directly and through proxies.

Conclusion

As it becomes increasingly apparent that the unipolar system has come to an end, the US seems to be settling for a bipolar world between itself and China, with the US the larger pole of the two. In the coming decade, the US seeks to invest in its allies while setting high expectations of them in competing against adversaries in the future contest between democracies and autocracies. For NATO, this means that although its foundation remains transatlantic, its ambitions, according to the US, should be global.

Comparing the most recent strategic documents of the US and NATO, it is clear that both identify Russia, China and terrorism as core security threats, but that they prioritise them differently. Both view Russia as the most acute threat and stand solid in defending 'every inch' of NATO territory and supporting Ukraine against Russia's full-scale invasion. However, in the longer term there is less convergence, as the US clearly prioritises the China challenge and, in addition, is withdrawing from international counter-terrorism to focus on domestic threats. NATO, although recognising China poses a multi-domain challenge, still has a more nuanced stance and is reluctant to go beyond its regional boundaries in defining or planning for military threats related to China.

Leading European allies, such as France and Germany, have still not accepted the Biden administration's bipolar pitch. On his way home from a visit to China in 2023, French president Emmanuel Macron said Europe faced 'the threat of becoming a vassal between the United States and

China, while it could be a third pole'. In addressing the European Parliament on 9 May 2023, German chancellor Olaf Scholz similarly argued that the world is 'multipolar and has been for a long time'. Public poll partly supports this line of thinking. It shows that most Europeans would prefer Europe to remain neutral in a conflict between China and Taiwan. While Russia nowadays is seen as an 'adversary' by an average of 62% of respondents, China is still viewed by most as a 'necessary partner'.

As the US struggles to remain the most powerful country in the world, albeit in a bipolar system, its only true rival, China, will continue to be a major preoccupation for Washington in the coming decade. Whether the US and Europe will find a way to align with China will provide the answer to the question of whether the transatlantic community is holding firm or drifting apart. This, in turn, will have implications for the formation of the international system in the future.

NATO exercises in Germany,
Canadian troops, October 1983.

THE TRANSATLANTIC ALLIANCE IN AN ERA OF STRATEGIC COMPETITION

Benedetta Berti

For almost 75 years, NATO has played an indispensable role in ensuring the freedom and security of its members, while contributing to uphold the rules-based international order. The Alliance's success remains grounded in its military strength, political unity and ability to evolve. Today, NATO is undergoing a profound strategic, military and political adaptation to ensure it remains effective in a world of growing strategic competition, persistent fragility and recurrent shocks. As part of this process, the Alliance is significantly strengthening its deterrence and defence posture. It is also stepping up support for allies facing non-military challenges, such as economic coercion, energy manipulation and other hybrid tactics. While refocusing on the collective defence of allies, NATO continues to invest in deepening cooperation with partner countries far and near. Maintaining this global approach remains essential, given the interconnected nature of many of the threats and challenges that the Alliance faces.

Visionary leadership and pragmatic statecraft: the making of NATO

The establishment of the North Atlantic Treaty Organization is a prime example of visionary leadership, combined with pragmatic statecraft. Back in 1949, the notion of establishing a defensive alliance that would bind together European and North American countries in an enduring way was nothing short of revolutionary. Building on the ashes of two devastating world wars, NATO founders wanted to bring together former adversaries and enable them to preserve their freedom and security through a collective defence commitment (article five of the Treaty). They also sought to establish and foster a community based on shared values – individual liberty, human rights, democracy and the rule of law – to promote stability and well-being in the North Atlantic area.

That strategic vision was accompanied by a strong dose of pragmatism and the understanding that the Alliance would require an institutional framework to organise and enable the collective defence of allies, by military and non-military means. NATO provided that framework for co-operation. It offered a permanent forum for allies to come together on a daily basis to consult and coordinate, and, in so doing, increasingly deepen and cement the transatlantic bond. NATO's function was simultaneously strategic, military and political. Its very existence sent a clear deterrence signal to potential adversaries, namely the Soviet Union. NATO's military structures enabled defence cooperation between allied countries, fostering not only military interoperability but also, just as importantly, strategic convergence. At the same time, NATO's political and administrative headquarters facilitated regular political consultations, helping to further build and solidify transatlantic relations.

The assumption about the critical value of transatlantic cooperation still holds true today: the bond remains central to ensuring the security of all NATO allies and to contributing to peace and stability in the Euro-Atlantic area. What is more, in a context of growing strategic competition, where assertive authoritarian actors are increasingly putting pressure on the rules-based international order and challenging the security of allies, the need for Europe and North America to cooperate closely is stronger than ever.

NATO in practice: seven decades of adaptation
Building on this sound strategic vision and clarity of purpose, NATO has been able to evolve over the past seven decades to respond to changes in the broader strategic landscape. Indeed, while the Alliance's purpose has endured, its tasks and priorities have adapted significantly over time.

During the Cold War, NATO's core focus was ensuring the credible deterrence and defence of Western Europe, in order to prevent a conflict with the Soviet Union. It was essentially a one-adversary, one-theatre focused defensive alliance. Its activities were centred on protecting and defending the territory and population of allied countries against potential attack: in other words, 'article five contingencies'.

In the period following the fall of the Soviet Union and the end of the Cold War, NATO embarked on a deep transformation. It began undertaking crisis management and response operations outside the territory of its member states, driven by the understanding that serious 'non-article five' crises and conflicts in the Alliance's broader geographic neighborhood could bring insecurity and instability to members, and that NATO could be a useful mechanism for upholding international peace and security. NATO's focus on responding to asymmetric threats and challenges deepened after the 9/11 terrorist attacks against the United States, which led to the only invocation of article five in NATO's history. Throughout the 2000s, NATO developed tools to support its members and the broader international community in fighting terrorism, including through its deployment in Afghanistan.

Beyond crisis management, the 1990s also brought significant change for NATO. A focus on building dialogue and cooperation with non-member countries in its broader vicinity – particularly former Warsaw Pact adversaries in the aftermath of the Cold War – was key. In addition to this reaching out and building bridges, partnerships with countries who wished to become members of the Alliance were formed. This process of enlargement not only strengthened the Alliance but also served a key political role, supporting the countries' integration, and in many cases contributing to their future accession into the European Union. Throughout the 1990s and 2000s, NATO continued to deepen its work with non-member countries, progressively developing partnerships across the broader Euro-Atlantic area, the Middle East and North Africa, and further across the globe, including in the Indo-Pacific.

NATO's adaptation in the post-Cold War era and its rationale are articulated clearly in the 2010 NATO Strategic Concept. This explains how the Alliance re-oriented itself to operate in a security environment where the Euro-Atlantic area was essentially seen as a region of relative peace and stability, and where the possibility of conventional threats against member countries was perceived as relatively low. It emphasises the importance of being able to counter asymmetric, unconventional threats and challenges, such as terrorism, including through the deployment of forces at strategic distance, as in the case of Afghanistan. To ensure allied security in a world of diffuse threats, the Strategic Concept also stresses the importance of cooperating with partners in the Euro-Atlantic area and beyond. This shift in priorities served the Alliance well in the post-Cold War decades, but has required a significant adjustment in recent years, in line with the progressive deterioration of the broader Euro-Atlantic and global security environment.

Back to the future: preparing for a more contested world

Over the past ten years, NATO has evolved to meet the needs of a significantly more complex and contested security environment. Put simply, many of the overarching assumptions that drove the 2010 Strategic Concept no longer hold true, and NATO has had to adapt. These changes are clearly explained in the 2022 Strategic Concept.

First, the Concept states NATO has to operate in an environment where the Euro-Atlantic area is no longer 'at peace' and where the Alliance cannot discount the possibility of an attack against allies' sovereignty and territorial integrity. In the Concept, NATO defined the Russian Federation as the most significant and direct threat to allies' security, peace and stability in the Euro-Atlantic area. Practically, this means that for the first time since the end of the Cold War, NATO has had to re-focus on strengthening its deterrence and defence posture and rebuilding its ability to ensure the credible protection of allied territories and populations against potential article five contingencies. This process of resetting began in 2014, in the aftermath of Russia's illegal annexation of Crimea, and was significantly accelerated after Russia's invasion of Ukraine brought full-scale war back to Europe and further undermined the stability and predictability of the post-Cold War European security order.

In the same vein, the Alliance has been reiterating the importance of supporting Ukraine as it exercises its right to self-defence against Russian aggression, recognising that a strong, free and independent Ukraine is essential for stability and peace in Europe.

Practically, since 2014, the Alliance has implemented the largest reinforcement of its collective defence in a generation, including investing in eight multi-national battlegroups now deployed across NATO's eastern flank, backed by pre-positioned equipment and capabilities. The Alliance's ability to credibly deter and defend has also been boosted by upgraded NATO defence plans, strengthening command and control structures and ensuring the Alliance has a larger pool of forces across land, air, sea and cyber domains able to respond swiftly to any threats. To implement this historic reset, NATO allies, and especially those in Europe and Canada, have had to invest more in defence. Since 2014, these countries have added an estimated $600 billion to their defence budgets, in line with the pledge made in 2014 to make progress towards meeting the benchmark of spending 2% of GDP on defence by 2024. At the 2023

NATO Summit, NATO countries reiterated this commitment and stressed the importance of spending a minimum of 2% on defence, recognising that in some cases more resources are needed to deliver forces and capabilities required to fully execute agreed plans.

Secondly, the Concept stresses that the Alliance's security environment is extremely complex and contested, and that, in this context, NATO has to be able to deal with potential simultaneous threats and challenges, both military and non-military. Specifically, the Concept stresses how rising strategic competition, pervasive instability and recurrent shocks all define NATO's tactical landscape, requiring the Alliance to maintain a broad and global approach to security.

Rising strategic competition is a key feature of the Alliance's operating environment, playing out across the ideological, political, technological and military dimension. Assertive, authoritarian actors – led by Russia and China – are putting constant pressure on the rules-based international order. The Concept recognises that China's 'stated ambitions and coercive policies challenge our interests, security and values'. In this sense, the 2022 assessment underlines the importance of building transatlantic convergence to address systemic challenges, while emphasising the importance of building resilience against coercion.

More broadly, NATO recognises that, in a context where strategic competitors and adversaries increasingly use both military and non-military tools, it is essential to enhance both national and collective resilience. This is why the 2022 Strategic Concept defines resilience as a key enabler of collective defence and security. It also stresses the importance of investing in resilient physical and digital infrastructure, as well as societies. In the same vein, the strategy recognises the need to work together – as a transatlantic community and with like-minded partners – to identify and mitigate strategic vulnerabilities and dependencies.

In addition, NATO has to remain able to tackle enduring asymmetric threats to allied security, such as terrorism. More broadly, the Alliance's neighbourhood remains characterised by pervasive fragility and conflict, which continue to fuel terrorism, violent extremism, and transnational crime. In turn, these dynamics have the potential to directly undermine the security of the Alliance, making clear the importance of working with partner countries to contribute to security and stability beyond the Alliance's borders. Finally, NATO needs to able to absorb, operate effectively and respond to systemic shocks, whether global pandemics or the direct and indirect impact of climate change on security. Dealing with these global challenges also calls for strengthening cooperation with other partner countries and organisations.

In sum, over the last decade, NATO has embarked on a significant process of military and political adaptation to ensure it can effectively enable the collective defence of allies in a competitive, contested and unpredictable world.

Prime minister Margaret Thatcher's (1925–2013)
state visit to the USSR, 29 March 1987.

MARGARET THATCHER:
THE OPTIMISTIC CONSERVATIVE

Charles Moore

Margaret Thatcher once attended an anniversary dinner of a think-tank where its senior staff kept congratulating one another in their speeches. When, finally, it was her turn to speak, she was fed up. 'I've just listened to seven speeches by men,' she began, 'and all I want to say is that the cocks may crow, but the hen lays the eggs.' Those words express very well the attitude, character and unique position in British public life the Conservative prime minister occupied at that time.

I shall concentrate on Thatcher in the Cold War. I want to go back to 1975, when she first became Conservative leader – four years before she reached 10 Downing Street. On the Cold War, as with economic and many other issues, she wished to make a break with the dominant orthodoxies, which she saw as things of the past. The fashion then was for 'détente'. She worried that the West was engaging with the Soviet Union from a position of weakness. She feared what was then called 'Finlandisation'. This meant the danger that the rest of the West might imitate the policy that circumstances and geography had forced upon Finland. In order to survive without Soviet attack, Finland had to lie low and adopt a position of neutrality, rather than being an active member of NATO. She thought such an attitude was spreading throughout the West.

Thatcher immediately tackled this. She sought to deal with the issue both in terms of great power and defence relationships, but also on a more moral plane that showed concern for the actual citizens who lived under Soviet rule. In her first major speech on the subject, in Chelsea, London, in 1975, she said: 'When the Soviet leaders jail a writer or a priest or a doctor or a worker for the crime of speaking freely, it's not only for humanitarian reasons we should be concerned, for these acts reveal a regime that is afraid of truth and liberty. It dare not allow its people to enjoy the freedom we take for granted, and a nation that denies this freedom to its own people will have few scruples in denying them to others.'

She saw the question in terms of trying to reach the people oppressed by the Soviet Union as well as the more traditional interstate power relationships in which she was also very interested. She shared this view with a man called Ronald Reagan, whom she met for the first time that year and who held no office, having ceased to be governor of California. In her next big speech devoted to the subject, in January 1976, Thatcher said the Soviets were 'bent on world domination'. This speech absolutely enraged the Soviet regime. *Red Star*, the newspaper of the Red Army, duly attacked her. They satirised her by calling her the 'Iron Lady'. They meant this as an insult because, sarcastic and sexist as Russian propaganda has often been, it was obvious that a woman could not be iron. It was to the Soviets a comical idea to be an iron lady. They made the comparison with Bismarck: you can be an iron chancellor, but an iron lady was a joke.

Thatcher immediately seized on this. She could see exactly how this intended insult would help her standing as a still new and inexperienced leader. And so, for a dinner in her constituency, she deliberately and unusually wore red, the colour (though not in the United States) of socialism, rather than the customary Tory blue. 'I stand before you tonight,' she said, 'in my *Red Star* chiffon evening gown…[you should watch it on YouTube, it's good]…my face softly made up and my fair hair gently waved, the Iron Lady of the Western world, a Cold War warrior. Yes, I am an iron lady. After all, it wasn't a bad thing to be an iron duke [the Duke of Wellington, the victor over Napoleon at Waterloo]. Yes, if that's how they wish to interpret my defence of values and freedoms fundamental to our way of life.'

She thus stole from her opponents the best sobriquet she could possibly have to make herself known across the world. It was one which dramatised not only her views and strength of character but also her sex, which was always important in the way she approached politics – men being weak and women, in her view, being strong. She won her first general election as leader in 1979 and, in January 1981, Ronald Reagan became president of the United States. The two of them were determined to confront the Soviet menace by redressing the balance of nuclear power. Helped by Helmut Kohl in Germany, they succeeded in installing cruise and Pershing missiles in Europe and leading the political defeat of the Campaign for Nuclear Disarmament and other unilateralists.

In 1982, under Thatcher's leadership – and, after some delay, with President Reagan's help – Britain won the Falklands War, a victory that mightily impressed the Soviets. They began to believe that, after a period of weakness, Britain had recovered the will and capacity to project military power. In 1983, Thatcher won the general election partly on the disarmament issue, with the biggest majority any Conservative government has ever achieved in the era of universal suffrage.

After these successful first four years in office, Thatcher decided that, because she had achieved these things, alongside Reagan, it was time to bargain from strength. Ideological though she was, she was also realistic. She loved to say she was a conviction politician, and she was, but she was also cunning, and that was something she did not love to say. She could see it was time to start a dialogue, but the question was, with whom?

She went to the funeral of the Soviet leader Yuri Andropov in Moscow in February 1984 and stood stoically in the freezing cold. She despaired because the Soviet leaders hanging around mourning the dead man were all very old, including his successor, Konstantin Chernenko. On the plane home, she sank into her seat and exclaimed, 'For God's sake, find me a young Russian.' The Foreign Office, though not her favourite institution, obliged. They found Mikhail Gorbachev, not at that time Soviet leader nor formally anointed as such, but clearly in the ascendant.

Thatcher invited Gorbachev to Chequers, her country residence, and there, that December, took place an extraordinary set of conversations. Her press secretary, Bernard Ingham, told me the very first thing she said to Gorbachev as she took him into the room was 'I want you to know that I hate communism', intending to set the tone. Extraordinarily, it was successful. Both host and guest liked the frankness. They were talking rather like students debating. She was saying capitalism and liberty are superior, and free markets are great. Gorbachev was saying, 'No, yours is a cruel system. In the Soviet Union, people live joyfully.' Thatcher immediately took to him. It was always important in her relationships with world leaders – virtually all men – as to whether she liked them personally. It mattered whether she thought they were 'manly men'. She thought this very much of Reagan and of Gorbachev, who, in her words, had 'wonderful sparkly eyes'. In the time taken for this meeting – it was scheduled for three hours, but took twice that – a trust built up. Afterwards, she immediately authorised the famous words: 'This is a man we can do business with.'

Once Gorbachev had left, Thatcher suddenly threw up her hands in exclamation and said, 'Goodness, tomorrow's China and I haven't had my hair done!' In that extraordinary week, she flew from London to Beijing to settle the Hong Kong Agreement with Deng Xiaoping, before proceeding to Hong Kong to sell the agreement in the former colony. Thence, via Pearl Harbor and Honolulu, she went on to visit Camp David, the US president's country retreat in Maryland, before flying home. At Camp David, she talked to Reagan, introducing him to the idea that Gorbachev would be important.

When Gorbachev came to supreme office the following year, he 'quickly saw Mrs Thatcher', in the words of one of his aides, 'as the shortest way to send a message to Washington'. This established a remarkable relationship of very deep trust with Reagan, though by no means always agreement; and a respectable level of trust with the Kremlin. This developed as *perestroika* did and everyone became interested in Gorbachev. Perhaps the apex for Thatcher, along with her visit to the shipyards in Gdansk in 1988, was her visit to Moscow in March 1987. There, she made a great physical impression with her hats and camel hair coat and suede boots. Because Gorbachev wanted to embody the mood of change, it suited him to give her great freedom never before granted to a visiting Western leader. She was allowed to move around the streets, meet people without total prearrangement and, above all, to be interviewed at length on Soviet television, where she completely wiped the floor with the two apparatchik interviewers, who were rude to her.

The Soviet people had never seen anything remotely like it. Thatcher spoke bluntly, criticising the regime, while at the same time supporting its reformist tendencies. As at Chequers, she also had endless private arguments with Gorbachev. At one point, they moved rooms. Probably so he could show her a painting of a rural scene, the sun shining on a drenched landscape after a storm. 'Look, prime minister,' he said, 'this picture is like our conversation, with the light breaking through.' Thatcher looked and replied, in a line she could not have prepared, 'Yes, Mr President, but the light is coming from the West.'

It is not an exaggeration to say that from 1983 to early 1989, the double act of Gorbachev and Thatcher was so powerful, alongside Reagan, that Margaret Thatcher played a principal part in changing the global situation and the outcome of the Cold War.

Then came a curious and conflicted period for Thatcher, where she got what she had always wished for, yet also what she did not want at all. When the Berlin Wall came down in November 1989, although she had worked so hard for that day, she privately described it as 'the dagger in my heart' because she was so frightened of German reunification.

She had two reasons for this; one, I think, disproportionate, the other more powerful. The first was her fear – she was very much a child of the Second World War – of the return of German nationalism. This was certainly not a trivial matter, but she allowed personal prejudice against Germany and her consequent dislike of Helmut Kohl to exaggerate it.

Her second fear was that if East Germany collapsed suddenly, the Soviet Union, and Gorbachev, with whom she by now had a close relationship, would not be able to contain it. There would be a conflagration; there might even be a war, and Europe might end up with a united Germany neutral between Russia and the West, and therefore very dangerous. She also feared old Soviet communist or Russian nationalist revanchism, which did indeed nearly happen with the unsuccessful coup against Gorbachev in August 1991, after she had left office. This fear was not unreasonable. Thatcher also contemplated the rising issue of the nationalities which started to come through with the break-up of the Soviet Union, and whose consequences for good and ill we all witness today. She was very conflicted: she believed in the liberation of Poland, Hungary etc., and was also highly sympathetic to the national aspirations of the Baltic states, Ukraine and other components of the Soviet Union. But she was also very worried that, in the latter cases, violence and chaos might break out. In June 1990, she went to speak to the parliament in Kyiv and was given a rapturous reception, but she did not tell its members what they most wanted to hear. She did not say, 'Yes, go off and be independent.' She said words to the effect of 'Please give Gorbachev more time; try to support his reforms.'

By 1990, which ought to have been the apotheosis of her Cold War policy, Thatcher remained incredibly popular in the east of Europe, but was frozen out by President George H W Bush, with whom she did not have such a close relationship as she had with Ronald Reagan, and by Helmut Kohl. You could say she got caught by the hinge of history.

What might it tell us about where we are now? One of the strengths of Margaret Thatcher was that, though she often preached optimism, she always retained a conservative sense of threat. She always understood that free institutions, markets and liberty itself are threatened by people who dislike them. This was the key reason for her constant preoccupation with a high level of defence preparedness and her unwavering belief (in contrast to Reagan's more idealistic stance) in the nuclear deterrent. In January 1990, she received a notable memo from Charles Powell, her closest and most important private secretary. This was during an era dubbed 'the end of history'. Powell told her that, on the contrary, the 1990s and beyond 'will mark the return of history, and the West will once again be confronting nationalism'. Thatcher heavily underlined this note, her most common way of showing approval.

We can surely see that, in the years soon after her resignation, and with the rise of Putin, the West became lackadaisical in this regard. The Germany of Gerhard Schröder and Angela Merkel, in particular, and perhaps the America of Barack Obama, seemed to act as if history had ended. Such a belief, so comprehensively disproved every day since 24 February last year, and indeed, since the invasion of Crimea in 2014, has allowed Putin to get away, literally, with murder. I hope we are now witnessing something much closer to what Thatcher always hoped for: a Europe active in defending its freedom. That Europe is the sort of Europe that she preferred to the tight, small, Western European Community of old. It is a Europe whose dynamism is coming from the Atlantic and from the east of the continent.

I revert to a word used at the beginning – 'Finlandisation'. Fifty years on, as Finland joins NATO, it is reversing its meaning. It now stands for being strong in the Western alliance. Perhaps we shall soon have 'Swedenisation' to make the same point even more strongly.

Galileo Galilei showing his telescope to the
Doge of Venice. Engraving from a painting by
De Scantis. Published in *L'Illustrazione Italiana*,
no. 41, 6 August 1876.

FREEDOM OF SPEECH AND THE LEADERS
OF TOMORROW

Claire Coutinho

The quest for truth has long provided humanity with the moral coordinates for technological and scientific progress. History is littered with examples of institutions trying to censor the exchange of ideas considered heretical by restricting the rights of individuals to discuss, publish and engage with ideas that run counter to the established consensus. In the battle between the pursuit of truth and a devotion to dogma, we in the West plant our flag firmly on the side of those who fought against the governments and organised religions that tried to suppress the free exchange of ideas.

The father of modern science, Galileo Galilei, embodies this battle between truth and dogma. Galileo made improvements to the refracting telescope which earned him financial success in early seventeenth-century Venice, but his invention also led to something considerably more valuable. By using the new telescope to create topographical charts of the Moon, discover the four phases of Venus and, most importantly, view several moons in the orbit of Jupiter, he was able to prove that Copernicus's theory of heliocentrism was, in fact, true.

The rest of his story is well known. Having mortally offended the Catholic Church, he was tried, found 'suspect of heresy', banned from publishing and ordered to recant his findings. His most enduring punishment was a lifetime of house arrest. During this exile he continued his ground-breaking work, subverting censorship by sending his works to be published in Holland.

This was a critical moment in the development of the scientific rationalism that continues to underpin our Enlightenment values. Through the work of Copernicus, Galileo and others, nature moved out of the realm of the theological into the realm of the quantifiable – in Galileo's own words, 'the book of Nature is written in the language of mathematics'. But Galileo also knew that this triumph of reason is predicated on the necessity of discussion. It requires people to put ideas forward freely, to test them and to pass them between minds so that they can be constantly refined. The truth cannot be reached if certain predetermined ideas are considered to be unquestionable.

Centuries later, we now give thanks to the Galileos, the Keplers and the Newtons for pushing forward the frontiers of human thought. These visionary thinkers have shaped our understanding of astronomy, mathematics, natural history, biology and more. They, along with innumerable other scientists, have built the modern world – creating extraordinary technologies which have not only improved our health but given us access to information and experiences our ancestors could only dream of. None of this would have been possible without the rigorous application of the free exchange of ideas. Yet, in twenty-first-century Britain, we have seen the free exchange of ideas under threat in the very places where the most controversial debates should be taking place – on university campuses.

Aristotle believed that everything can be reduced to a *telos* – a purpose, aim or goal. Alongside a university's core telos of pursuing truth, the modern university is also tasked with creating independent thinkers who are equipped with the tools to think about the world critically. Universities are training grounds for the business, political and cultural leaders of tomorrow, and this is especially true in Britain, which is home to four of the world's top ten universities. The generation currently studying at university will need the skills of critical thought more than ever before; the pace of technological change is transforming the world at a speed none of us can be fully prepared for, and we will need leadership that can meet this pace of change.

Take the onset of AI, for example. What role should large language models, like ChatGPT, play in education? How do we navigate copyright disputes between human artists and AI? How do we integrate AI into the workforce without displacing human workers? These are all challenging ethical dilemmas with no easy answers, and we are doing the leaders of tomorrow a disservice if we do not encourage them to expose themselves to other points of view and develop their critical thinking skills.

The importance of the process of debate in arriving at a solution is not just limited to the sciences and the natural world, but also influences the social order and our political governance. Britain's constitutional settlement has been reached largely through considered debate, persuasion and reform, rather than violent revolution or upheaval. Great reformers like William Wilberforce and Benjamin Disraeli recognised that in order for these reforms to be sustained, they must be implemented with the consent of the people. The best way to achieve this consent is for free and open debate to act as a safety valve, where grievances of all kinds can be discussed in good faith before settling on a route forward.

This perspective was shared by J. S. Mill, who said that depriving ourselves of the chance to debate also denies us 'the clearer perception and livelier impression of truth, produced by its collision with error'. In Mill's view, the process of debate was valuable as both a means and an end. Yet this process is exactly what students are being deprived of in British universities.

How does this trend manifest itself on campus? Curious students who want to open their minds by listening to other points of view are shouted down or barred from attending debates. Visiting speakers who do not conform to an omniscient progressive monoculture are intimidated into submission by aggressive protests. In the worst cases, academics are losing their livelihoods, and their reputations, for the crime of expressing mainstream opinions.

All of this is driven by a small group of vocal activists who fire off a lot of tweets and draft open letters to create the impression that their view is shared by the majority. Many readers will be familiar with the case of Kathleen Stock, a professor of philosophy at the University of Sussex, who felt the sharp edge of a campaign of this nature in 2021. After expressing mainstream views on the status of biological sex, Stock was subject to a toxic, organised campaign to get her fired. In a free society, people are perfectly entitled to counter those views if they disagree with them. Yet instead of using persuasive arguments to oppose Stock's views, these activists centred their campaign on intimidation and aggression. Stock was forced to install CCTV in her home, hire bodyguards for when she was present on campus and, ultimately, was left with no choice but to resign from her position at the university.

Despite losing her job, Stock is now a successful author and public speaker on sexuality and gender identity, but many of the other victims claimed by this culture of intimidation do not want to spend the rest of their career absorbed in the rough and tumble of professional political commentary. Many of them simply want to carry on with the jobs they love – as they did before they dared to dissent from the monoculture. This is especially the case for those working in disciplines as far from politics as possible, such as mathematics.

In the course of my work as an education minister I was astonished to speak to a group of university mathematicians who were being pressured into 'decolonising' their curricula – by suppressing the work of 'white mathematicians' and elevating the work of 'non-white mathematicians'.

Mathematicians use a decimal system created in India, algebra derived from the Arab world and complex analysis based on imaginary numbers forged in Europe. There is perhaps no discipline which is more rooted in global cooperation than mathematics. It was mathematician David Hilbert who said: 'Mathematics knows no race or geographic boundaries; for mathematics, the cultural world is one country.' These academics were deeply concerned by the politicisation of their subject at the behest of university administrators who were pushing contested ideology as unquestionable fact. The message I heard from them was one I have heard countless times since: 'We are fearful of speaking out because of the potential for a backlash that could put our jobs at risk.'

The experience of these mathematicians is one shared by many, but it is an experience which differs greatly from the overt, top-down censorship of centuries gone by. It is an insidious *self*-censorship which bubbles away under the surface, where students and academics with mainstream views don't say what they think because they're scared of the consequences for their studies or their careers. Research shows that one third of all academics in the UK self-censor and there are similar reports from across Europe. In the US, a third of academics self-censor during interviews or lectures. Often, it's academics approaching the end of their careers who are more likely to feel they can speak openly than their junior colleagues.

This self-censorship is not limited to those on the political right. While those who are right wing are more likely to self-censor, 42% of left-leaning academics in the social sciences report that they don't express their views due to social pressure from their colleagues. This has material consequences, too, as we now have evidence that academic freedom boosts innovation. One study found that when academic freedom rises by one standard deviation, the number of patents filed two years later grows by two fifths.

What is to blame for the culture of censorship that has infiltrated so many aspects of civil society? The answer lies, at least partly, in the rise of social media. Social media has created tangible connections between individuals on an extraordinary scale. In some ways, speech has never been so free. However, in breaking down the barriers to communication, social media has also encouraged us to lock ourselves away in echo chambers, surrounded by tribes of people who share our own beliefs. The more we use these platforms, the more their algorithms feed us *what* we like to see, from *who* we like to see. It's far too easy to get hooked on the drip of dopamine hits from people who agree with us.

This form of connection is a far cry from how we used to get to know each other, which was often in congregations where communities would be brought together through communal spaces and shared experiences. Whether it was at church, local community events or walking to the village pub, we would naturally collide with people of all different backgrounds and viewpoints – young and old, rich and poor, conservative and liberal. Now, as our interactions have moved online, we are encouraged to find communities of people who think just like we do. The allure of these online communities is compelling: you will never be challenged, you will never encounter dissent and your virtue will always be affirmed.

We now see these expectations bleeding into real life and onto university campuses. Activists have become so immersed in the cultural conformity of online communities that they believe it is righteous to silence anyone who dissents from their worldview. Using the language of tolerance and emotional safety to justify this oppression, words become violence, and contested social issues are declared 'beyond debate' in order to protect those who might be offended. Yet this approach misunderstands how we become a tolerant society. A tolerant society isn't one where everyone must fit into a narrow, preconceived idea of moral virtue – where only those who take a certain point of view are allowed to speak their mind – but one which allows us to understand those we disagree with, and where minority views have a place in the debate. It is only through open discussion, in good faith, that we can begin to bridge divides and understand those we disagree with.

If we had allowed this culture of conformity to continue, we would have been consenting to an intellectual sedative being injected into the university experience. That is why, in the UK, we chose to act. Through the Higher Education (Freedom of Speech) Act, we made sure to protect the principle of free speech which has been at the centre of so much of our progress in the West.

The Act holds universities accountable for the state of free speech on their campuses and protects staff, students and visiting speakers who advocate viewpoints of all kinds. Through a new complaints scheme, students, academics and speakers will be able to have a complaint independently investigated. The creation of a new statutory tort means that anyone who feels that their free speech rights have been wrongly infringed will have a clear path to redress through the courts. Crucially, in circumstances where urgent action is needed, an injunction can be sought from the court to prevent a breach of the new free speech duties before it occurs.

The Act also creates a powerful Director for Freedom of Speech and Academic Freedom at the universities regulator, the Office for Students. The director will be a torchbearer for freedom of speech in higher education, with the power to investigate and take action against providers who are found to have breached their duties to uphold free speech.

While no legislation by itself can change culture, our new duty to protect and promote freedom of speech – backed up by accessible means of redress – is already starting to have an effect. I have spoken to vice-chancellors who are making plans to embed an appreciation for free speech at the beginning of a student's academic journey, and we have seen an emboldened approach from university leaders who are fighting back when cancel culture rears its head.

I am delighted that Kathleen Stock – despite the best attempts of some – did, in fact, speak to curious and respectful students at Oxford University recently, backed by strong action from their vice-chancellor. I am also pleased that students who disagreed were allowed to protest outside. Both are important.

It may be a while before the current generation of students are sitting in boardrooms and legislative chambers, grappling with the pressing issues of their time. But if they are to develop the skills they need to make informed decisions, they must immerse themselves in views they find distasteful and, crucially, engage with people they disagree with. A desire to hear other opinions – not to silence them – is the most effective way to sharpen our own thinking and make our beliefs more robust. Our Freedom of Speech Act is how we will protect this culture within our universities.

I believe in the principle of freedom of speech because I believe that the fundamental well-being of our society rests on our ability to tolerate each other. In the words of the late philosopher Sir Roger Scruton, one of the lecturers I was lucky enough to have during my own time at university: 'Free speech is not the cause of the tensions growing around us, but the only possible solution to them.'

Romulus and Remus, oil on canvas
by Peter Paul Rubens, 1615–16.

IN PURSUIT OF GREATNESS:
FROM TROY TO WESTMINSTER

Daisy Dunn

The peoples of Greece and Rome were inspired by the idea of 'Great Men'. These men were envisaged as having lived hundreds if not thousands of years before in a more glorious age. They were tall and strong and ate so much meat it is a wonder they were not afflicted by gout, and they consorted with women who rivalled goddesses in looks and strength. Many of them were said to have possessed divine blood. Both the mortal and divine ones fascinated the gods, who were described by the poets as orchestrating their lives. They were the sort of characters who populated classical foundation myths.

Every culture has produced foundation myths. These usually take the form of elaborate stories woven to explain the origins of a people and its customs. The Romans, including the historian Livy, wrote of Romulus overthrowing his twin brother Remus to establish his city on the Palatine Hill. The boys were the sons of the war god Mars and Rhea Silvia, the Vestal Virgin he raped, which accounted for the Romans' bellicosity. They were famously nourished by a she-wolf, hence their unnatural strength, before being raised by a shepherd and his wife.

The Romans also venerated Aeneas, who, on a timeline quite incompatible with this story, fought in the Trojan War and escaped the burning citadel with a band of refugees to establish a new home in Italy. Aeneas brought with him his son Ascanius, known to Virgil as Iulus and thus imagined as a founding member of the *gens Iulia*, the family to which Julius Caesar and his great-nephew, the future emperor Augustus, belonged. Virgil's epic poem the *Aeneid* was, at its most basic, an extended foundation myth intended to legitimise, but also subtly critique, the new mode of rule introduced under Augustus following the collapse of the Roman Republic.

In the poem, Aeneas is made to travel through nascent Carthage on his way to Italy and witness for himself the development of a Carthaginian foundation myth. The people of Carthage, situated in the area of Tunis, had recently relocated from Phoenician Tyre (now in Lebanon) and were still in the process of building their new city. It was said that Dido fled her homeland after her brother, Pygmalion, murdered her husband out of desire for his treasure. She led a boatful of disaffected Phoenicians to North Africa, where she requested a patch of land only so big as to be covered by a single ox-hide. Dido cleverly cut the hide into the finest shreds, which she laid end to end upon the ground, thereby encompassing the perimeter of Qart Hadasht – the 'new city' of Carthage. The hill around which Dido supposedly laid her hide is still known as Byrsa, from the Greek for ox-hide. In the *Aeneid*, Dido prays that Aeneas will stay and become part of Carthage's development, but the gods have other ideas for the heroic escapee of Troy.

The Trojan War was a foundation myth of another kind. Most people living in the classical world believed that a war had truly been fought at Troy, situated near the Hellespont in the west of Turkey, and that it marked the separation between old times and new. The war was believed to have been fought about 400 years before the Homeric epics were first written down. The warriors of this period, around the twelfth century BC, were envisaged as far superior to the men who came after them. They were very much of the Great Men mould – Diomedes, a Greek warrior, could lift a boulder that no one living in Homer's generation could – and in many cases boasted divine parentage. We think especially of Aeneas, Achilles and Odysseus.

These fictional characters were on a superficial level the ancient equivalents of modern superheroes. It was not simply children who worshipped them, but grown men, particularly men with political ambitions. Throughout classical history, political leaders strove to claim them as ancestors. Until the sixth century BC, the Greek island of Lesbos was ruled by the Penthilidae, a noble dynasty with origins in Thessaly, northeast Greece. According to Aristotle, the Penthilidae authorised the use of violence against their citizens, who could be flogged or struck with clubs. They might have been far from heroic in their conduct, but the Penthilidae aspired to heroism and declared themselves to be descendants of Orestes, son of Agamemnon, who led the Greek army to victory over Troy in the *Iliad*. In drawing this connection, they perhaps intended to present and justify their heavy-handedness as a legacy of their warrior ancestry. Hundreds of years later, Julius Caesar promoted his alleged lineage via Iulus from Venus, which readers acquainted with Caesar's romantic life might agree was appropriate.

There was clearly much to gain from forging connections with people who had founded thriving cities. Myth and early history were so closely intertwined that some of these lineages even carried a degree of credibility. Some people, such as the historian Thucydides, who claimed descent from the Homeric hero Ajax, probably believed their heroic connections to be real. The Penthilidae of Lesbos did not rest on the laurels of their own nobility. Their name might have been famous on the island and in their native Thessaly for generations, but it had nothing on that of Agamemnon. Claiming to share blood with a hero was not always simply an exercise in establishing legitimacy to rule. It was a way of instilling confidence in voters or in the public they represented. If their ancestors were successful then there was every hope they might be, too.

Foundation myths were often of personal as well as political interest to world leaders. Alexander the Great took a detour in Troy while on campaign to perform honours for Priam, king of Troy, as well as Athena and Achilles, to whom he believed he was related. Alexander kept an edition of the *Iliad* produced by his former tutor Aristotle under his pillow at night. The poem that gave life to the mythical heroes served as a sort of bible. It might have echoed true events to a small degree – the veracity of the Trojan War is still much disputed – but for the most part it would be defined in modern terms as a work of fiction. The distinction between fiction and non-fiction was not drawn in antiquity. The poem contains eternal truths about ruling, serving, fighting and existing that transcend history. It was not wholly opportunistic to seek to establish authority through it.

Modern politicians would be hard-pressed to sustain the tradition and claim allegiance with any figure of the mythical past. Genealogy is now a highly developed discipline. Ancient heroes nevertheless continue to be namechecked. Boris Johnson kept a bust on his desk of Pericles, the populist *strategos*, or general, who oversaw the development of democracy in Athens in the fifth century BC, and has hailed him a personal hero. Born circa 493 BC, Pericles, who held the position of *strategos* every year between 443 BC and his death in 429, helped to direct the adornment of the Parthenon and served as a *choregos* (financial sponsor) of important plays in Athens. He was nevertheless far from perfect, and was, for example, implicated in accusations made against the Parthenon artist Phidias, condemned for impiety after allegedly inserting portraits of himself and Pericles into a sculpture of Athena. To the modern reader, Pericles can also seem a curiously prosaic figure. One of the most egregious quotes attributed to him is: 'Great is the glory of the woman who is least spoken about, whether for good or for ill.'

In his final speech as UK prime minister in September 2022, Johnson referenced another classical hero, Lucius Quinctius Cincinnatus, a politician of fifth-century BC Rome. According to Livy, Cincinnatus had retired from his political life as a senator to tend his modest farm when he was summoned to return to frontline politics. An Italic tribe, the Aequi, had invaded Rome and the situation had become so desperate it was decided a dictator be appointed. Cincinnatus agreed to step into the breach and reportedly brought the conflict to a satisfactory conclusion in just 15 days. Having saved his city, he returned to his plough. Cincinnatus's (alleged) return to power led some quarters of the media to speculate that Johnson intended to do precisely the same. His classical reference was overanalysed and taken as evidence that he believed his work in Downing Street was far from complete. The theory was tempered only slightly by his resignation as an MP in June 2023.

Johnson's successor, Liz Truss, certainly a much spoken-about woman, chose to quote Seneca the Younger in her own parting speech as prime minister in autumn 2022. 'It is not because things are difficult that we do not dare,' she said. 'It is because we do not dare that they are difficult.' Her words were believed to refer to the daringness of the mini-budget introduced during her record brief term. Seneca may lack the heroic cachet of Achilles, but in the Roman world he was idolised for the strength of his convictions. In opening his veins at Emperor Nero's request, he died, according to the mores of the time, a hero's death. Truss's resignation fell far short of being recognised as a heroic act.

Cincinnatus and Seneca are no longer so famous as to constitute part of a universal language. Today's politicians do not quote ancient figures in order to clarify their thoughts. They in fact risk obfuscating their points and driving a wedge between themselves and the public by having recourse to a world that comparatively few now study. So why look to antiquity at all?

Many in Westminster today are naturally aligned with the politicians of the ancient world. They are not seeking to impress with the loftiness of their learning, still less confound with references that many would find oblique. Rather, they reach into antiquity for affirmation of their own authority, in much the same way the rulers of Lesbos did when they promoted their alleged connections to Agamemnon. Contemporary political figures cannot pretend to be blood relations, but they can evoke the spirit of a glorious, now mysterious past. Figures from antiquity, even mythical ones, still have weight in the modern world. The eternal truths that Alexander found in the *Iliad* have come to be attached to antiquity more widely. Ancient wisdom seems almost oracular owing to the mystery that envelops it in the modern imagination. One does not need to understand it to believe that it carries some kind of long-lost truth.

It is in this way that foundation myths continue to grow. There was a tacit assumption in antiquity that *kleos* – an immortal reputation aspired to by Homeric heroes and the politicians who sought to emulate them – could outweigh human flaws. Agamemnon continued to be admired in spite of having sacrificed his own daughter, Iphigenia, to secure a fair wind for his voyage to Troy. His wife Clytemnestra murdered him after he returned home from the war. Cincinnatus was by no means a hero to the plebeians or less wealthy members of Rome, whose interests he did little to champion. One might have expected such factors to render these figures *personae non gratae* in today's flagrantly judgemental society, but we are perhaps more realistic in our approach to the classical world than we are to many later periods of history. Our quest for some hallowed truth in the mists of time propels us to take the bad with the good.

Most importantly, we implicitly understand that heroism is a valuable fiction. This is arguably the most useful lesson to draw from the worlds created by Homer, Virgil and other classical authors. Aside from the flaws individual to each hero – from sulking Achilles to autocratic Augustus – there are flaws inherent to the concept of heroism itself. In the first book of Homer's *Iliad*, Nestor, the elderly king of Pylos, tells Agamemnon and Achilles they are inferior to some of the men he has known in his lifetime, the likes of which, he says, he is unlikely ever to encounter again. It is striking that even Homeric heroes could be outshone by earlier champions. That there is nothing truly 'super' about heroes of the past is important. People embrace them today knowing that they are, in many cases, as flawed as they themselves are and thus fundamentally human.

There is an emptiness to instilling greatness in figures of the past, then, because those self-same figures instilled greatness in their own ancestors, giving rise to a continuous cycle of projecting virtue onto people one can never truly know. This is what Hesiod, Homer's near-contemporary poet, was describing when he outlined the five ages of man in *Theogony* and *Works and Days.* The first of these, the Golden Age, gave way to an inferior Silver Age, which was succeeded in turn by an even worse Bronze Age. There was some respite in the development of the Heroic Age, in which the Trojan War was said to have been fought, but then began a depressing and seemingly endless Iron Age. We recognise in this lineage the fallacy of 'golden-age thinking' and, through this, the fallacy of foundation myths. As fortifying as it may feel to forge connections with the past, in doing so we lay ourselves bare to accusations of not being good enough, not because we fail to measure up in this long descent of man, but because the quest for absolute greatness is ultimately impossible to fulfil.

Seeing as this is so, there is an argument for keeping the ancient foundation myths alive by embracing even their most flawed and double-edged characters, for we are unlikely to find any better. These myths and their reception highlight the fruitlessness of seeking perfection. This is a particularly pertinent consideration in an age of so-called cancel culture, which frequently holds historical figures to account for failing to live up to modern standards of behaviour and ethics. Politicians, ancient and modern, who associate themselves with classical figures for public or private affirmation of their authority provide a useful service. For all that their adoption of classical exempla may seem purely opportunistic and arrogantly fanciful, it serves to remind us that it is possible to distinguish good qualities where bad exist, and to push against the false narrative of eternal decline. The quest for greatness, doomed though it may be, constitutes an essential part of history and our efforts to situate ourselves within it.

'Epicurus', detail from *Scuola di Atene*.
Fresco by Raffaello Sanzio da Urbino, 1511.

EPICURUS, LUCRETIUS AND THE MYTH OF MYTHLESSNESS

David Butterfield

Leadership and statecraft are intimately intertwined. After all, you cannot craft a state without knowing how to lead. And, rather more fundamentally, you cannot lead any populace into crafting a state unless there is some sense of common identity or purpose. The germane question for good and sustainable statecraft therefore lies farther upstream: what is the process whereby a society comes to feel that it is communally associated – and somehow 'in it together'?

This is a large and complex question, and certainly not one that can be answered succinctly. Given the scope of this essay, I do not propose to wade out ill-advisedly into anthropological or sociopolitical waters. Instead, I wish to explore the most primitive and primary catalyst for binding people together and creating the stable environment from which states can emerge: myths.

Just what are myths? To the modern reader, this word seems to be the polar opposite of history proper – historical fiction, not fact. The Greek *mūthos* meant 'story', and was often opposed to *logos*, 'rational account'. On such a model, myths are mere tales, forged by design or happenstance. They are told and retold, either to give people a sense of place in their world or to peddle and propagate some religious or ideological dogma. Nevertheless, it is a mistake to regard such myths, however true or false, as divorced from the daily realities of people's lives, then and now.

In actuality, these shared stories frame and tailor the past in a way that can ground and stabilise a community, however large or small. By situating them within the fabric of history, myths provide a sense of tradition and belonging to rally around. Whether they are preserved orally, or via literary texts, or sacred scripture, they are a tradition that orientates and steers the community. Such is the binding value of myths that they will be kept alive, refreshed and renewed as and when the times require.

Yet we can only progress so far with generalisations like these. In order to find the specifics that will illuminate these claims, my instinct as a classicist is to delve back into the world of ancient Greece and Rome. Among the colourful and conflicting ideas of that age, I will turn to a particularly radical and controversial philosophy, one which will give us serious pause for thought in our modern era.

Myths had multiple modes in antiquity, some more fundamental than others. Among the most important and essential were the fantastic founding myths that ancient cultures told themselves. Athens, for instance, was founded by the goddess Athena, when victorious over her sea-god brother Poseidon; Thebes was founded by the Phoenician king Cadmus after he slew a dragon and generated warriors by planting the dragon's teeth; Rome was founded by Romulus, after his fellow wolf-raised brother disagreed about whose hill should host the new city – and, in a yet earlier sense, the Roman race was founded by the exiled prince Aeneas, fleeing Troy after the Greeks had prevailed. Each of these foundational tales placed citizens in a shared narrative of divine favour, connecting them with larger-than-life figures from the past. Such stories were kept vibrant and relevant by their recurrence in literature, art and religious cults. For ancient Greeks and Romans alike, the lines between myth and history were always blurred: most people did indeed believe in the heroic cast of ancient literature as historical figures, directing their debates instead to questions about which particular tales were the truest. Even if there was always intellectual scepticism from some quarters, that rarely ranged far outside the ivory towers of academia.

Yet these tales, so implicated in each city's identity, were not without political consequences. When Julius Caesar started claiming that he was ultimately descended from Rome's founding father Aeneas, and thus from his mother Venus, he did so by depicting the goddess on his coinage and placing that connection in the literal hands of Romans. Not long after, he broke the age-old taboo and displayed his own face there, too. Such assertive acts of mythmaking laid the ground for his own godhood: after his dictatorship and assassination in 44 BC, his supporters chose to deify him – an act approved by the appearance of the Julian Star, as Halley's Comet did the rounds that July. In turn, this romantic forgery helped inaugurate the Julio-Claudian imperial line, from Divus Augustus to the no less 'divine' Nero. The convention, once established, was not abandoned thereafter – and so the Roman Empire advanced to shape most of Europe and the Mediterranean, and a millennium later much of the wider world.

Myths, then, change societies, for better and worse. But what happens, by turn, when myths are banished from a society, rejected as not just false but entirely meaningless? What happens when reason declares itself supreme over anything regarded as supernatural or irrational or unexplained? This is not the place to do anything more than cast a wary eye over to the French Revolution, and to wonder how much *liberté, égalité* and *fraternité* was bestowed on unwitting Parisians by the Enlightenment-inspired *Culte de la Raison*.

To answer these questions, I turn to a figure who was a countercultural radical in ancient Greece. His ancient influence was relatively small in his own day but would prove to be major some two millennia later. This man was Epicurus, who found his way to Athens from the Greek island of Samos around the year 300 BC, where he established an intellectual community, the Garden. Just like his fellow Samian philosopher, Pythagoras, Epicurus's school was open to all comers, being one of the world's first educational institutions that accepted men and women on equal terms.

Epicurus's philosophy was formulated in a world replete with rival philosophies, after half a millennium of fervid Greek thought. The early philosopher-scientists (such as Thales, Anaximander, Anaxagoras) had sought to understand the world through its material elements; then Socrates and Plato, driven by logical argument and metaphysical speculation, reached beyond for transcendent truths; their ethereal ideas were reined in by the unremitting enquiry and experimentation of Aristotle's ever-revolving mind; and in his wake various rival Hellenistic schools cropped up and chopped up theory to forge the new philosophies of Stoicism, Scepticism, Cynicism and Epicureanism.

To take this account to where it matters, we should summarise the three radical beliefs of Epicurus. The first springs from physics: everything that exists is either matter (stuff) or nothing (void). And all existing matter is made of indivisible and invisible atoms – something we now take for granted but which was deemed an absurd theory in the ancient world.

Second, we humans, however special we may appear, are accordingly made exclusively of atoms and void: there is no third, immaterial part. So, when we die, our atomic bodies and atomic soul – and therefore all that is us – die and disappear, too. There is thus no afterlife, only the one life we experience right now.

Third, the multiple traditional gods do materially exist but they do so remotely, having no interest in our world. Since they do not interact with our daily lives, there is no providence, no divine plan, and no goal for the random amalgam of creatures we call the human race. So, all religion and superstition are not just a waste of time but a harmful delusion.

These three Epicurean tenets – that nothing is immaterial, that no human lives beyond death and that there is nothing divine in or about human existence – were incredibly controversial in the Greco-Roman world, in almost all places and periods. Epicureanism was genuinely eccentric.

As for the devotees of Epicurus and his worldview, what were they to make of their lives? Simple: they were to devote themselves to pleasure – but not the sensuous pleasures of a dissolute life. Rather, true pleasure was secured by the removal of pains, both physical and psychological. Most importantly, comprehending the rational workings of our universe would dispel the mental miseries of misunderstanding. Epicurus's teachings sought to reveal the rational everywhere and to exclude the irrational.

The major cultural obstacle to this mission was myth, especially as preserved in literature. Epicurus did not hesitate to dismiss the *Iliad* and the *Odyssey*, those great epic poems of quasi-biblical status, as the mere 'babblings of Homer'. Since these tales told untruths, Epicurus sought to understand how these superstitious tales emerge and have such a hold on society.

Epicurus's answer does not survive. But we can reconstruct it by turning to his most famous Roman adherent, the poet Lucretius, who was active in the Republic in the 50s BC. In the hope of captivating and converting his fellow citizens to the counterintuitive philosophy of Epicureanism, Lucretius crafted a remarkably ambitious, almost hubristic, work of literature: a six-book, 7,500-verse Latin poem *De rerum natura* (*On the nature of things* – ie *On Everything*).

This stubbornly dogmatic – and stunningly beautiful – poem pursues its graduated curriculum with remorseless logic. It journeys from the microscopic movement of atoms, through the workings of our human bodies, up to the macroscopic survey of subterranean regions and the heavens above. Despite being a technical poem based on atomic physics, it is replete with Lucretius's personal passion.

At repeated points in his poem, Lucretius dismisses popular myths as foolish misunderstandings of the rational truths of an atomically ordered world. In the latter half of Book Five, we encounter his famous account of how and why humans evolved. They were a chance creation – anthropo-morphic but animal-like, primitive humans who were able to survive in their challenging environment. According to Epicurean theory, it was pure chance that they existed as they did, and that they were able to survive for an unknown number of generations.

Lucretius is curiously ambivalent about whether human societies are in progress or decline. The ingenuity of humans meant that innovation was inevitable, and that new and advantageous technologies would accrue. Yet the arrival of these crafts – metalworking, seafaring, militarisation – did more harm than good, encouraging commercial greed, power-lust and widespread slaughter. Lucretius's strong message is that society does not progress hand in hand with the passing of time.

Crucially, Lucretius includes among the mixed blessings of human ingenuity the creation of superstitions about our world. He argues that myths about the gods were devised and propagated by early humans because they failed to understand the phenomena of their lives – be they wondrous events in the natural world, or the bewildering experiences of the human mind awake and asleep. Having made this fundamental error, they made the much more harmful misstep of assuming that the gods were actively in control of human life, and that they demanded sacrifice and appeasement to avoid wreaking their vengeful wrath.

So, for Epicureans, humans are utterly devoid of purpose. They are neither created for anything nor going anywhere. Worse than that, the tales they tell about mankind's origin, divine providence and future glories are false and pernicious. Epicurus's solution was to retreat from the misguided world and to spend his life in quiet philosophical contemplation with friends.

We may sympathise. The outcome for any society that believes itself to be unrooted from any broader frame of purpose is inevitable. It immerses itself in the vivid present: the current moment, here and now, is paramount in the absence of any shared duty to the past or communal hope for the future. This presentism has a feedback loop: it inevitably distracts people from active participation in broader structures – the nation, the civic community and even the family – and instead turns the focus reflexively onto the individual. Two outcomes soon follow from such a stance.

First, there is a withdrawal from politics. After all, why have a stake in shaping the public sphere when your concerns do not extend beyond yourself? The ancient Greeks, in Athens and elsewhere, had a name for such apolitical figures: an *idiōtēs*, which – rather revealingly – lies behind our own 'idiot'. To give up on the activity of your *polis*, or city, was to behave like a self-absorbed fool. In turn, if citizens chose to withdraw from the public sphere and band together around a new, private entity, they would soon retreat into a cult; unfettered by wider community restraints, and with no mooring in the grand historical frame, they could rapidly find themselves spinning out of control.

Second, if all people are reduced by such an outlook to mere individuals, bereft of shared traditions and any civic grouping between single persons and all humankind, then everyone is in practice reduced to mere identical units in the body politic as a whole. This creates the void of meaning in which authoritarian figures can not just emerge but reach for totalitarian solutions. The populace at large is primed to receive a new binding ideology – not one organically formed and shaped over generations from the bottom up, but one imposed anew from the top, and perhaps based on nothing real at all.

Both of these outcomes – forgoing any stake in the political sphere to retreat into an orthodox cult or opening the door and ushering in a dictatorial ideologue – are manifestly societal failures.

To take the position that societies are harmed by their socially constructed myths is not just unhelpful but empirically unsound. What is more, it is untrue, but told to give certain ideological groups their legitimacy. In other words, it is a myth. The fact is that cross-culturally, throughout the human world, myths are ubiquitous, both in the present and in the past. In almost all societies they help embed a sense of meaning and belonging. And for that purpose, the truth or falsehood is largely irrelevant, so long as it serves to ground and bind a community. While many of these mythic traditions may – if misapplied or distorted – emerge to be harmful or deleterious, in all cases they do forge a body politic that leads to a coherently crafted state.

To close, we may return to Lucretius as a sobering case study of my argument – for his rational philosophy adopted the very irrationality it feared. Epicurus had argued that living a life free from pain could give you a life 'worthy of the gods'. Remarkably, Lucretius not only accepted this, but came to regard his master as godlike. In fact, in one famous line he declares *deus ille fuit, deus* – 'that man was a god, a god!' Withdrawn from the sociopolitical fray of life in late-Republican Rome, Lucretius relapsed into a fundamental devotion to Epicurus as the sole gospel;

ignoring the many philosophical and scientific developments in the quarter-millennium between his master and himself, Lucretius sought out the words of Epicurus alone, and with the zeal of a fundamentalist. Despite the rational truths that had been revealed in the world outside, the intellectual shutters of Lucretius's mind remained closed.

We know nothing of the man's own life. Perhaps he lived the life of a rebel, perhaps that of a recluse. At any rate, this astoundingly beautiful poem – one of the most arresting artistic achievements in world literature – failed to change the world as he hoped. Its chief influence, evidenced most notably in the Augustan poets Virgil, Horace and Ovid, was *literary*. No surviving author from the first hundred years after Lucretius's death cited the work directly, and no Roman testimony survives praising the *poem's* intellectual achievement. On the contrary, the Christian Church Fathers, most prominently Lactantius, mocked and vilified it as the dangerously misconceived undertaking of a delirious author. In a similarly malicious spirit, tales circulated in later chroniclers, such as St Jerome, about Lucretius committing suicide by drinking a love potion. Lucretian *ratio*, or reason, was defeated by human reality.

Perhaps this is the idea with which to close: societies without myths – without those tales we each tell ourselves for all manner of reasons – are without meaning. And such societies can and will be misled, steered towards certain disaster and destruction. The only uncertainty for these deracinated communities is when, not if, that sad fate comes.

Officer cadets at the Passing Out Parade at
Sandhurst Royal Military Academy, Surrey, UK.

HEROIC LEADERSHIP:
ITS TIME IS OVER

Edward Stringer

This essay is less a rigorous academic treatise and more of a personal reflection after a 39-year military career where I undertook almost every command and leadership course a 'baby general' could before owning the campus myself during my final tour as Director General of the UK Defence Academy. In between these mostly enjoyable bouts of academic leisure, I had a varied career split between operations overseas and tours in Whitehall, including being the MOD's director of military operations for nearly three years. Across that time, I had much exposure to the most senior ranks, both home and away, and so could correlate what we taught our putative general class as an ideal, and what we actually got in return as learned behaviour. I was guided throughout by the old family wisdom passed on by my mother: if you want to know what people really think, look at what they do, don't listen to what they say. This is, in essence, just the concept of revealed preference. And this short think-piece is my assessment of what is revealed by what we teach and then measure – because you get what you measure…

Rather than look at examples of individual leadership in practice and try to generalise from them, this paper looks at the interaction of doctrine – what we teach – and promotion pathways – how people actually progress – in order to try to assess what we are likely to encourage. It will then look at real world outcomes to see if there is any evidence for the hypothesis. Finally, it will suggest why our current doctrine, which has a defensible rationale, might be wrong for the age we are now entering: the digital age, a world where data rules, and where quantum computer-powered artificial intelligence (AI) might be able to provide military intelligence such as we have never had before. If it does, this must have a bearing on decision-making; military leadership at its core is about making difficult decisions in challenging circumstances.

Myths and symbols persist, and the most persistent myth of UK military leadership is that of military genius, symbolised by the kingfisher bird. It is the chosen emblem of the pivotal course in any general's career: the Higher Command and Staff Course, undertaken at the main Defence Academy campus at Shrivenham. The kingfisher was selected as the course's symbol as it provides the metaphor at the heart of T. E. Lawrence's quote on generalship: 'Nine-tenths of tactics are certain, and taught in books, but the irrational tenth is like the kingfisher flashing across the pool, and that is the test of generals.'

And there is a secondary symbolism because Lawrence is an almost uniquely romantic, individual and heroic figure of military folklore. A man achieving great success against the odds, not through leading a team of brother officers (this was pre-gender neutrality) but through his own foresight, brilliance, energy, dash and ability to impose his will.

His quote is explicit. Any competent officer can be taught 90% of what he needs to know and be; that is but rational assessment and studied management of a headquarters and its battle rhythm. But there remains that last 10%, 'the irrational tenth', that is beyond such prosaic language. This is the unteachable but unmissable quality of poetry in motion. It is the vision that pierces the fog of war, to discern what no other mortals can see. This even has a military term: *coup d'œil*, the sweep of the eye that takes in the essence of the tableau in front and subliminally makes immediate sense of it. And having done so the general can then display the 'kingfisher moment' when, intuitively understanding the mind of his opposing general, and with his own troops firmly believing in his vision, he produces, *deus ex machina*, the unexpected but brilliant checkmate manoeuvre. There is even a name for this: operational art. And the unofficial but widely used associated term to define those so naturally gifted: an operational artist.

All this is defensible. Who wouldn't want imaginative commanders with drive and energy who, through personal charisma and effort of will, can command the loyalty of the fighting troops beneath them and win? And if a commander uses their staff appropriately, then they can add such personal value while maximising the talents of the whole – in support but also in challenging, loyal opposition that works through the options. This is the ideal of the wise general, but we must go back to the beginning of a career to look at how officers get to be selectable for the senior courses and highest positions, and so what is likely to transpire in reality.

Every officer cadet arriving at the Royal Military Academy Sandhurst will quickly have drilled into them the mantra that 'the only thing worse than a bad plan is no plan at all!' For someone about to become a junior officer in direct control of troops this is but common sense. If you have just received a panicky message that the enemy is about to descend on you in 20 minutes, you have 19 minutes to cobble together a plan that is good enough, and one minute to sell it to your troops in such a way that they believe in you and, by extension, it. And so will fight with belief.

Such situations for a junior officer are rarely likely to pose wicked problems, and so rules of thumb, heuristics and common sense dictate the plan. Salesmanship, looking confident even if you harbour some doubts, help you sell the plan as you brief your subordinates. Competence in these two capacities will see you through much of your time as a junior officer. Add in published doctrine's emphasis on 'tempo' and 'offensive action', and you have a culture where he who darts in first with something plausible wins.

And which senior officer doesn't want smart juniors who can be thrown a fast ball when in a hole and deal with it? Such juniors do well, and so they get promoted at the first look, for our quite rigid promotion hierarchy only allows promotion of the cohorts who left Sandhurst within a set window. Those who leap through the window as it opens are openly referred to as 'first look promotees' and their cards are marked accordingly. The best jobs follow (known as 'black bag' jobs), which are likely to gather the strongest performance report tariffs, and so this cohort is the one in the van when the second window opens, and so on. (This is not unique to the military – see Malcom Gladwell's *Outliers* for the unwitting bias in outwardly meritocratic systems.) It is all but impossible to catch up if you are a late developer. Or unlucky. Or don't do everything you can to game the system.

So we now have the seed-corn to make senior, strategic rank. And the qualities that define them are not necessarily the abilities required in more senior posts where challenges are more intractable and complex 'wicked' problems present themselves. This cohort are likely to include those who can throw something together off the cuff (cuffers), those who can style it out (bluffers) and those who seized the moment with elbows sharpened (chancers). Which is not to say such streetwise attributes aren't useful, and it is good to have leaders focused on outputs and winning. But it doesn't necessarily make you Eisenhower.

Having completed unit command as a major discriminating event, the pivotal selection is the one for the Higher Command and Staff Course.

Indeed, this is such a venturi for higher rank that failure to be selected can be the make-or-break moment that sees some officers deciding to leave their service. And this is the course that has the kingfisher as its motif, already discussed, the symbol of brilliance so emblematic it features on the tie that graduates are allowed to wear.

Repeated attempts by the college directing staff to make this course genuinely educational, a curious and questioning period of reflection on doctrine, tend to founder on the established view that it must be a selection course too – it must have winners and losers. Being expressly competitive, and of quite short duration at four months, the behaviour encouraged has been described, in modern parlance, as 'toxic'. Indeed, a graduate from one of the security services recently returned to her service and recommended that no one be sent next year as she had found the experience so draining. Not all courses are like that – but the incentives are always there, pushing it that way.

And it is on this course that the idea of military genius is rehearsed most energetically, and from it our leading graduates will emerge as fully fledged generals. They will have studied the major role models of wartime generalship, and those from the UK still hail from the Second World War. They will have studied the political-military interface. And so Churchill and the relationship he had with his Chiefs of Staff committee and his field generals will have featured. It is worth, then, looking at Churchill's own assessment of what makes a great general. The following quote from Churchill was cited by Field Marshal Carver in his monograph on Montgomery. It came from Churchill's biography of his ancestor, the great general John Churchill, Duke of Marlborough, that he wrote just before the Second World War.

'[The war's] highest solution must be evolved from the eye and brain and soul of a single man', and, dismissing the efforts of 'almost any intelligent scribe [who] can draw up a lucid and logical treatise full of laboriously ascertained facts and technical phrases on a particular war situation', he asserted that 'Nothing but genius, the daemon in man, can answer the riddles of war, and genius, though it may be armed, cannot be acquired, either by reading or by experience.'

The language here is emotive. Through it, Churchill can be seen to be an evangelical advocate of the 'general as born genius' theory. Add in General Alanbrooke, whose wartime diaries are still a bible for the modern, ambitious general and who, despite their airing his frequent frustration with Churchill, also reinforces the charismatic, genius general trope, and a pattern to emulate starts to emerge.

'Getting on' still hinges on giving your superiors the impression that you have 'it'. 'It' is undefined, and, indeed, unmeasurable. But it clearly suggests you are one of Napoleon's 'lucky generals', a charismatic practitioner of the operational arts. You have the mark of genius, an intuitive capacity to win that transcends rational explanation. And all this bolstered by the fact that the superior general assessing whether one has 'it' or not doesn't himself have to justify it either – this too being an intuitive judgement. No wonder that the military's senior leadership tends to follow tribal cycles.

Why should we worry about any of this? Why would we not want our generals to be charismatic, flair players? There are two answers to this, one general and one specific to today.

The general point I shall hurry over. In short, it is striking that when one lists the impressively competent generals from the Second World War, Churchill tried to have several of them removed. Usually for not being swashbuckling enough and providing, instead, realistic assessments of often dire situations; sometimes, one senses, for simply not having what Churchill considered to be 'the right stuff'. Thus, for example, both Tedder and Slim were on the receiving end of Churchill's ire and desire for them to be replaced. History finds no two better commanders than these two. Meanwhile, some pretty monstrous egos, such as late-era Montgomery, were tolerated long after replacing them might have been wise. And those upon whom Churchill had a professional crush based more than a little on 'appearance and bearing', such as Alexander, were always favoured regardless of results.

In linking to the specifics of today we might first, paradoxically, go back to the transition into the current era, the age of industrial warfare – commonly accepted to begin with the rapid evolution of warfare during the American Civil War of 1860–65. The macro-observation is that the Southern states are widely considered to have had the best battlefield commanders, in Jackson, Longstreet and Stuart, but they lost the war. And it was lost for many geostrategic reasons that demonstrate that war and warfare are not the same thing. Among them are the finances of war and the use of modern methods of production and communication, against which fighting with tactical flair and charisma in set-piece battles did little more than stave off strategic defeat for a while.

The linking figure that brings us back to the specific arguments of today is Ulysses S. Grant.

When the war started, Grant was a struggling figure, having left the army after an unremarkable career largely spent in the back-room divisions of supply and administration. A reserved character, he had, as John Keegan writes, always lost out to 'bustling, bonhomious, chance-grabbing optimists'. But come the war, civilian-led advances in these vital logistic capacities, in which he had specialised, were fundamentally rewriting the character of war. He promoted rapidly to senior rank officers who had only recently joined up but who brought in expertise in the railway and the telegraph. One hundred and sixty years later, as we move from the Industrial to the Information Age, we find ourselves in a similar position of warfare being in a state of flux, as it ineluctably follows the socioeconomic transition.

As Director General Joint Force Development, in 2018 I wrote this introduction to a primer that sought to explain what Information Age warfare could look like:

> Rapid evolution of the internet and the global market in data it has created are altering the fabric of society, its economy and its labour market. This is usually described as the dawn of the Information Age. Businesses that saw the possibilities early and adapted have thrived; those that clung to the ways of the Industrial Age, even with a veneer of modernising 'IT', are withering. We are still coming to terms with its ramifications: the influence of the echo chambers of social media; the effect on markets of companies that can eavesdrop on the fears and desires of its customer base, and manipulate them; the philosophical implications of an artificial intelligence that can tell us what to do but cannot tell us why.
>
> Just as the factory, telegraph, railroad and machine-gun ushered in industrial warfare and wars of production, the information age will bring in information warfare in turn. We have seen how the introduction of cyber, space, electronic warfare and drones has altered the 'ways' of the final chapter of industrial warfare. It has been a rapid evolution. But the convergence of four key technologies of the information age – cloud computing, robotics, artificial intelligence and big data – promises to revolutionise warfare as surely as the Industrial Revolution did.

In the five years since then, Ukraine has revealed what a country with a peacetime defence budget one twelfth of that of the UK, or less than 1% of that of the USA, can do when it applies just some of these largely civilian, or 'dual-use', technologies to reimagine modern warfare. Behind the horrors of Industrial Age warfare that persist, the brutal battles of artillery, the advantage that Ukraine has crafted is built on better, more imaginative and flexible organisation of its fighting forces. Musk's Starlink, Palantir's data-analysis tools, myriad civilian drones – all have all been repurposed and integrated via the cloud into a slick system of advanced military command and control.

It has happened as well and as fast as it has because Zelensky has employed civilians with tech backgrounds to digitise the whole of the government's executive branches, including the military. Mykhailo Fedorov was a 28-year-old tech entrepreneur when he was appointed as the minister in charge in 2019. Even more remarkably, they have rebuilt not from an already advanced Western baseline, but from a recent post-Soviet one. It has been a stunning achievement.

Even so, it has achieved but a fraction of what is theoretically possible, were the combinations of AI, data-at-the-edge and autonomous systems to be unleashed by a NATO budget. What can be said is that command and control already looks different. The networks are flatter and faster, less hierarchical, more adaptable. They require more cooperation across traditional command boundaries, which often have a simple hierarchical and geographic framing. Understanding how these networks function in practice will become a vital command skill. And that is before you further enhance a commander's understanding with the products of artificial intelligence. AI will alter decision-making and, as military leadership is ultimately about making decisions under pressure, it should alter our approach to leadership too.

As yet it is unclear how, but a glance at some analogous areas is illuminating. The world of chess is centred on competitive strategy and it has been upended by AI. Two decades ago the greatest grand master (Kasparov) was beaten by a machine, and machines have advanced exponentially since those relatively crude programmes that with brute force amalgamated all previous human game knowledge. Now, such machines as built by DeepMind – AlphaGo and AlphaZero – can teach themselves from first principles in hours and can produce moves humans had not previously considered. It is now axiomatic that no grand master can beat a machine; a good one playing very well might draw.

This has caused some to lament what has been lost, and in shades redolent of operational art: Oliver Roeder of the *FT*, in noting that 'Chess used to be an art', appears to be accepting that science has taken over. Some grand masters decry that intuition and brilliance have been lost to mechanics. Others, though, have used the machine to make them better players. Kasparov himself has cautioned that too many young players have gone the other way and now always uncritically follow the machine. But to understand fully what is going on requires a team of chess coaches, data scientists and programmers. This man-machine team becomes a better chess player. Better than one relying on practice and the odd flash of instinctive brilliance – even if they might be more naturally talented.

The febrile world of finance provides intriguing parallels, not least in the persona of the fund manager as lucky general. As Nicholas Taleb notes in *Fooled By Randomness*, if you analyse the performance of multiple hedge funds over time, then they produce slightly fewer successes than should be the case if random decisions were taken. But we don't tend to see it that way; we create backwards narratives that explain why some financial geniuses have been successful so that we may follow them. Whole industries are created around emulating what author Tom Wolfe characterised as the 'Masters of the Universe'. And they are only slightly dented when a 'Master' then falls spectacularly, so atavistic is our longing for compelling narratives and to explain success in heroic terms.

In reality, much trading is now driven at frantic speed by algorithms. To seek an advantage for a while was to understand the data latency in fibre-optic transmission of laser pulses. Physical geography had more of a bearing than the intuitive genius of the guru. In reality it is the 'quants', the mathematical and computational 'nerds', who have made companies fortunes while the public front remains Wolfe's Masters.

There is another argument to be explored here: is being good at the stock market dependent on being good at the fundamentals of business and economics, or more concerned with understanding, and perhaps manipulating, the herd mentality of investors? If the latter, then it makes perfect sense to create a persona of confident invulnerability, as your own words and deeds might well shape that market to profitable effect. Is this not a similar argument to that made of our generals: all victories in the end come down to battles between the moral components of each side, and so a belief in, or fear of, the genius general could sway both sides profitably? Soviet generals used to scoff at their British counterparts, noting that every German the British came up against was 'a genius', while they had no trouble beating them all. There is evidence of this 'Rommel Effect' in the behaviour of some British generals of the Second World War. In peacetime, of course, such manoeuvrings can be useful in Whitehall funding battles.

There must be some truth in the idea of charismatic generals bolstering the belief of troops under their command and, therefore, their essential morale. The argument of this think-piece is not that such attributes are harmful per se. It is that if we fetishise the idea of good generalship being an innate product of genius – one the general himself might not be able to explain – then we risk a version of moral hazard: in their desire to demonstrate these qualities our officers might be encouraged to gamble, overreach and, perhaps, cover up until they can make good. And when they do finally make general rank, then they can inhale their own smoke and believe they don't have to justify decisions that may in reality be little more than whimsical. The heroic school of leadership can lead to superheated command systems where competitive personalities and egos dominate.

There is current evidence for this, which one doesn't want to explore in too much detail as it gets personal very quickly. But one notes that the government has had to instigate many formal inquiries recently: from Chilcot through the withdrawal from Kabul to the waste of billions of pounds within the Ajax programme and the RAF's recruiting scandal. Core themes are optimism bias and failure to transmit reports of failure upwards for resolution, even unto dissembling. Staffs are used to make so the general's 'vision and intent' as much as to analyse from first principles, or provide constructive challenge. Around this time, in separate cases, several senior officers were cashiered – one even sent to prison – for offences whose roots were in high-handed arrogance or entitlement.

In 2021, Simon Akam wrote a long book on recent command failings in the British Army: *The Changing of the Guard*. While some critics found it may have over-reached, many other credible voices saw the kernels of truth in it. Frank Ledwidge's generally well-reviewed *Losing Small Wars* made similar points. It is hard to boil the arguments down to a single sentence, but the essence of them is that the Army is a complacent, tribal organisation living on its reputation, the 'can do' attitude, and fooling itself. Indeed, that very fetishising of established shibboleths prevents necessary reform. Throughout, there is a sense of career competitiveness intruding on what should be purely operational matters. Such accusations are not invalid.

These general criticisms of heroic leadership apply in any era, and are countered to an extent by the argument already raised that we need decisive generals able to function in the fog of war. But as we move into the Information Age our generals will have quants of their own. AI will chew over many orders of magnitude more data – Top Secret to Open Source – than any previous 'mandraulic' system could hope to have assimilated, let alone cross-referenced. Its algorithms will have self-trained by endlessly churning mass data such that they are now beyond the initial programmer's understanding of how they 'think'. They will generate both counterintuitive analysis and options for action. How then is a system predicated on the intuition and instinct of a single genius general going to cope?

The answer is we don't know. But I will offer that we ought to approach the question in a spirit of open-minded enquiry and curiousness, not with an instinctive sense of the answer before we start. We need to be like savvy bank bosses who can see the nerds might make better bets. Or the chess grand masters who realised that the man-machine team might make them better players. In short, it is time to revisit the fetishes of our current teachings on command and generalship. The demands of the future are not those of the past. Those whose success was built on an intuitive sense of how to game the previous era's incentives are the least likely to be able to adapt to the counterintuitive possibilities of tomorrow.

The conclusion of this essay is not that the UK military has got everything wrong, nor that it cannot produce some excellent commanders across all three services. It is one of shade and emphasis. If you fetishise a leadership style centred on the genius of the individual, within a peacetime structure that is explicitly competitive, then you must expect to get more of the behaviour that plays explicitly to such incentivisation. It also has a self-sustaining quality that makes it hard to shift. These traits can be corrosive at the best of times, even if considered necessary in some circumstances. In the emerging epoch, where the general's intuition might be trumped by the collective wisdom of a man-machine team, they may be actively regressive.

Thomas C. Schelling receives the Nobel Prize in
Economic Sciences from King Carl XVI Gustaf of
Sweden during a ceremony at the Concert Hall in
Stockholm, 10 December 2005.

DETERRENCE AND COMPELLENCE
IN FOREIGN POLICY:
THE IMPORTANCE OF UNDERSTANDING
A COUNTRY'S ADVERSARIES

Elisabeth Braw

Convincing countries not to engage in destructive actions ought to be straightforward: a group of other countries simply point out that doing so would come at a substantial cost. The same principle applies to the criminal justice system. But the challenge in deterring nation states is that a country's leaders may not be deterred by the prospective punishment – because the announced punishment may not bother them in the way that, say, a long prison term bothers a prospective murderer. Indeed, war is once again raging in Europe because a country's leaders were not deterred by the punishment outlined by other countries. That's a painful reminder that deterrence (preventing negative actions) and compellence (enticing positive actions) are not an absolute science: they have to be targeted not just with a country in mind but with its leaders in mind too.

In January 1991, after Saddam Hussein's Iraq had invaded Kuwait and refused all international pleas to withdraw, President George H W Bush wrote him a letter, which Secretary of State James Baker delivered to Foreign Minister Tariq Aziz. 'Iraq is already feeling the effects of the sanctions mandated by the United Nations. Should war come, it will be a far greater tragedy for you and your country,' the US president wrote to his Iraqi counterpart. 'The American people would demand the strongest possible response. You and your country will pay a terrible price if you order unconscionable acts of this sort.'

Aziz refused to accept the letter. In a subsequent interview for a documentary about the war, he explained what transpired after Baker handed him the letter. 'I read [the letter] very carefully. And then when I ended reading it, I told him, "Look, Mr Secretary, this is not the kind of correspondence between two heads of state. This is a letter of threat, and I cannot receive from you a letter of threat to my president", and I returned it to him.' Aziz then told Baker: 'Mr Secretary, Iraq is a very ancient nation, we lived for six thousand years. I have no doubts that you are a very powerful nation, I have no doubts that you have a very strong military machine and you'll inflict on us heavy losses, but Iraq will survive and this leadership will decide the future of Iraq.'

Despite reminding Saddam of its superior armed forces and fearsome weaponry, the world's undisputed superpower had failed to force the hand of his economically struggling mid-sized power in the Middle East. The United States failed because it used the wrong threats: Aziz knew that Saddam would not be fazed by a US military attack.

Would Aziz and Saddam have reacted differently if Bush had threatened, say, permanent Western entry bans and asset freezes for Saddam and his extended family? We'll never know. But we do know that in issuing his threats to Saddam, Bush engaged in mirror-imaging: he issued threats of a kind that would have caused him to reconsider prospective actions. But the motivations of a democratically elected leader are highly likely to differ from those of an autocrat, because the democratically elected leader cares about his or her country, at the very least because he or she would face being voted out of power if they put the country in serious jeopardy. Autocrats habitually argue that they act on behalf of their citizens, but in reality they act in a manner that serves their interests or ideology, usually at the expense of most of their citizens. That's what Saddam did, not just in invading Kuwait but throughout his decades-long rule. That's what Adolf Hitler did, what Josef Stalin did, what Muammar Gaddafi did, what autocrats behind the Iron Curtain did and what other autocrats around the rest of the world have done and are still doing. It's no coincidence that Vladimir Putin and his top advisors have spent years pursuing aggression that brings their citizens economic hardship and isolation, while their own family members have been enjoying life in the West and, in many cases, own properties there.

So, what if an invasion of Ukraine prompts Western governments to impose sanctions that make Western consumer goods more expensive or unavailable in Russia? What if such an invasion triggers visa bans for ordinary Russians? That's what has happened since Putin ordered Russia's invasion of Ukraine. He knew it would happen because Western leaders had said that was the sort of punishment he could expect if he invaded Ukraine. But he invaded anyway.

Deterrence theory, as perfected by Thomas Schelling and others during the Cold War, rests on punishment. The deterring side has to signal to a potential aggressor that the prospective aggression will be avenged with punishment so severe that the benefit of the aggression will not be worth the cost. The question is, what's severe enough to alter the prospective aggressor's cost-benefit calculus? When I first started working on deterrence of grey-zone aggression (aggression in the grey zone between war and peace, which includes disinformation and cyber and economic subversion), a radio interviewer asked me what kind of punishment Western countries should signal they'd impose on countries engaging in such activities. I mentioned a couple of ideas, whereupon a military analyst who served as the channel's expert commentator declared my ideas nonsense, 'because we have nukes'.

Yes, nuclear weapons are the ultimate punishment, but as George H W Bush found out, they don't work as a deterrent if the prospective aggressor doesn't take the threat of them seriously. Saddam didn't think the United States would drop nuclear bombs on Iraq if his forces remained in Kuwait, and countries engaging in grey-zone aggression certainly don't believe Western countries will avenge such acts by firing nuclear missiles at them. That's because, as Schelling never ceased to point out, deterrence by punishment has to be proportionate in order to be credible. If the threatened punishment is disproportionate to the act it seeks to deter, the prospective aggressor will rightly conclude that it won't be used.

Deterrence by punishment also has to be specific. If the prospective punishment causes harm to large numbers of people, including the leaders, the leaders may consider it tolerable. If, however, the prospective harm concerns only the leaders, they may think twice. That's why many homeowners put angry-dog warnings on their front doors, and that's why liberal democracies have a criminal justice system that sends offenders (but not their families) to prison. We know that the prospect of being bitten by an angry dog or spending time in jail discourages a fair amount of people from engaging in criminal acts. No criminal justice system in a democracy can, of course, threaten or use collective punishment, while leaders act on behalf of their countries, which can be punished as a result of their leaders' actions. Nevertheless, the threat of punishment targeted at a country's leaders is more likely to change their cost-benefit calculus than the threat of punishment spread evenly across the population.

Countries wanting to change foreign leaders' cost-benefit calculi thus need to understand what motivates them and what matters to them. During the Second World War and especially during the Cold War, the CIA and other agencies assembled psychological profiles of world leaders ranging from Adolf Hitler to Saddam Hussein. Because the profiles were written by psychologists, not deterrence specialists, they unsurprisingly focused on character traits. The psychologists found Hitler to be an insecure, impotent, masochistic and suicidal narcissist; regarding Saddam Hussein, the psychologists declared that 'in pursuit of his messianic dreams, there is no evidence he is constrained by conscience; his only loyalty is to Saddam Hussein'. Fidel Castro was deemed 'so highly neurotic and unstable a personality as to be quite vulnerable to certain kinds of psychological pressure'.

Such findings about foreign leaders, however partial – it was clearly not possible for American government psychologists to examine the leaders in person – are crucial as countries try to deter aggression by hostile countries. Yet the CIA profiles and similar profiles other Western governments may have assembled don't seem to have been used in deterrence planning. It wasn't just Saddam Hussein who was presented with deterrence-by-punishment signalling that seemed to Western leaders extraordinarily compelling but failed, because the Iraqi leader was unfazed by such threats. Time and again other regional autocrats have faced similar punishment and disregarded it. Indeed, one might argue that the only power on which NATO's nuclear-based deterrence signalling has had an effect was the Soviet Union and its Warsaw Pact allies because they were led by mostly rational individuals and the nuclear threat was proportionate and thus credible. We don't know whether NATO's nuclear-based deterrence signalling did change any minds in Moscow. Did Moscow consider military attacks on a NATO member state but reconsider after taking the expected retaliation into account? We don't know. After the end of the Cold War, historians and political scientists had a unique opportunity to measure the effect of Western deterrence signalling by interviewing officials and leaders in charge of Warsaw Pact countries during the Cold War. That was not done. There seem to have been no such interviews with Saddam Hussein either.

What's clear, though, is that most deterrence and compellence signalling is far more complicated than it was with the relatively straightforward case of the Warsaw Pact, precisely because in order to work it needs to be based on the to-be-deterred countries' leaders' motivations and desires. The leaders' motivations and desires, and their loyalties and weaknesses, will differ from person to person, just as we all have different motivations and desires. And as we have seen, autocratic leaders are unlikely to be motivated by what's best for their country. As Joachim Wiegand, the highly successful head of the Stasi's church division, explained to me (for my book *God's Spies*) when we discussed how his department identified which pastors might be suitable prospects for recruitment as agents: 'First you need to understand what makes him tick.'

Indeed, first you need to understand what makes the person tick. Instead, Western governments habitually take a, dare I say, Marxist approach to deterrence. That approach is based on a mechanistic understanding of human behaviour that assumes that if condition A exists and the government responds with B, the result is C. But precisely because humans have a range of motivations and desires, and because those motivations and desires differ from one person to the next, it's indispensable to understand the foreign leader whose actions are to be deterred (or compelled) and tailor the messaging correspondingly.

Take the mindset of the invasion of Ukraine. Once it was clear that Putin was preparing for an invasion, Western politicians energetically did their very best to deter it. They did so by imposing economic sanctions and by other threats. But Putin has never given the impression of primarily wanting to improve the lot of the Russian people, and in recent years he hasn't put their interests first. The Russian president and his top lieutenants also knew that Western governments were likely to impose visa bans and asset freezes on them, but since they rarely holiday in the West they clearly considered this an acceptable price.

What makes Putin tick? That's what governments would have needed to establish in order to threaten punishment that would hurt or frighten him. A promising option would have been to focus on Alina Kabaeva, Putin's rumoured girlfriend of a decade, and her young children, of whom Putin is thought to be the father. Over the years, she and the children have lived in Switzerland for long periods of time; Kabaeva indisputably enjoys a Western lifestyle. By threatening an end to that glittery life, and the associated right to travel within the Schengen area, if Putin invaded Ukraine, Western governments could have triggered a brutally honest conversation between Putin and Kabaeva. Other family members and associates of Putin and his top lieutenants, too, have for years been enjoying a glamorous life in the West. Foreign Minister Sergey Lavrov's 26-year-old stepdaughter Polina Kovaleva owns a £4.4 million apartment in the swanky London neighbourhood of Kensington, and his daughter, Ekaterina Vinokurova, lived in New York for many years.

Any threat involving sanctions on Kabaeva or other well-connected Russians living in Switzerland would admittedly have had to be led by Berne, which has been slow to take action against Russia. But it would have been worth a try, just as threatening to impose sanctions on Kovaleva, Vinokurova, Putin's daughters and other Russians connected to the leadership would have been worth a try. In the end, the UK sanctioned Kabaeva in May 2022, the EU sanctioned her in June and the United States in August. After the war began, a combination of sanctions were imposed on Kovaleva, Vinokurova and Putin's daughters. As punishment, the sanctions were justified and necessary. But they could have been tested as a deterrent before the invasion.

What makes a foreign leader tick is indeed the central question for Western governments to ask as more and more countries retreat into autocracy and as the rules-based international order continues to crumble. With the United Nations no longer able to keep order the way it was designed to, countries committed to peace and democracy will need to collectively compel other countries to do the right thing – compellence – or at least deter them from taking aggressive action against other countries. It has never been more important to understand how leaders and their top lieutenants tick.

Take Xi Jinping, who is rumoured to have designs on Taiwan. Under Xi's leadership, China has also been engaging in increasingly frequent hostile behaviour towards Vietnam and the Philippines. While the country is unlikely to attack them militarily, it's likely to continue harassing them, especially at sea. What makes Xi tick? It's not the prosperity of the Chinese people, or otherwise he would be a more attentive steward of his country's economy. It may be the well-being of the Chinese Communist Party, or of his phalanx of the CCP. Or it may be the well-being of Xi, his wife and their daughter, who has also enjoyed life in the West as an undergraduate at Harvard.

What makes Iran's supreme leader Ali Khamenei tick? What motivates Niger's new leader, who at the time of writing has just been installed by a military coup? To prevent a further deterioration of countries' coexistence on our planet, Western governments need to deter a fast-growing number of threats. That doesn't mean that Western countries should appoint themselves as a global traffic police force. And yes, Western countries including the United States and Britain have in the past engaged in precisely the kind of action – an invasion – that they should seek to deter. But precisely because there is no global traffic police force, today countries committed to an orderly world must use both deterrence and compellence to try to limit war and conflicts.

Threatening a smaller country with a mighty military force may not seem like being a good global citizen. But if doing so is done in the service of a peace, it's certainly acceptable and indeed desirable. The question, once again, is around when such threats work and when other threats are needed. With deterrence and compellence becoming more crucial than they have been in over three decades, understanding what makes foreign leaders tick is of the utmost importance.

Trinity Test Site, Manhattan Project
Alamogordo Army Airfield..

THE TERRIBLE DILEMMAS OF LEADERSHIP
IN A THERMONUCLEAR WORLD

Francis J. Gavin

How should we think about the dilemmas of leadership in a thermonuclear world? And what can history – especially the history of how American presidents wrestled with the enormous responsibility of nuclear decision-making – tell us about our contemporary nuclear dilemmas?

Let me begin with a story from the past. Former Secretary of State Dean Acheson purportedly advised President John F. Kennedy that his most important responsibility was to think long and hard about nuclear weapons. Acheson told JFK that he had to decide whether or not he would ever use nuclear weapons, and once he had, to never tell anyone.

Kennedy appeared to heed this advice. Declassified documents reveal that few presidents in the nuclear era made as great an effort to understand the nuts and bolts of how a nuclear war could unfold. He asked searching questions of his advisors, and even authorised a closely held study of how a pre-emptive nuclear attack on Soviet nuclear forces would play out and what it would accomplish. And, of course, he faced perhaps the most dangerous period in world history, when a nuclear exchange seemed frighteningly possible. Beginning with the disastrous Vienna summit and the building of the Berlin Wall in the summer of 1961, and culminating in the terrifying 13-day Cuban Missile Crisis, no American leader ever came closer to a thermonuclear war.

What did Kennedy think of nuclear weapons, and did he ever seriously entertain using them? I can argue it either way. The risks he took and the strategies he embraced were quite aggressive. America's nuclear war plans followed a certain logic – go first, go fast, go hard – so that the Soviets would be left with little or nothing in reserve to reply with. He authorised a speech by Roswell Gilpatric in the autumn of 1961 which Soviet leader Nikita Khrushchev interpreted, with some justification, as a first strike speech. The Soviet secret placement of nuclear-tipped warheads was a grave affront. And time was not on the US's side – in the autumn of 1962, the United States had such overwhelming strategic nuclear superiority that a pre-emptive attack might neutralise the ability of the Soviets to respond. This window – which opened up with new American satellites allowing it to target Russian forces that were far smaller and more vulnerable than had been recognised – would close quickly. Indeed, in less than a year, military planners would tell the president that the US lived in a state of mutual vulnerability with Russia and that a pre-emptive nuclear strike would invite unimaginable devastation upon the United States.

Does that mean, if the Russians had not pulled their nuclear forces from Cuba in the fall of 1962, that JFK would have risked nuclear war in an assault on the island? Not necessarily. There is as much, if not more, evidence pointing in the other direction – Kennedy worked diligently to make sure nuclear weapons were under firm American and civilian command, installing permissive action links and increasing civilian controls over the bomb. During the Cuban Missile Crisis, he sought political solutions that avoided the risk of escalation, which he feared any military attack on Cuba would bring. He used his brother, the attorney general Robert F Kennedy, to negotiate with Soviet representatives, going around some of his more hawkish advisors. While it is impossible to prove, there is evidence that JFK would have gone to great lengths to avoid any military clash, which might have led to rapid escalation.

The evidence of his desire to avoid nuclear use becomes even clearer after the United States compelled Khrushchev to remove Russia's medium-range ballistic missiles from Cuba. When the crisis was over, he worked very hard to reduce nuclear dangers. Instead of seeking to further punish the Soviets after their irresponsible deception, he instead decided – at great domestic political cost, and to the consternation of his allies – to work with the Soviet Union to reduce nuclear dangers. He pursued the first major nuclear arms control agreement, the partial test ban treaty, signed less than a year after the Cuban Missile Crisis ended.

Why does this matter today? Russia's brutal invasion of Ukraine has, for the first time since the end of the Cold War and, arguably, for the first time since Kennedy's presidency, brought back the spectre of nuclear use. I want to briefly highlight several often-underappreciated dilemmas history reminds us a nuclearised world visits on international politics. This is especially important as we wrestle with the carnage in Ukraine and the highly irresponsible nuclear threats President Putin and his associates have made.

How seriously should we take such threats, and what does the past reveal about individual leaders who made – or received – them? Reactions have ranged on a spectrum, from those who have dismissed Putin's nuclear threats as bluffs that should be ignored, to those who argue they must be taken with the utmost seriousness.

Who is right? This highlights firstly what I suggest are at least six puzzles and dilemmas about individual leadership in a thermonuclear age. The truth is, we cannot know, *ex ante,* how to best evaluate nuclear threats. Most of these arguments are about nuclear deterrence, which is about preventing something from happening. And given how much we argue over things that actually do happen, figuring out why something like nuclear use does not happen – until it does – is very hard.

For example, consider the question of whether nuclear weapons made the Cold War more or less stable. Did America's nuclear weapons prevent the Soviet Union from taking over Western Europe during the Cold War? Or did the Soviets never have any intention of coming, or were they deterred by other Western actions? Did nuclear weapons provide for what the military historian John Lewis Gaddis called 'the Long Peace', or, as the Berlin and Cuban crises indicate, did they bring the world close to a catastrophic thermonuclear war?

A second dilemma: thermonuclear weapons have transformed the international system, yet the decision to use them typically lies in the hands of a single individual. Great power wars of conquest and invasion, which shaped world politics for a millennia, made no sense in a thermonuclear world after the early 1950s. The consequences of nuclear use are overwhelming and catastrophic, and would affect millions, including many outside the battle zone. There was not a political goal that was worth this cost.

Such a capability, one might think, could only be used if it went through a serious, complex process, where every stakeholder had a say. But in fact, as far as we know, the decision to use nuclear weapons usually lies in the hands of one person at the top of the system – a Biden, a Sunak, a Xi, a Macron, a Modi, a Putin. This concern about the extraordinary concentration of power in one person's hands was heightened, understandably, when Donald Trump was US president. Indeed, the concentration in the American case is more pointed than in others because the history of American war plans – marked by pre-emptive elements – requires incredibly fast decision-making. Regardless of the reason, the idea that one person can make a decision that affects the fate of the entire planet is, to say the least, deeply concerning.

Which leads to a third dilemma. While it makes literally no strategic sense to use these weapons to achieve political ends, there is an enormous incentive to make others think you might use them to generate coercive leverage. In such a world, it is very tempting for a leader to bluff; simply a polite term for lying. This creates an incentive system where bad behaviour is possibly rewarded and responsible behaviour punished.

Compare this dynamic with the non-nuclear world. If Country A has 50 tanks, and takes on an adversary with 500 tanks, its threat to attack is not credible. But the same is not true with nuclear weapons, where the possessor of 500 nuclear weapons may be a responsible actor and signal that they will never use these terrible weapons. The person with fewer weapons may, however, be willing to make irresponsible threats to get their way. Who can tell if the person is serious or not? Given the consequences of nuclear use, doesn't it make some sense to pay attention to the threat? Indeed, if you look at the details of Soviet premier Khrushchev's threats of nuclear blackmail in the late 1950s and early 1960s, one can imagine circumstances where he got away with his bluff, where the US simply conceded to avoid the danger of a nuclear war.

To be clear, this bluffing dynamic is not simply the act of dictators and despots. The United States has long based its grand strategy on signalling a willingness to use nuclear weapons first. It was arguably the threat to use nuclear weapons by Eisenhower and Kennedy that prevented Khrushchev from taking Berlin or keeping his missiles in Cuba. And President Richard Nixon on several occasions tried to put forward strategies and positions that made it appear he would be willing to use nuclear weapons. Tapes reveal he often considered the 'madman' theory, or the rationality of an irrational approach. The idea that his adversaries might think he was crazy enough to use them might force them, against their interests, to back down. One wonders if Nixon embraced this strategy as a result of watching how close Khrushchev came to getting away with nuclear bluffing at the end of the Eisenhower presidency.

Indeed, this highlights a fourth dilemma. One of the reasons the United States signalled a willingness to go first was in order to keep the states it protects – like Japan, Germany and other allies – from acquiring their own nuclear weapons. It is forgotten how radical America's nuclear non-proliferation policies are: when, in human history, has one state been able to convince another state not to acquire a technology that meets its most important, difficult goal – protecting its sovereignty and largely eliminating the danger it will be invaded and conquered? Yet American presidents have entered into a number of security arrangements to offer to protect allies from assault by nuclear-armed enemies and, in return, expose the American homeland to nuclear attack in order to protect some far-away country. These commitments drove the United States to acquire expensive nuclear delivery forces possessing accuracy, stealth, mobility and speed, deployed in strategies that were quite forward-leaning. The radical nature of extended deterrence is rarely appreciated, though it is at the heart of the debate over Ukraine's accession to NATO.

This highlights a fifth dilemma: nuclear weapons are tools of the weak. They flatten out other forms of power, be it conventional military power, economic prowess or cultural attraction. No one in the US would ever think about North Korea for a minute if they didn't have the bomb. But the fact that they do means a sixth-rate power with a barely functioning economy commands the attention of the United States.

Which leads to a final dilemma, one that it's difficult to prove but that I believe to be true. If any American president could wave their hand and make the world non-nuclear, with one possible exception – Richard Nixon – they would surely do so.

Why? First, imagine the terrible individual responsibility. You possess the power to use a weapon that could incinerate countries and kill tens of millions, if not end life on the planet. Your adversaries are often ruthless, authoritarian tyrants. And the choice to use the weapons will likely not come over a direct threat to the American homeland – neither Mexico nor Canada will invade you, and the Atlantic and Pacific Ocean provide protection from overseas invaders. Your choice to use the bomb, and expose your own citizens and society to destruction, will be made when some far-away ally is attacked. Just as bad, you strongly sense that at the end of the day, you would never authorise nuclear use, short of a direct nuclear attack upon the American homeland, and even then, you aren't sure.

Consider Presidents Eisenhower and Kennedy in the late 1950s and early 1960s, facing an aggressive, ruthless geopolitical and ideological adversary, committed to aggression and world revolution, led by men willing to do terrible things to their own citizens, all within living memory of another brutal regime, Nazi Germany. This, in a world where surprise attacks similar to those launched in 1941 by Japan and Hitler's

Germany, though with thermonuclear weapons, seemed plausible. Eisenhower and Kennedy's reticence came at a time when the United States actually possessed overwhelming nuclear superiority, which both understood was a 'wasting asset'. Still, neither president came close to using them during a dangerous crisis. In retrospect, one wonders if America's nuclear promises were, in fact, a giant bluff.

A world without nuclear weapons would be one where you slept better at night and could deploy other forms of America's power more easily. If you are an American president, why would you want a world where terrible weapons empowered your otherwise weak enemies, and gave you sole responsibility for doing something horrendous, essentially based on the lie that you would use these weapons to protect far-away allies? Yet, needless to say, nuclear weapons exist, are likely to be part of the leading powers' arsenals for quite some time, and the dilemmas and puzzles around them are unlikely to be resolved.

Presidential candidate John F. Kennedy (1917–63)
is greeted by hundreds of people as he campaigns
in 1960, in Charlotte, North Carolina.

JOHN F. KENNEDY AND THE CHALLENGE
OF DEMOCRATIC LEADERSHIP

Fredrik Logevall

My topic is America's 35th president, John F. Kennedy, and his meaning for us today. Six decades have passed since Kennedy's assassination, as his motorcade crept slowly along Elm Street, beneath the Texas School Book Depository, in Dallas, on a sunny fall day in November 1963. Yet he remains an outsized persona, not only in the United States but abroad, an iconic figure, a man known universally by his initials, more remembered than all but a small number of twenti-eth-century world leaders.

Born in 1917, during one world war, and at the dawn of the so-called American Century, he came of age in a second world war, then rose all the way to the presidency, only to be cut down at 46, while leading a United States that stood at the apex of its power. He was a man of privilege and affluence who endured chronic ill health and pain as well as colossal personal tragedy, and whose story-book life captivated millions of people – not merely in the United States but overseas, not merely in death but in life. Known for his handsome looks, cool and elegant demeanour, and continuous womanising, Kennedy was gifted and flawed, as a politician and as a person, and his thousand days in the White House witnessed mistakes as well as successes. But through his captivating leadership and inspirational rhetoric he elevated Americans' belief in the capacity of politics to solve big problems and speak to society's highest aspirations, while in foreign affairs he showed it was possible to move from sharp hostility toward the Soviet Union to coexistence. The American public responded. By the middle of 1963, close to 60% of Americans claimed that they had voted for Kennedy in 1960, although only 49.7% had in fact done so. After his death, his landslide grew to 65%. Kennedy's average approval rating of 70% while in office puts him at the top among post-Second World War US presidents, and later generations would rate his performance higher still.

What explains the enduring hold of John F. Kennedy's legacy, his lasting appeal? Does it have something to do with his youthful and dignified bearing, his handsome looks? Yes, in part. What about the glamour of his White House, his beautiful family? That too matters, as does his inspirational speechmaking. And no doubt he retains a hold on Americans partly because of the timing and nature of his death, which was captured on film and plays on an endless loop in our minds. He is forever in his mid-40s, seemingly in the prime of life.

All those things matter. But as I research and write a two-volume study of the man and his times, I'm increasingly convinced that, more than anything, it was Kennedy's abiding faith in his nation and its brand of democratic politics that explains most fully his abiding legacy. I'd like to examine that issue in the pages that follow, in the process touching upon why I believe Kennedy's example matters for us today.

From a young age, John F. Kennedy was fascinated by the problems of democratic leadership in politics. The interest was there in his undergraduate papers at Harvard as well as in his senior thesis, which was published as a book, *Why England Slept*, just a few weeks after his graduation, in 1940, when he was 23. The animating question of the study was why Britain was so poorly prepared when war broke out in 1939. To read the book is to see that its young author is fascinated by the challenges of leadership, and the dilemmas that confront officials who seek to do what is required of them while not alienating their temperamental constituents. It's a theme Kennedy would return to in a later book, *Profiles in Courage*, and a conundrum he would confront to the end of his days.

Let us linger a bit on *Profiles in Courage*, which appeared in 1956 and featured profiles of eight US senators who showed notable courage and risked their careers in taking political stances unpopular with their constituents, their parties and in some cases their regions. Here, the challenges of democratic politics are front and centre. The introductory chapter is notable, not least for its current resonance. Its title is 'Courage and Politics', but more than anything the chapter argues for the vital importance in a democracy of political compromise, of having 'the sense of things possible'. To condemn all compromise as immoral is short-sighted, Kennedy insists, for decisions of public policy often involve difficult choices, often from a menu of lousy options.

> The fanatics and extremists and even those conscientiously devoted to hard and fast principles are always disappointed at the failure of their government to rush to implement all of their principles and to

denounce those of their opponents. [But] some of my colleagues who are criticized today for lack of forthright principles – or who are looked upon with scornful eyes as compromising 'politicians' – are simply engaged in the art of conciliating, balancing, and interpreting the forces and factions of public opinion, an art essential to keeping our nation united and our Government to function. Their consciences may direct them from time to time to make a more rigid stand for principle – but their intellects tell them that a fair or poor bill is better than no bill at all, and that only through the give-and-take of compromise will any bill receive the successive approval of the Senate, the House, the President and the nation.

The concluding chapter returns to these broader themes. It matters to us today for what it says about Kennedy's view of political leadership, and for serving as a kind of eternal antidote to the cynicism about politics and politicians that periodically courses through American political discourse. Here, Kennedy extols both compromise and courage (the courage he most favours is that of moderates who resist extremists). At the same time, he stresses that his book is not intended to laud independence for the sake of independence, or to suggest that there is on every issue a right side and a wrong side. 'On the contrary,' he writes, 'I share the feelings expressed by prime minister Melbourne, who, when irritated by the criticism of the then youthful historian T. B. Macaulay, remarked that he would like to be as sure of anything as Macaulay seemed to be of everything.'

He then quotes Abraham Lincoln: 'There are few things wholly evil or wholly good. Almost everything, especially of Government policy, is an inseparable compound of the two, so that our best judgment of the preponderance between them is continually demanded.'

Here Kennedy may have been influenced by a conversation he had around the time of the publication of *Profiles* with his long-time British friend David Ormsby-Gore. From his reading of American history, Kennedy told the Englishman, he had drawn the lessons that there were usually two sides to every serious political problem. The radicals of the right and the left, in their constant demand for simple solutions, didn't grasp this fundamental point. 'Now, this didn't prevent him being capable of taking decisions,' Ormsby-Gore later said of the conversation, 'but it did always prevent him saying, "I know that I have got nothing but right on my side and the other side is entirely wrong," and he never would adopt that attitude. He said that one of the sad things in life, particularly if you were a politician, was that you discovered that the other side really had a very good case. He was most unpartisan in that way.'

In divisive times, such as the one the United States is living through today, this emphasis on the need for compromise is often derided, mistakenly, as naive. On the contrary, the naive view is the one that dismisses the need for bargaining with opponents, the need for compromise based on mutual concessions. Neither then nor later was Kennedy above bareknuckle politics or partisan sparring, but he understood that honest bargaining was necessary to a well-functioning democracy, and that civility in the public realm prevented dehumanisation and helped Americans to see political opponents as adversaries, not enemies. He understood that *dignity* – acting in a dignified manner and treating others appropriate to their dignity – is a core value of democracy.

Closely associated with Kennedy's interest in the demands of democratic leadership was his frequent exhortation to Americans to commit themselves to a life of public service. As he put it in his 1961 Inaugural Address: 'Ask not what your country can do for you – ask what you can do for your country.' This was no new idea in his mind; it had been drilled into him at Choate, his prep school alma mater. Even before that, his parents had implemented in their nine children the importance of thinking beyond oneself, of doing something for the greater good. When, in 1946, Kennedy returned to Choate to give a lecture, he urged the students to be engaged citizens and to serve their country in some way. On the stump that year, in his maiden election campaign, he fleshed out the argument, sounding notes that seem especially resonant in our own time. Beware lazy cynicism about politics and politicians, the skinny young candidate implored audiences, for the survival of democracy depended on having an informed and engaged citizenry, committed to reasoned discourse and accepting of good-faith bargaining between the parties. In that campaign and in his later ones, including in his run for the White House, Kennedy employed the language of empathy, emphasising Americans' common goals and common fate as a people, and he embodied a kind of patriotism that doesn't transcend partisanship, but enriches partisan struggle, making it always an invitation to others to join you.

It's a powerful political philosophy, one that has lost none of its salience in the ensuing years. And though it cannot be said that Kennedy ranks among America's great presidents, alongside Washington, Lincoln and Franklin Roosevelt – he didn't live long enough, didn't accomplish enough – one feels he had the capacity for greatness. Through his visionary leadership and inspired rhetoric, he summoned the narrative of American hope, as he challenged people to believe in a better society at home while embracing the nation's leadership position abroad. He approached his job as president with earnest resoluteness – a fundamental test of political leadership. He had the discipline and maturity to discern matters that transcended self-interest, and he was able and willing to set aside immature ego and emotionalism, and to act with prudence and self-restraint. Beneath all the style and glamour, Kennedy was basically a serious man on a serious mission.

He was at once a realist and an idealist. Like all philosophic liberals – whether on the right side of the political spectrum or the left – he understood that people have selfish interests, but he believed in democracy and robust conversation because he had faith in the capacity of people to pursue their own lives, to respect and be mindful of people unlike themselves, to keep society progressing. In other words, Kennedy embodied what my colleague James Kloppenberg in his book *Toward Democracy* refers to as an 'ethic of reciprocity' – a mutual respect, a recognition and tolerance for one another, even if we do not all share the same moral commitments. Politically, Kloppenberg writes, it means the willingness to accept defeat, to allow your worst enemies to govern if they win an election.

Kennedy reminds us that there was an age, not so long ago, when it was possible to believe that politics could speak to society's moral yearnings and be harnessed to its highest aspirations, when it was possible to think in terms of the social whole, of the public good, of the need to emphasise what Americans had in common over what set them apart.

Whether that message can work in today's world is one of the crucial questions of our time. No doubt the United States is different today than it was 60 years ago. Voters are more cynical, more suspicious about politics, about institutions, more likely to question one another's motives. And the media environment is different too – the nation now has a much less deferential press corps, and an incredible expansion of opinion makers and influencers in which everyone weighs in with little accounting of their expertise or their credibility.

Imagine if one of the legendary Kennedy press conferences were held today. The instant he was off the air, zealous partisans would be debating and disputing every word and undoing what he attempted to convey directly to the public. Social media would be afire with haters and sceptics and trolls.

We don't know how JFK would have navigated any of that. He surely would have felt frustrated and irritated by it. But he would have been as likely as anyone to cut through it, to appeal to a fundamental sense of decency and fairness that didn't persuade everyone but did carry along a great many people, both at the time and since. As much as anyone, Kennedy could have persuaded the mass of his compatriots that, through engagement and good will, we can make real and lasting connections across differences, that society is not a zero-sum war, but a conversation and a negotiation. He could have convinced them that, in the house of democracy, there can be no enemies, and that when politicians treat each other as enemies, honest bargaining becomes impossible, and debate within the halls of power in Washington becomes as venomously personal as it is politically meaningless.

Finally, a Kennedy alive today would insist upon another essential ingredient of democratic governance: rational, fact-based discourse. One can have one's own view about why the facts are the way they are, but all must agree on the facts if there's going to be a sensible conversation about problems and how to solve them. Consider here Kennedy's remarks in a speech planned for the Dallas Trade Mart on 22 November 1963, a destination he never reached:

> In a world of complex and continuing problems, in a world full of frustrations and irritations, America's leadership must be guided by learning and reason, or else those who confuse rhetoric with reality, and the plausible with the possible, will gain popular ascendancy, and with their seemingly swift and simple solutions to every world problem. We cannot expect...that everyone will talk sense to the American people, but we can hope that fewer people will listen to this nonsense.

Finnish field marshal
Carl Gustaf Emil Mannerheim (1867–1951)
in Lausanne, Switzerland, 10 February 1947.

GUSTAF MANNERHEIM: THE LEADER WHO HELPED SHAPE A FREE FINLAND

Henrik Meinander

Political and military leaders operating at the highest level have always attracted interest, given that their decisions often have far-reaching consequences for a huge amount of people. This is not only due to their original intentions – events often tend to turn out otherwise than planned, which is a challenge for historians trying to explain how leadership or statecraft has been executed.

Up until the nineteenth century, written history was mostly about how rulers and military commanders won or lost battles due to personal strengths and weaknesses. The genre is still thriving, but gradually more structural and generalised approaches to the theme have appeared. One interesting study is the wide-ranging survey from 2004 in which the psychologists Steven L. Rubenzer and Thomas R. Faschingbauer compared the personalities, characteristics and leadership decisions of all the American presidents since the formation of the republic in 1776.

The duo asked historians, writers and journalists to evaluate the leadership of the presidents. The outcome of the almost 600-question-long survey was not straightforward. While the sources were very heterogeneous, respondents could nevertheless recognise eight leadership types: dominators, introverts, 'good guys', innocents, actors, preservationists, philosophers and extroverts. And the highest scores for good leadership, according to this comparison, went to extroverts Franklin D. Roosevelt and John F. Kennedy, who were not only clever but also master manipulators.

Do these claims have any relevance when we focus on the leadership and statecraft of Finland's most renowned public figure, Gustaf Mannerheim? Yes and no. Certain features in decision-making are universal, others are historically and geographically specific. Despite being born in 1867 in the north-eastern periphery of Europe, in the Grand Duchy of Finland, at that time one of the poorest countries on the continent, during his career Mannerheim would take part in, and in some cases be solely responsible for, decisions that would have a formative impact not only on Finnish but also European history.

After a three-decade-long career in the Russian army, Mannerheim returned to Finland in late 1917, which, due to the increasing chaos in the Russian Empire after the Bolshevik coup, had declared its independence. When the Russian Revolution of January 1918 spread to Finland, he was appointed commander-in-chief of his country's counter-revolutionary army and led it to victory in May 1918. After a comfortable private life during the interwar period, he was called back to the same position in late autumn 1939, when Finland was dragged into the Second World War, staying in post until ending his career as president of Finland from 1944–46.

An analysis of Mannerheim's career shows us, if nothing else, that while we are all born with certain talents and in a specific socio-cultural framework, how these strengths or weaknesses are revealed over our lifetimes depends to a large extent on societal and geopolitical factors that we can have no impact on.

Mannerheim's biologically inherited gifts were favourable but not exceptional. With his six-foot height, resilient health and attractive looks, he certainly caught attention. As the offspring of one of Finland's leading noble families, his background was also privileged, but his early educational records were less convincing. As a teenager he was relegated for bad behaviour both from his grammar school and the Finnish Cadet Corps. Through his family's ties to the imperial elite, he got a new chance at the Nicholas Cavalry School in St Petersburg, which gave his motivation a needed boost, and his career took a positive turn.

His adolescent shortcomings might have been a psychological reaction to his father's bankruptcy and scandalous escape with a mistress to Paris. On the other hand, his six siblings seemed to have carried the social shame much more ably, and they all got decent civilian educations. A more plausible explanation could be that the young Mannerheim, due to his wild nature and often foolhardy bravery, simply needed more hardship and discipline to get on the right track.

Mannerheim passed the exam at Nicholas Cavalry School with a high score and, in 1889, started his first military appointment in the small Polish town of Kalisz. This only intensified his ambition to be admitted to the prestigious Chevalier Guards in St Petersburg. This goal, once again thanks to his family's close links to the imperial court, soon bore fruit. During his first years in this regiment, who were the life guards of the

Russian empress, he was introduced to court life and married a Russian noblewoman with a substantial fortune, Anastasia Arapova, who gave birth to two daughters. He also made a name for himself in prestigious equestrian competitions. The marriage brought him wealth and influence, but ended a decade later in divorce due to his adultery.

Mannerheim's professional advances were, at that stage, unimpressive. He failed the entrance examination to the Russian military academy, and his promotions remained imperative until 1904, when he enrolled as a volunteer in the Russo-Japanese War. The war was lost, but the skilful horseman showed his ability as a frontline officer and was sent on a two-year espionage expedition through Central Asia – an extremely demanding task on horseback – which he completed so successfully that his military career took off.

When the First World War broke out, Mannerheim had reached the rank of major-general, and during the war he rose to commander of a cavalry corps before the revolutionary chaos in the summer of 1917 began to disintegrate the Imperial Army.

All these turning points would transform the flamboyant life guard officer into a resilient commander with a realistic understanding of great power politics. He was thus well equipped when, in January 1918, he was appointed commander-in-chief of the troops of the newborn state of Finland, now in a state of revolution due to the country's rocky transition to independence. The Finnish socialists were strongly encouraged by the Russian Bolsheviks to win power and acquired weaponry from Russian soldiers left in Finland.

In March 1918, after the Bolshevik government had been forced to sign the Treaty of Brest-Litovsk with Germany, in which Lenin promised to stay aloof from the Finnish conflict, the war tipped over in favour of Mannerheim's White Army. The Treaty also resulted in the Whites receiving decisive support from the German army; within two months the Finnish revolution was crushed. Mannerheim, however, was not at all happy to be working with his former enemies, the Germans, and resigned. He was convinced Germany would lose the war, and when that happened he was called back to function as regent in the wake of the resignation of Frederick Charles of Hesse, brother-in-law of German emperor Wilhelm II – a position he held until the summer of 1919.

During that short era, he advocated energetically for Finnish involvement on the counter-revolutionary side in the Russian Civil War. This awoke suspicions that he was less interested in Finnish independence than in the restoration of former Russian rule. After having signed the republican constitution of Finland, he stood as a candidate in the presidential election, but in large part due to these suspicions, he lost and retreated to a comfortable gentleman's life on money raised by his devoted supporters.

His shortcomings in domestic politics between 1918 and 1919 convinced Mannerheim to stay aloof from parliamentary intrigues. But when tensions in great power politics in the 1930s grew sharper, his expertise and networks became more appreciated by the Finnish political elite than before. As chairman of the National Defence Committee, Mannerheim warned European governments repeatedly of the growing threats of a new war. He had maintained his contacts with leading European military and diplomatic actors, and claimed the only way for Finland to avoid becoming a battlefield was a military alliance with Sweden, which could calm down invasion plans by the Soviet Union and Germany.

The Swedish government was not prepared to bind its destiny to the risky borderland. Finland was thus thrown again into a world war, and Mannerheim was called to function once more as the commander-in-chief of the Finnish Army. Due to his age – he was 72 in 1939 – Mannerheim's style of military leadership was in many ways out of date. But his geopolitical understanding and diplomatic experiences compensated for most of these shortcomings, and when the Second World War ended in 1945, Finland was the only country in Eastern Europe that had avoided occupation and maintained its independence as well as its democratic institutions.

During this period, a crucial impact on Mannerheim's military leadership was his trustful cooperation with Risto Ryti, Finnish prime minister during the Winter War – a three-and-a-half-month battle against Soviet invaders in 1939 – and president during a second Soviet war, known as the Continuation War, between 1941 and 1944. They were both Anglophiles, but after the Winter War each came to the conclusion that Finland's only way to survive was through a military alliance with Germany, since Stalin was not prepared to leave Finland untouched.

The decisive moment came in late summer 1940, when Soviet pressure on Finland increased and Hitler secretly began to plan an invasion of the Soviet Union. Hitler was well-informed of the Soviet stress on Finland and offered its leadership first weaponry and goods, then diplomatic support, and finally, in December 1940, a military alliance. Could

Mannerheim and Ryti have declined these offers? In principle yes, but in practice not. The Stalin and Hitler pact from 1939 was still in force. Even if their secret protocol, in which Finland was defined in the Soviet sphere of interest, was not known about by the Finnish leadership, it was easy to interpret Stalin's intentions concerning Finland, not least after the Baltic states had been brutally incorporated into the Soviet Union.

All realistic alternatives had by then been thoroughly checked and ruled out. A Finno-Swedish alliance was bluntly denied by Moscow and Berlin. British military support was not an option after the Wehrmacht occupied Denmark and Norway. As so often before and thereafter, the Finnish leaders were forced to play the weak cards they held – in this case, they had to swiftly decide what great power to join before their country once again became dragged into a military conflict.

In that specific situation, an alliance with Hitler's Germany was the only safe choice. If the German invitation had been declined, Finland would certainly have been occupied either by the Wehrmacht or the Red Army and would have lost any chance of manoeuvring through the clash between the two dictatorships with its independence intact. But instead, due to this skilful balancing act, Finland was able to cut its ties to Germany in September 1944 and sign the Armistice Treaty with the Allied Forces, which became the Paris Peace Treaty of 1947.

The German support for Finland had remained substantial throughout the war 1941–44, but an official alliance treaty was never signed. President Ryti could thus claim that Finland fought its own defensive battle to maintain its reputation among Western countries. Despite this, he and seven of his cabinet were brought to trial for war responsibility. The accused denied any responsibility for the alliance, but received jail sentences in February 1946. Ryti was given ten years, his seven officials shorter terms. The sentences were less harsh than those imposed on the guilty during the Nuremberg and Tokyo trials, and were widely understood as unfair, due to the difficult circumstances in which the politicians had taken their decision. But in many ways the sentences stigmatised their legacy.

Mannerheim's fate was luckier. He had consciously avoided specific declarations about the nature of cooperation with Germany, and one month before the alliance ended he had finally been elected president – which in practice gave him immunity against any charges. Directly after the sentences were handed down to the politicians in March 1946, he resigned as president and spent most of his remaining life focusing on working on his memoirs.

In them, Mannerheim followed tightly the defence arguments put forward by the accused politicians. He played down the importance of German military support for Finland in 1941–44, and described his own position in the decision-making as subordinate to President Ryti and his war cabinet. Those claims were clearly not honest. The alliance with Germany had been crucial for the survival of Finnish independence, and Mannerheim's geopolitical views had strongly informed Finnish strategies throughout the war.

Hidden agendas; leadership profile
The truth about the Finno-German alliance was not politically convenient to reveal when the crimes of the Nazi regime became public and Finland's relationship with its former enemy, the Soviet Union, needed to be improved. In fact, it took a couple of decades before Finnish historians began to uncover the full extent of the alliance, and many Finnish citizens would stick much longer to the memory of a separate war.

Once this more critical picture of Finland's role in both world wars began to unfold, it would reflect on Mannerheim's legacy. Among many Finnish socialists, Mannerheim had, since the crushed revolution of 1918, been remembered as 'the white butcher', and as the Finno-German alliance was scrutinised more closely he was even accused by some of being Hitler's lackey. His reputation has experienced a veritable rollercoaster ride over the years, but gradually a calmer and more diversified picture of him has taken shape, which offers space for considering the different dimensions of his leadership.

Returning to the eight leadership profiles characterised by Rubenzer and Faschingbauer, it is safe to claim that Mannerheim had a lot in common with the extroverts Franklin D. Roosevelt and John F. Kennedy. During his career in Russia, he learnt how to perform in public and build up an aura of heroic motives. He lacked the moral scruples to hide his own ambitions and strategic calculations, which might arouse condemnation but is in fact a quality required by every politician and decision-maker with any longevity.

Examples of the latter are the hidden motives behind Mannerheim's calculations and decisions in both 1918 and 1941. Had he, in January 1918, told the Finnish government that he saw himself fighting the Reds primarily for Russia's former rulers, he would not have been appointed. And had he, after the Second World War, admitted to being crucially responsible for Finland joining the German attack against the Soviet Union in the summer of 1941, he would have been accused of cowardice – or worse, considering President Ryti and seven government colleagues received jail sentences for the alliance with Germany.

Yet the consequences of these two hidden agendas were in the end favourable both for Finland and for Mannerheim himself. Mannerheim understood the military conflict between the Whites and Reds in Finland as part of the broader arenas of the Russian Revolution and the First World War, and he had no illusions about German motives for supporting the Finnish Whites. Thus he maintained his distanced attitude towards the Germans and could, after their capitulation, be called back to government to repair Finland's damage in relation to the victorious Western powers.

The same geopolitical macro perspective was also typical of Mannerheim's leadership during the next world war. As emphasised earlier, his decision to join the German offensive in the summer of 1941 was certainly not taken without hesitation. But it paid off. Finland managed to avoid a Soviet invasion, then cut the alliance with Germany, and finally secured its independence. Even if these were unintended chain reactions in the context of the larger war arena, things could easily have gone gravely wrong for Finland without Mannerheim's leadership.

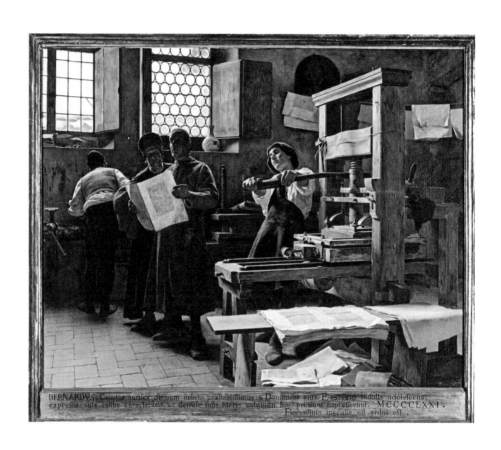

La stamperia di Bernando Cennini,
oil on canvas by Tito Lessi, 1906.

INFORMATION OVERLOAD AND POLICYMAKING: INSIGHTS FROM THE EARLY MODERN ERA

Iskander Rehman

When I was five years old, my grandparents took me to Hamleys. The largest toy shop in the world, Hamleys is a beloved London landmark stretching over seven floors. I entered its cavernous halls in a state of dazed bewilderment, nervously clutching my grandmother's hand as she and my grandfather instructed me to choose a birthday present. Surely, this must have been one of the happiest moments in my young life.

Instead, somewhat puzzlingly, subtle changes in my general demeanour began to slowly unfold. My palms grew sweaty, my breathing accelerated and my initial elation soon curdled into some deeper form of existential angst. How could I possibly choose just one toy amid such mind-numbing abundance? There were thousands of bright, shiny objects to examine, categorise, evaluate and meticulously cross-reference. The Teenage Mutant Ninja Turtle section alone appeared to yawn into infinity. It was all too much for my five-year-old brain. I broke down crying and we had to leave. Later that day, my patient grandparents took me to another, much smaller, toy shop where I rapidly made my pick.

Why share this mildly embarrassing childhood memory? It points – albeit on a micro level – to some of the decisional quandaries that come from living in a time of unparallelled plenty. We live in an era of abundance and distraction, of shrinking attention spans, 'content shock', and of seemingly endless quantity over elusively finite quality. Thanks to the internet, we have never had access to so much information, and yet somehow, we appear to be less collectively well-read, less well-informed and more intellectually febrile, fragmented and jittery. The statistics are depressing – Americans now touch their smartphones an average of 2,617 times a day. As digital databases expand, attention spans shrink. The average time spent on a web page is 15 seconds; reading an article, approximately one minute. We're also witnessing a slump in general reading – Americans now claim to read, on average, 12.6 books a year, which is two to three fewer than between 2001 and 2006 – and this decline is most pronounced among university-age individuals. Part of this is due to the ease and ubiquity of continuous digital distraction, but also, one might contend, due to sheer, overwhelming, awe-inspiring – and ultimately terrifying – abundance.

We all struggle to collect and process the ever-growing mounds of information at our disposal. What should we privilege or prioritise during our limited time on Earth? What should we merely skim, and what should we read in depth? Do I really need to read all of Proust or Dostoevsky to be a truly educated, well-rounded individual, as I repeatedly— and vainly—remind myself at the onset of each summer holiday? And yet this is hardly a new phenomenon. Writing in a state of cranky isolation from his cottage in mid-nineteenth-century Massachusetts, Henry David Thoreau lamented the fact he had never got around to reading Plato: 'His *Dialogues*, which contain what was immortal in him, lie on the next shelf, and yet I never read him.' And then comes that all-too-familiar self-flagellation, as the misanthropic New Englander griped: 'We should be as good as the worthies of antiquity, but partly by first knowing how good they were. We are a race of tit-men [runts], and soar but little higher in our intellectual flights than the column of the daily paper.'

When it comes to history, which periods should we endeavour to truly grasp and why? After all, history keeps on expanding – not only in temporal scope, but also historiographically, and even geographically, as we become ever more aware of alternative historical traditions outside the bounds of the West. Should an American ruthlessly prioritise the American Revolution over antiquity? Are the most recent periods of our history always the most relevant? Conversely, can one truly understand the history of the American Revolution and the thought processes of the founding fathers without delving into the writings of Sallust, Livy, Plutarch or Cicero? Not necessarily. As the famed historian and French Resistance hero Marc Bloch once noted, when reaching for a deeper understanding of complex phenomena, linear chronological prioritisations don't always make the most sense:

> What would one think of the geophysicist who, satisfied with having computed their remoteness to a fraction of an inch, would then conclude that the influence of the moon upon the earth is far greater

than that of the sun? Neither in outer space, nor in time, can the potency of a force be measured by the single dimension of distance.

Perhaps more importantly, how do these issues of information management and cognitive overload affect intelligence gatherers and policymakers? These vast and complex issues will no doubt only gain in salience in the coming years. It therefore might prove helpful to focus briefly here on two core themes.

First, our latent anxieties around informational abundance and complexity – which may appear exacerbated by technological advances – are not new, and were particularly prevalent during the so-called 'information explosion' of the early modern era. That epoch, spanning the early Renaissance to the late baroque period, remains rich with insights for applied historians. Second, and perhaps most importantly, the historian's endeavour should be viewed not solely in terms of rich empirical content, but also in terms of intellectual processes. Indeed, the process of historical enquiry itself provides a form of calisthenics for the mind, one which strengthens its capability to process information, boosts its ability to detect shifting patterns amid tangled skeins of concurrent events and more generally helps it rise above the crushing mass of everyday phenomena. In so doing, it greatly enhances what the ancients would have termed prudence: practical wisdom in the classical Aristotelian sense – what we would now perhaps refer to as intuition or good judgement.

The early modern period is particularly interesting for scholars of information management and policymaking. It was a time of enormous political, intellectual and diplomatic upheaval. The increased sophistication of the early modern state, its growing centralisation, the heightened intricacy of its bureaucratic apparatus – complete with teetering mounds of paperwork and endless reams of epistolary exchanges – all required chronically overworked rulers to find safe and effective ways to delegate authority, administer newly sprawling domains and implement their increasingly far-reaching reforms. Institutionally, this led to the mushrooming of small governing councils composed of tight cadres of ministers and royal counsellors across Europe, and to the rise of the figure of the secretary – the discreet and dedicated public servant at the heart of the new 'letterocracy', whose dry tendrils extended across the chancelleries, ministries and embassies of the Continent. Paperwork had become, in the words of historian Paul M. Dover, 'the demon of early modern statecraft'. Kings, popes and doges all found themselves gasping for air under a veritable deluge of memoranda and correspondence. Philip II was frequently driven to despair by 'these devils, my papers', with up to 16,000 separate petitions sent to his desk over the course of a single year. Similarly, in France, Cardinal Richelieu, behind his wintry and steely exterior, was in fact often a neurotic mess, according to scholar A. Lloyd Moote, a 'bundle of nervous energy' drowning in work and suffering debilitating migraines. In the face of this avalanche of correspondence, new bureaucratic solutions were devised, as were new methods of communication. In fact, some of the more fascinating documents from the period could be described as early versions of shared online documents – manuscripts or memoranda where the sovereign would write in one margin, the advisor in the other, both communicating back and forth through these jointly annotated briefs. Counsellors and ministers would sometimes draft short daily memoranda for their rulers which compiled key intelligence findings, point-by-point summaries and select excerpts of diplomatic dispatches – early versions of the Presidential Daily Briefings, which first officially came into being during the Lyndon Johnson administration in the 1960s.

Within this densely saturated information environment, the role of the newly empowered secretary, ambassador or counsellor was not only to filter, distil and interpret incoming torrents of data, but also to provide clear and actionable guidance to overwhelmed rulers. This required, noted many commentators at the time, a distinct set of skills: clarity of style and expression, the ability to be detail-oriented while not losing sight of the big picture, and the capacity to combine careful reflection with decisiveness.

Many readers will be familiar with Winston Churchill's 1940 memorandum touting the virtues of 'short crisp paragraphs' in government communications and calling for an end to bloated, unnecessary verbiage. Many sixteenth- and seventeenth-century writers argued along similar lines, and even more forcefully. The Spanish Jesuit Baltasar Gracián was characteristically direct in his hugely popular *Pocket Oracle and Art of Prudence* (1647), berating his fellow court apparatchiks in the following terms: 'Don't be tedious. Brevity flatters and opens more doors: it gains in courtesy what it loses in precision. What's good, if brief, is twice as good.'

Meanwhile, writers such as the Florentine historian and statesman Guicciardini warned against getting bogged down in detail, writing in the *Ricordi* in 1530 that trying to absorb too much information could exert something of a paralysing effect: 'At times, I have seen a man who knows only the general facts of the case judge well, whereas the same person will judge poorly when he has heard the details.'

With the advent of the printing press and the rediscovery of long-lost works from antiquity, historically inclined counsellors and legislators faced a daunting new problem –overwhelmingly abundant source material. Some of this cognitive burden was newly offloaded in the form of florilegia, compendia and encyclopedias. After all, noted Samuel Johnson, it was time for scholars to acknowledge perfect omniscience was impossible, and knowledge was ultimately of two kinds: either we perfectly knew a subject ourselves or – more realistically – we knew where we could find information about it. And indeed, this was when some of our more recognisable methods of academic practice came into being, such as the footnote – devised primarily as a means of assisting seventeenth-century bookworms to burrow through increasingly dense layers of scholarship.

Figures including Johnson and Francis Bacon also spoke of the necessity of adopting new, more differentiated reading strategies. For example, Bacon had this to say in 1597: 'Some books are to be tasted, others to be swallowed, and some few to be chewed and digested; that is, some books are to be read only in parts; others to be read, but not curiously; and some few to be read wholly, and with diligence and attention.' And indeed, this metaphor of reading as a form of intellectual digestion, or careful rumination, had become exceedingly commonplace since the late Middle Ages, and was liberally employed by figures ranging from Petrarch to Bacon, Montaigne, or William Drake. Meanwhile, satirists from Jean de La Bruyère to Jonathan Swift fiercely lampooned contemporaries who never actually metabolised great works in full, but rather sampled ready-made summaries, with Swift jesting that, after all, 'to enter the palace of learning at the great gate requires an expense of time and forms, therefore men of much haste and little ceremony are content to get in by the back-door'.

History was still considered the wet nurse of prudence, and its study an essential prerequisite for sound statecraft. Not only did it serve a moral function – encouraging legacy-obsessed legislators to act virtuously – it also allowed for the vicarious acquisition of experiences extending far beyond the fleeting span of mortal life. At the same time, however, writers started to warn of history's potential – through its sheer bloated mass – to confound, daze and overwhelm. 'How much is the sight of a man's mind distracted by experience and history?' wondered Bacon. When it came to the study of the rise or fall of great nations, it was perhaps not wise, he said, to 'look too long upon these turning wheels of vicissitude, lest we become giddy'. To be overly fascinated by history, Philip Sidney argued in his influential *Defense of Poesy* (1595), was to run the risk of being 'captivated to the truth of a foolish world', mired in grubby, unedifying sequences of events rather than engaging in more elevated forms of philosophical or poetical reflection.

To which thinkers could – and did – respond that it was not so much the dull cataloguing of events themselves that mattered, but rather how one chose to make sense of them. Central to the process of historical enquiry is the notion of discernment, a word first entering common usage in the late 1500s. What does it mean precisely? A modern dictionary definition might say 'keenness of intellectual perception, insight, acuteness of judgment'. More prosaically, one might simply suggest it is the ability to engage in critical thinking. Its etymology can provide some clues – it derives from the Latin *dis-cernere*, which means to separate, divide or, more accurately, sift apart. Thus, writes Montaigne in his *Essays*, a true student of history should 'pass everything through a sieve and lodge nothing in his head on mere authority or trust'. Famously, the French humanist wrote it was better to have a 'well-made rather than a well-filled head'. Beyond a sometimes overzealous quest for immediate parallels, history can be almost equally useful when highlighting moments of ruptures and discontinuity. For, as Juan Luis Vives rightly observed in *On Education* (c. 1531):

> Even a knowledge of that which has been changed is useful; whether you recall something of the past to guide you in what would be useful in your own case, or whether you apply something, which formerly was managed in such and such a way, and so adapt the same or a similar method, to your own actions, as the case may fit.

To sift through history with ease also requires avoidance of the common pitfalls or pathologies of the discipline. French historian Emmanuel Le Roy Ladurie once mused that all too often his academic colleagues appeared to be 'either truffle hunters, their noses buried in the details, or parachutists, hanging high in the air and looking for general patterns in the countryside far below them'. Arguably, this issue has only become more acute since Ladurie made this observation in the 1980s. The historian-cum-policymaker must avoid stumbling into such artificial, academically imposed binaries, for it is precisely the telescopic quality of historical work – its ability to zoom in and out of the factual weeds while retaining sight of panoramic societal or geopolitical vistas – that renders it so uniquely valuable to policymakers.

Indeed, the best historians tend to be the best sifters, sorters and processors – honing a manner of approaching the world which may at first glance appear rooted in relatively unconscious thought processes, but in reality flows from a much deeper intellectual predisposition. As Herbert Butterfield once observed, a profound understanding of the past can often prove salutary, uncorking an almost alchemical process within formerly leaden psyches:

> It seems true…that many of the errors which spring from a little history are often corrected as people go on to study more and more history…A little history may make people mentally rigid. Only if we go on learning more and more of it…will it correct its own deficiencies gradually and help us reach the required elasticity of mind.

Malleability, adjustability and a certain wilfully acquired intellectual limberness: these aspects of the cognitive process inherent to historical examination are most relevant to our era, along with the associated ability to engage in what the Greek historian Polybius termed the *'interweaving of events'* – that is, the ability to scry the riotous flow of world affairs with the hope of spotting, amid its eddying whirls, underlying currents of cause and effect.

This intuitive sifting and sorting ability, gradually accreted over years of study, allows one to identify chains of causation more rapidly and fluidly, to draw attention more easily to the interconnections between theatres, actions and events, and to more seamlessly analyse geopolitical developments horizontally as well as vertically. Neuroscientists might refer to this as the ability to engage in associative processes across multiple planes simultaneously. And, indeed, neuroscience shows that the brain region most consistently engaged during analogical or relational reasoning is the left frontal lobe – the same part of the brain long postulated to play a key role in creative innovation. It's perhaps for all of these reasons the Harvard historian John Clive once openly wondered whether 'historians, especially those dealing with abstract entities like groups and classes and movements, have to possess a special metaphorical capacity, a plastic or tactile imagination that can detect shapes or configurations where others less gifted see only jumble and confusion'.

Isaiah Berlin, in his skilful essay on political judgement, evokes something very similar, albeit with his characteristic iridescent eloquence; an ability that entails, above all, 'a capacity for integrating a vast amalgam of constantly changing, multicolored, evanescent, perpetually overlapping data, too many, too swift, too intermingled to be caught and pinned down like so many individual butterflies', thus conjuring an acute sense of 'what fits with what, what springs from what, what leads to what', and so forth.

In short, applied historians should perhaps be somewhat more optimistic as to the prospects of their chosen field. Yes, history departments may be closing; yes, tenured job prospects may be dwindling; but somewhat paradoxically, in our information-drenched, distraction-filled and data-drowned world, the historian's hard-earned mental navigational skills may actually prove to be among those most useful for harried, cognitively overwhelmed policymakers.

Washington Crossing the Delaware,
oil on canvas by Emanuel Leutze, 1851.

MYTHS OF ORIGIN: THE UNITED KINGDOM
AND THE UNITED STATES

J. C. D. Clark

What is the problem?

The myths of origin that become hegemonic within states can be immensely influential. The most famous foundation story in Western culture has been that of the Jewish people, set out in the first five books of the Bible. These books are largely remembered in post-Christian cultures for the stories of the Creation, the Garden of Eden, and Adam and Eve. All are indeed present. But the repeated theme throughout these five books is the exhortation of Moses to 'the children of Israel' that they take by force their God-given land.

These books relate the story of Moses leading his people out of their 'bondage' in Egypt; their passage through the Red Sea, as the waters parted to allow them to cross; their sufferings in the Sinai desert. Throughout, Moses urged them on to military conquest of the land 'that floweth with milk and honey'. As to the existing inhabitants, the people of Israel were commanded in some places in the text to drive them out, in others to 'utterly destroy them', or to 'smite every male thereof with the edge of the sword; but the women, and the little ones, and the cattle, and all that is in the city ... shalt thou take unto thyself'. (Genesis 35.11; Exodus 3.8; Leviticus 14.34, 25.1; Numbers 10.29, 14.8, 15.2, 32.21-22, 33.53; Deuteronomy, 7.2, 20. 13–14, 20.17, 31.2–34.5) It was a powerful myth of divinely-sanctioned conquest.

More recently, myths of origin have been validated by Christian churches rather than by direct and audible divine commands (as when God spoke to Moses). Vladimir Putin's 5,000 word essay 'On the Historical Unity of the Russians and Ukranians', published on 12 July 2021, provided a rationale for Russia's invasion of Ukraine on 24 February 2022. In that essay Putin contended that Russia and Ukraine occupied 'essentially the same historical and spiritual space'. 'History' revealed the existence, 'over more than a thousand years', of foreign 'forces that have always sought to undermine our unity'. Spiritual space was identified by 'the Orthodox faith', expressed in Russian Orthodoxy's 'unified church government', clashing with the Catholicism of Lithuania and Poland.

Putin's essay largely analyzed churches as political phenomena, as definitions of identity. But as historical concepts, these churches proved to be powerful explanatory devices. Such an approach was used to show, in a remarkable rejection of Bolshevik internationalism, that 'modern Ukraine is entirely the product of the Soviet era' as the Bolsheviks' expectations of the demise of the nation state led to their 'bestowing territorial gifts'. The break-up of the USSR meant a large reduction in Russia's rightful population: 'Our spiritual unity has also been attacked.'

But are myths of origin more widely shared? Here I shall pose some basic general questions, and then ask how these issues are found in operation in the histories of the United Kingdom and the United States. First, what are myths of origin? Why do people devise them? How do they work?

Turning to these two states, I shall then ask: when and how did their national myths arise? Did those myths experience trajectories over time? Were they subjected to revision as a result of historical research, or of events? Finally, if myths of origin are such dangerous things, how should they be dealt with?

What are myths of origin?

A much longer chronological perspective may help to explain recent events. At the end of the last ice age in the northern hemisphere, the glaciers retreated and the snowfields melted. They were replaced by woodland and grassland. At that point tiny bands of people moved in and began to grow grain, and to keep livestock on the meadows. They were the last innocent generation. But their farming practices created the idea of private property in land, which could hardly develop among hunter-gatherers or herdsmen. Subsequent mass migrations therefore had to entail forcible dispossession.

Since that time, all polities of which written record survives began in the same way: with enormous episodes of murder and theft. Such sanguinary realities then had to be re-described, turned into episodes that were ethically justified, initially often divinely sanctioned. Stable, peaceful societies were derived from unstable and violent origins. The evolution over only a few thousand years of the sophisticated and complex societies of today was never inevitable. In their evolution myths of origin played an important part, by promoting positive practices but also by continuing to camouflage negative ones.

If polities typically arise as a result of episodes of extreme violence, it can be appreciated that they do not have 'founding principles' (unless murder and theft count as principles). These episodes are not ones revealing, let alone driven by, the working out of general principles of government or of universal human rights. Instead, they are episodes of chaos. Out of the chaos step forward individuals claiming to interpret those episodes, to explain what they mean. Those meanings are, at the outset, heavily disputed. Over time, certain interpretations often emerge as hegemonic. But they are never uncontested and never immortal: they change over time.

If so, historically stable values and practices can never be inferred from claimed 'founding principles'. These founding principles have to be expressed in terms too general to be meaningful, like the written constitutions to which they sometimes relate. The US and the UK are often claimed to be 'democracies', but their political systems work in different ways. They are often held to pursue 'liberty', but liberty to do what?

A myth of origin is therefore unlikely to be decisive. To be effective, it has to contain elements of truth. It will also contain elements of false-hood: to make the falsehood palatable is the purpose of the myth. To make myths of origin plausible, they are expressed as histories. They can better be examined through the discipline of history than through the discipline of philosophy.

What do the histories of the UK and the US show?

A comparison between the UK and the US confronts a paradox that his-torians outside the US have had little success in resolving, since their historical theories often contradict hegemonic US myths of origin. The riddle is the nature and causes of the American Revolution itself. For the American war of 1776–83 was quite unlike wars of national liberation: the new nation was an outcome of the Revolution, not its cause. It was not a war between a Catholic and a Protestant country. It was not between a capitalist and a socialist society. It was not between militarists and pacifists. It was not centrally a conflict between people of different skin colours. On the contrary, the two cultures were similar. The myth of origin of the new United States, then, does not explain the American Revolution.

My own contribution has been to suggest that the American Revolution contained some elements of a war of religion. The reality of the Revolution was not republicanism, or universal human rights. Instead, these made up the subsequent myth of origin. This explains parts of the myth of origin that won acceptance subsequent to the Revolution, in the new republic. Remarkably, that Revolution was not preceded by any substantial reflections in the American colonies on democracy, or on the nature and merits of republican forms of government. Instead, the reality had major elements of sectarian conflict. The outcome was a polity that the Protestant Dissenters made (as politicized Islam now reveals). It glorified a notion, or notions, of religious destiny, in Biblical imagery a City on a Hill. That Revolution had to be misrepresented if it was to be sanitised.

What of the UK? In recent centuries, one influential myth of origin derived from the Revolution of 1688. The reality of that Revolution was that it was an armed rebellion, backed by a foreign invasion, intended to destroy a Catholic monarchy and replace it with a Protestant one. This element had to be incorporated into, but misdescribed in, the myth of origin that succeeded 1688: that myth claimed that England, then Britain, then the United Kingdom, was essentially dedicated to liberty. This libertarian myth of origin was resisted by peoples that the English conquered and in countries thereafter held by force: Ireland and Scotland; then the American colonies; then a third world empire.

The meaning of the Revolution of 1688 was lastingly contested by Tories and Jacobites in England, and by some Scots and some Irish on the English periphery, but these challenges were beaten off. Britain fought the American war of 1776–83 with a firmly entrenched belief that it was consistent with a free constitution for the Westminster Parliament to legislate for the colonies, a principle that survived defeat. The American Revolution did not have decisive consequences in England.

At home, the regime in England was challenged by a series of revolutionaries, as in the early years of the French Revolution, such men often invoking the anti-monarchism of the 1640s; after 1815, sometimes invoking the idea of an Anglo-Saxon free constitution. English socialists planned the achievement of a socialist society by armed revolution, sometimes invoking an idea of the prosperity of workers, in the late Middle Ages, before the rise of capitalism. None of these threatened revolutions happened. Instead, English, then UK, history has been deeply modified by historians, not by ideologically-inspired revolutionaries.

The new myth that the historians have lately made is that the UK was built on the values of pluralism and diversity, a myth claiming to be based on the further myth that universal human rights were a creation of 'the Enlightenment', itself a myth of origin that rose to its present hegemony only in the 1960s.

What happened in the new United States? Since its myth of origin was premised on a justified revolution, the notion that a second revolution was needed to bring about a just society (as, notably, a socialist revolution) had no space in which to develop. The hegemonic myth of origin of the US was therefore powerful and long-lasting. Victory for the southern States in the civil war of 1861–65 would have destroyed it; the victory of the northern States confirmed it. It emerged greatly strengthened from the military victory of 1945.

Its alleged components were argued over by academic historians, who chiefly explored the options of 'Lockeian liberalism' and 'classical republicanism' (each largely a myth; for example, 'liberalism' was the proper name of an ideology coined more than a century after Locke's lifetime), but this historiographical contest ended in a stalemate that left the familiar myth of origin of the United States, as embodied in popular culture, largely intact.

When myths of origin are contradicted, challenged, modified or discarded, it is mostly because of major military defeat. In the United States the major modifier was military defeat, although a lesser military defeat, in the Vietnam war.

That myth of origin was fundamentally changed not by historicizing it, subjecting it to historical analysis, but by changing its owners, by including others within it, notably women and African Americans (but not until very recently, for example in the work of Ned Blackhawk, Native Americans). In that new form it is still powerful. The myth of the career open to talents is still hegemonic, despite the fact that social mobility in the US is little different from social mobility in other similarly advanced societies: inherited wealth is still a powerful determinant of the fortunes of individuals in successive generations, and many poor groups are trapped in material and cultural poverty.

But the myth has been secularised. The white settlers of the Thirteen Colonies that achieved independence in 1783 expanded by force across the North American continent, their republic growing by the annexation of Texas in 1845 and the military defeat of Mexico in the war of 1846–48.

In that decade ill-defined but evocative ideas of 'manifest destiny' were developed by some in the United States. These ideals, assumptions and assertions became however normally secular. Initially contested, the idea became widely diffused.

John Gast's famous picture *American Progress* was painted in 1872. It showed parties of white settlers moving westwards across the continent with Native Americans fleeing before them. But the scene was presided over and urged on not by God but by the figure of an airborne female representing Columbia, a personification of America itself. Thanks to the myth of origin, the land empire of the USA is not allowed to stand as an instance of imperialism; the USA is described as an exception. In 1998, a conference organized in Rome by the United Nations considered a document establishing an International Criminal Court; the United States voted against, and in 2002 a US Federal Act asserted the immunity of the US from the jurisdiction of that Court, which was then being constituted.

In 1920, President Woodrow Wilson used the phrase 'manifest destiny', but only to designate the drive to extend 'democracy'. US power is no longer projected with a missionary zeal, as it was by Wilson, the Presbyterian president of a Presbyterian university, Princeton. Instead, a secularized 'democracy' is used as the justification for the use of force by the US around the world. The contradiction between these democratic ideals and the actual working of US politics at home is almost never an issue in daily US politics: 'the Constitution' still has mythic status.

What, then, should be done?
How, finally, should myths of origin be dealt with? As an historian, I suggest that these things be analyzed historically. I focus on two parts: 'myths' and 'origins'.

First, 'myths'. These are partial untruths, used to claim authority: something (partly a fiction) happened in the past, therefore it should happen (in reality) in the future. Traditions are different: they are practices, acted out voluntarily by individuals. Myths are ideologies, imposed on individuals by ideologists. Traditions are what people do; myths of origin are what people are told to do. But the choice of what view of the past to which such authority is given must inevitably be arbitrary. Germans might prefer the Germany of Goethe and Schiller to the Germany of

Hitler and Goebbels; but why not prefer the Germany of Luther to that of Goethe and Schiller? Putin's myth of ancient and shared Russian and Ukrainian identity was contested by Norman Davies, a British scholar of Polish history. But he argued, in a review of the same thousand years of history, that 'Ukraine was part of the Polish state for longer than it was inside Russia': even if so, why this should dictate an outcome in the present was as unclear as it was in the case of Putin's argument.

Second, 'origins'. What people choose to call the origin of their state is equally an arbitrary choice. Citizens of the United States look back to 1776 as its Founding (with a capital letter); but each individual colony was much older, sometimes a century and a half older; the founders of each colony, had they survived, might have disagreed profoundly with the rejection of transatlantic unity in 1776. Each colony had been constituted by killing or ejecting the earlier occupants: their myths of origin were deleted. So 'history' is an infinite regress. There is no 'it', no History with a capital H, to justify any present-day decisions. Traditions, that is, unideological practices, may be safe guides; myths of origin may be deeply dangerous.

World chess champion Garry Kasparov stands
during a match against IBM super computer
Deep Blue in New York, 6 May 1997.

WHY HUMAN ART MATTERS
IN THE AGE OF AI

James Marriott

In Roald Dahl's short story 'The Great Automatic Grammatizator', an inventor named Adolph Knipe constructs a novel-writing machine. Knipe's fantastical and perhaps excessively gothic contraption can be manipulated by various pedals, levers and organ stops to produce detective stories, historical fiction, Westerns, tales of the sea and so on – in the style of Hemingway, Faulkner, Joyce or whoever you like. The Grammatizator's owners plot to supplant the world's novelists – 'squeeze 'em out', 'exactly like Rockefeller did with his oil companies', one of them enthuses. This being a Dahl story – and therefore dark and cynical – the plan is a virtually unqualified success. Dahl writes that in 'the first full year of the machine's operation it was estimated that at least one half of all the novels and stories published in the English language were produced by Adolph Knipe upon the Great Automatic Grammatizator'.

The Grammatizator is not quite here. But new generative artificial intelligence technologies, such as ChatGPT, are capable of producing plausible essays and pastiches of poems. Writers are understandably alarmed. In Hollywood, screenwriters are striking against studio plans to use large language models to write television scripts. Upsettingly, for those in my profession, AI already writes competent (if not always accurate) journalism. Some experts predict that a machine will be capable of writing a bestselling novel within decades or years.

If art and literature matter to you, no thought could be bleaker. To me, the prospect of a machine capable of writing a book seems almost unbearably sad. An assault on a profound aspect of what it is to be a human being. But need we be as pessimistic as Dahl? A machine may write books, but will it produce the higher form of writing we call literature? I am sceptical. For to believe a machine is capable of producing literature is to misunderstand what literature is and why we love it.

Let us take, for instance, this passage from Matthew Arnold's great poem 'Dover Beach':

Ah, love, let us be true
To one another! for the world, which seems
To lie before us like a land of dreams,
So various, so beautiful, so new,
Hath really neither joy, nor love, nor light,
Nor certitude, nor peace, nor help for pain;
And we are here as on a darkling plain
Swept with confused alarms of struggle and flight,
Where ignorant armies clash by night.

The profoundly moving poem records a familiar human sentiment. But no machine with access to the whole corpus of human writing should find it difficult to construct a description of despair – the subject crops up with melancholy frequency. And true, the final image is especially skilful. But we have no reason to believe literary skill will be permanently beyond the abilities of artificial intelligence already capable of writing a sonnet about spinach in the style of William Shakespeare.

But the poem is also a record of the noble, melancholy soul of Matthew Arnold. It matters as a human artefact, and an appreciation of Arnold's lines is inextricable from an appreciation of the human personality that created them. Even the reader's thrill at the poem's technical virtuosity is inextricable from the human intelligence that conceived it. You could give me a hundred years and I could not write the final lines.

One's appreciation of a work of art is often accompanied by the thought: 'Wow, how did they do that?' Part of the excitement of reading poetry or looking at a painting is the thrill of watching a human talent pushed to its utmost. The feeling is not dissimilar from the way an appreciation of athletics derives from our interest in what the human body can be made to do. Indeed, at the ancient Olympic Games there were prizes for poetry as well as sport. It is true that you could write a poem using artificial intelligence. Equally, the competitors in a 100 metre race could augment their physical skill by getting in a car and driving to the finish line – but that would be a different race. The existence of Formula One has not diminished the appeal of the foot race sprint.

There is an analogy here with chess. The game (or perhaps even the art) of chess was 'disrupted' by artificial intelligence almost three decades ago. Modern AI programmes make the best chess players look like pathetic amateurs by comparison. But this has done little to diminish the appeal of the game. More people play than ever before. And few chess players in history have achieved the fame of the greatest living player, Magnus Carlsen. Online, millions have watched Carlsen's greatest matches. Games between computers tend to attract much smaller audiences of dedicated nerds. Many more people have heard of Carlsen than have heard of the chess AI AlphaZero. But Carlsen is vastly the inferior player.

Human beings have a profound bias towards other humans. As the psychologist Steven Pinker puts it, 'we all have deep intuitions about causal connections to people'. It is for this reason, Pinker says, that collectors will pay a huge premium for JFK's golf clubs, for example, even if they are identical to those owned by a less well-known player. It turns out that chess fans are not purely (or even primarily) interested in the perfection of a game; rather, they are interested in the potential of the human mind and the drama of personality. Examples of this bias are everywhere. Any listener to a public phone-in show on the radio knows the callers are not principally interesting as analysts of current affairs. But their opinions fascinate us because they are the views of human beings. Even an AI so powerful that it solved the question of immigration or Brexit would be unlikely to abolish the radio phone-in show.

We may justly wonder: how interesting is intelligence to human beings? Interesting enough, certainly. But rarely the most fascinating thing. It is the same with art. Indeed, few people are as intriguing to us as famous singers, actors and writers. Newspapers are filled with gossip, sex scandals and speculation about the private lives of celebrities. Our fascination with art is deeply connected to our fascination with the human personality.

These personalities matter to us because art is profoundly human – as most great artists have understood. Philip Larkin once said: 'I write poems to preserve things I have seen/thought/felt (if I may so indicate a composite and complex experience).' Art, he wrote, is 'permanent communication'. In his treatise of 1897, *What is Art*, Tolstoy reaches a similar conclusion: 'Art begins when a man, with the purpose of communicating to other people a feeling he once experienced, calls it up again within himself and expresses it by certain external signs.' If a work of art does not preserve a human experience is it really a work of art at all?

'Dover Beach' is a consoling, not a depressing, poem because it preserves a human experience. I am comforted by it because it is a verbal artefact that has been skilfully constructed to connect me to another person. Alan Bennett puts it perfectly in his play *The History Boys*: 'The best moments in reading are when you come across something – a thought, a feeling, a way of looking at things – which you had thought special and particular to you. Now here it is, set down by someone else, a person you have never met, someone even who is long dead. And it is as if a hand has come out and taken yours.' Tennyson put it like this:

> So word by word, and line by line,
> The dead man touch'd me from the past,
> And all at once it seem'd at last
> The living soul was flash'd on mine

A feeling reconstructed by a machine cannot console in this way because it has no human hand to reach out to us. Perhaps even a conscious machine could not really make art, because its feelings would not be human ones. I can imagine a machine that could entertain. I cannot imagine one that could console.

This instinct for the human is not merely a philosophical abstraction. It is one of our most instinctive responses to art. Watching a YouTube video of the Mozart opera *Così fan tutte* recently, I was struck by the most up-voted comment: 'Absolutely moves me to tears every time I hear it. Whenever you see humans doing terrible things to each other or themselves I listen to this and realise what humans ARE capable of. People are making beautiful noises!'

I suppose one can imagine ways we might be duped into this response by means of deepfakes and so on. But the deception would have to be elaborate, and perhaps involve the faking of a human author along with their characteristic signs of existence – interviews with newspapers and so on. And if no legislation effectively compels publishers to state which content is made by humans and which by machine, we will have more urgent problems on our hands than the meaning of literature.

It is curious that machine art should have arrived at a time when our cultural obsession with the human personality in art is more powerful than ever. The writer David Shields's useful phrase 'reality hunger' describes the twenty-first-century yearning for the authentic and the real. As sales of literary fiction decline, the memoir flourishes. As soap opera viewership slumps, reality television booms. Even the novel itself has succumbed to this trend. Writers like Karl Ove Knausgård, Ben Lerner and Rachel Cusk have pioneered the new form of autofiction – novels that acquire their fascination and authority from their connection to life. The power of the novels that make up Knausgård's *My Struggle* series derives from the reader's suspicion that everything, or almost everything, in the book is real. Knausgård's genius for artistic banality – the long passages describing, say, the making of a cup of instant coffee, or a journey through the Swedish countryside with fractious children, rests on our belief in the authenticity of these moments. Knausgård could have made up more dramatic incidents, but boring reality is more interesting to his readers. Such is human nature.

Similarly, many reality television shows are significantly less eventful and artful than their fictional rivals. And yet, in the early 2000s, *Big Brother* enthralled the British public with its endless broadcast of people in a house not doing a great deal. What mattered was that these were real human beings.

In a future flooded with machine-produced content we may place a higher value on human art than ever before. In his classic essay 'The Work of Art in the Age of Mechanical Reproduction', Walter Benjamin speculated that the advent of machine reproduction of images would damage the almost magical aura of authenticity that surrounded original artworks. What is the point of Van Gogh's *Sunflowers* if you can buy a thousand cheap prints of it for a fraction of the price? Benjamin, of course, was wrong. Precisely the opposite happened. The proliferation of cheap prints increased the mystique of authentic artworks and caused their market value to rocket. In the latter half of the twentieth century art became obscenely expensive – its value deriving from its contact with the original human genius. Perhaps the advent of AI art will have a similar effect. A culture flooded with machine-produced content may be one that places an extraordinary premium on the human.

The future of many careers may turn out to depend on the value we place on that illusory, illogical human factor. Could we trust the justice dispensed by a robot judge, even if we were told it was measurably more reliable and less biased than that of a human? Will the opinions of a robot newspaper columnist matter? I sincerely hope not. Most of all, I hope we decide that human art still matters.

A world of machine art would be an eerie one. Art connects us to one another. We cannot, and we should not, replace that connection with an uncanny simulacrum of it. For without the art and literature of human beings we are left in the situation described in another great Matthew Arnold poem, 'To Marguerite: Continued':

> Yes! in the sea of life enisled,
> With echoing straits between us thrown,
> Dotting the shoreless watery wild,
> We mortal millions live *alone*.

Art and literature are the bridges between those human islands. Let us hope we keep them in good repair.

Relief depicting the Power of Government.
On the right is a figure of Statecraft flanked by
a defender of the Liberties and Rights of People.

THE COMPONENTS OF STATECRAFT:
PAST, PRESENT AND FUTURE

John Bew

Statecraft is called different things in different languages. And it has meant different things in different eras. To be regarded as a sound practitioner of statecraft is generally a thing to be welcomed. But what does that really mean in practice, aside from the accoutrement of sophistication which it assumes?

In French, statecraft is interchangeable with the concept of '*raison d'état*', or 'reason of state'. This was a term which became popularised from the early modern period, of which Cardinal Richelieu was perhaps the most famous practitioner. It was later juxtaposed awkwardly with the nobler ideas of the Enlightenment, when theories of governance took on a supposedly more idealistic turn.

In German, statecraft was sometimes seen as synonymous with something called 'realpolitik' – a more austere credo that sought to understand and adapt to the harsh realities of power politics. Realpolitik was born in the cauldron of the nineteenth-century European nation state, coined first after the 1848 revolutions in a period of class struggle, state formation, the surge of nationalism and great power competition. It was often seen as an antidote to excessive sentimentalism, Whiggish ideas of progress and liberal cant. In some respects, realpolitik was a direct response to infuriatingly pompous Anglo-Saxons and the insipid commercialism that some believed had infected their imperial mind.

In the English language, by contrast, statecraft has never been seen as something so crude as narrow realpolitik. It is a more elusive notion; but it is one that is nonetheless oriented to the 'national interest' and the practice of 'high politics', rather than the pursuit of high-minded universalist ideals. So defined, statecraft is an activity that normally applies to 'affairs of state' – core constitutional issues, security and foreign policy – as distinct from the general din of democratic politics. Likewise, good statecraft and populism are tricky to reconcile. Here, the emphasis is on the *craft* part of statecraft. English-language theories of statecraft began with privateers and courtiers in the early modern court but evolved alongside the professionalisation of diplomacy, espionage and military service in the British Empire and United States.

In my own preferred definition, statecraft is a little less austere than the German tradition – and perhaps a little less self-consciously professionalised than the English-language version. It sits somewhere in between, trying to strike a balance between wily self-awareness and burning fury at the hypocrisy or stupidity of others. It is an art rather than a science.

Good statecraft should encompass a creative as well as a critical impulse, leaving space for idealism and ideas. It is much more than a cult of the national interest, or the utilitarian application of ends, ways and means. It must build outward and upward, grasping the future rather than simply adapting to the circumstances in which it is practised. It must be optimistic in spirit, if sceptical in approach. It is, as the Federalist Papers reveal, about the *internal* coherence and functioning of the state – its parameters and internal mechanics – as well as great matters of international diplomacy overseas.

In other words, good statecraft starts at home with a careful nurturing of the needs of the state. And modern statecraft must not only adapt to the realities of democratic life, it should seek to harness and deploy them in the interest of the state.

But rather than giving you a history lesson, the intention of this essay is to do something new – or at least something that I haven't done before. And that is to *distil* rather than define the ingredients of statecraft, by bridging the gap between theory and practice.

First, I want to begin to synthesise some of the observations I have gleaned from an academic career studying statecraft (as a biographer, in particular) with the experience of working for four years in government. That is, to come to a sense of how those two worlds – the academy and the court – meld together.

Now, the mistake that academics who go into government sometimes make is to assume that they are bringing some sort of pure form of knowledge, to be carried into the political world hermetically sealed, opened carefully and laid out before the toothless scoundrels and philistines crowded around the table. To my mind, therefore, the idea that there should be an 'official historian' sitting at the shoulder of the king like an unsullied eunuch is not compelling. All good history is political in one way or another. Nonetheless, it is my firm view that the worlds of study and practice are more *sympatico* than is often assumed.

Second, in the next part of this short essay I want to outline the *components* of statecraft. Or, more precisely, I want to outline the components that I believe – from both historical study and some lived experience in applying this knowledge – are the essential preconditions of *good* statecraft.

Finally, there is a particular reason that the title of my paper refers to statecraft *past, present and future.* That is because the essay draws on ideas from a *deep past heritage* of thinking about statecraft; is *consciously present-minded* in how those ideas should be applied today; and, above all, argues that good statecraft cannot simply be based on eternal or classical wisdom but must always change to *adapt to the conditions of modernity.*

The last point is the one which I want to develop most in the course of my remarks. Because here is where I want to make a clarion call about the need to get better at the business of modern statecraft. While it is fashionable to say that there is a renaissance in the study of statecraft, it is also my view that the practice of statecraft is struggling to keep up with the world around it.

To be clear, my attempt to distil the critical components of statecraft is a first attempt. It should not be treated with biblical authority, therefore, and is certainly not intended as the last word. That said, they are presented here in the rather grandiose form of ten commandments. They come with some sense of hierarchy and, I hope, a logical progression between them. There are seven essential principles:

1. A grounding in history (or a reasonably developed sense of what has come before)
2. A good grasp of context (or fulsome appreciation of the parameters in which you operate)
3. A theory of change (how to move history along)
4. A creative as well as a critical mind (an ability to envisage something better rather than only engaging in critique)
5. An ecumenical approach to methodology (rather than privileging one analytical theory to the exclusion of others)
6. An appreciation of the spiritual over the hyper-rational
7. A wariness about the traps of presentism (including tech-utopianism)

And three additional recommendations to adapt to the modern world:

8. A willingness to extend the traditional arts of statecraft into new domains
9. A recognition that grand strategy is the highest form of statecraft
10. Embracing the centrality of planning (as a precondition of good statecraft in the twenty-first century)

To take each in turn:

1. A grounding in history (or a reasonably developed sense of what has come before)

Frank Gavin calls this a 'historical sensibility'. In its purest form, it is reflected in Machiavelli's view that one must understand the classical world (and its great historians) to navigate the early modern world.

One need not be a practitioner or an expert on history to achieve this. But one must have the ability to interrogate lazy assumptions about how we got to this point. And one must have a sense of what others think about what has happened in the past.

These narratives and stories have considerable political force in a way that does not depend on their veracity. History and analogy remain the language of government in almost every policy area – but none more so than in the areas of foreign policy and defence. It is therefore the starting point of any copybook of statecraft.

2. A good grasp of context (or fulsome appreciation of the parameters in which you operate)

This flows naturally from the first and again it should be helped by a grounding in history.

The parameters can be the system in which you operate. How does it work? Where do you sit within it? What levers can be pulled? In which ear must you whisper? It is obvious that life is easier at the apex of your system (or that you have more agency) and that you can wait your moment. It is also true that longevity gives you more opportunity to exert influence and to learn your trade on the job. The closer to the throne, I would also suggest, the easier it is for you to exercise influence and power through good manners, kind words and patience.

In a more precarious position, it may be wiser to scratch the occasional pair of eyes out or be noisy to be heard. But my own view is that raging against the machine gets you only so far. It can expedite the process of change, but it can sometimes lead you to exert your energies on the wrong things.

But far more important are the parameters beyond your system. People spend too long looking within. Edmund Burke said circumstances are the defining condition of any political scenario.

So how much domestic room for manoeuvre do you have? How firmly do you have your hands on the reins of power and how far can you stretch the logic of that? Where is it that you have authority? What appetite is there for risk?

The same applies to international politics. There are the obvious metrics of power (the size of the economy or proportion of GDP spent on military power); there are hierarchies; there are organisations that work and those that do not.

In sum, an appreciation of these objective realities is the baseline for any form of successful statecraft.

3. A theory of change (how to move history along)

The reason to know your history and to establish the parameters in which you operate is not to succumb meekly to them; otherwise, statecraft would only be about mowing the lawn and tending the plants.

Therefore, as the next evolutionary step, successful statecraft also requires a theory of change. This theory, I would also suggest, has to be constantly examined and re-examined.

It allows you to operate with and around, and sometimes even to defeat, the objective realities which you face. 'Respect the sea!', you are told when you are young. But a theory of change means you can swim in it and maybe even ride the waves.

I have experienced periods in government when you feel completely stuck in a box and unable to move left or right, only to burst free by accident, chance, opportunism and sometimes even acumen. I have seen Leninist approaches to change that have got very far very quickly – using the vanguard or trying to engineer a jolt in the pace of historical development. Yet I would also reflect that some forms of change can run out of momentum or leave themselves open to be reversed by other forces.

Raging against the machine is not always productive over a longer term. Sometimes it is better to redefine the existing lexicon and win over a wider grouping by speaking their language and showing that you are more attuned to their concerns.

The same goes for foreign policy. Good statecraft means that you can exert more influence than you might otherwise be expected to as a nation, on the basis of an objective assessment of the traditional metrics of power. That can be achieved by moving faster, being first, or by taking a disproportionate level of risk. But again, you must keep that under review and know when it is safer and more productive to fall back into the peloton, having set the pace.

4. A creative as well as a critical mind (an ability to envisage something better rather than only engaging in critique)

Statecraft has to be a creative effort. There is a balance to be struck here between the art of critique and analytical rigour and the ability to set out a vision for what may come next.

Critique is easier in government. Writing a strategy or vision statement, or making a choice to change course, is much harder. But the imagination, fortitude and willingness to do so is vital. The critical tools are essential, I should be clear. But the creative impulse, I would suggest, has been run down too much.

Academia is partly to blame here. The endeavour to expose power structures and use scholarship to challenge the system is laudable and a sign of a healthy society. But the balance in the scholarly world has become skewed toward critique, due to the expansion of critical studies and the atomisation of history and other disciplines. Government needs to free itself from these shackles.

5. An ecumenical approach to methodology (rather than privileging one analytical theory to the exclusion of others)

Here is a useful starting point for the adoption of knowledge in government – everything is true and nothing is true. The greater the variety of insights you can digest, the greater nuance and subtlety you will bring to your statecraft. One of my reflections in government is that the idea that one should approach complex questions with a pre-cooked way of looking at something is remarkably self-limiting.

That is why we should be ecumenical in the tools of analysis. Relying on one form of analysis – a single theory or overarching methodology – is dangerous. You can't afford to be picky. In fact, it is essential that you try to see the world through the eyes of others.

This is also one of the great insights of Henry Kissinger and indeed George Kennan before him. You not only need to 'think in time' yourself but also to think of how others think in time. This applies particularly to rivals and adversaries. What is *their* conception of historical change? What is their conception of time and how long are they prepared to wait to get their way?

6. An appreciation of the spiritual over the hyper-rational

Governments are obsessed with metrics. Political science has slipped into government – not helped by an over-reliance on polling. I have talked about objective realities. But objective realities are not just structural – they involve imponderables like mood and tone.

Ludwig von Rochau, the creator of the concept of realpolitik, noted that the art of politics in the democratic age was to distinguish between momentary fashions and impulses and settled and received wisdom. He also said the zeitgeist is the defining feature of any age.

The more that an idea or ideas became settled in the mind of a nation, the more political force they gained. Their inherent truth was secondary to that. Again, my lived experience of political life is that an ability to tap into the mood (or even to shape and guide it) is a remarkably powerful thing to do in support of statecraft.

7. A wariness about the traps of presentism

Good statecraft should also be based on a sense of perspective. It should mitigate against something else that I have seen in government, which is the assumption that there is something particularly unique or new about the age in which we exist.

This is ever-present in a number of prevailing notions that we often hear (or have heard) in the last few years:

'Technology will change everything.' Every generation has said the same.

'The global middle ground may not be fully with us on Ukraine.' When was it ever fully with us?

'The authoritarians do grand strategy better.' They said the same in the 1930s and through much of the Cold War.

We must beware the idea that the problems of the present are uniquely different to the same types of dilemmas we have faced in the past. And we must beware the siren call of modernism and tech-utopianism to cure the ills of the age in which we live.

And yet, this is not an argument for thumbing one's nose at modernity. On the contrary, today's statecraft requires a quantum leap to keep up with it. So, to that end, this essay concludes with three more commandments (or humble suggestions) for statecraft in the modern age.

8. Keeping pace with new forms of power

Our understanding of what national security is has expanded exponentially in recent years. Traditional defence and security are but one part of a nation's ability to ensure that its interests are protected and promoted. Trade and economic security are regarded as increasingly important. Science and technological development are now central to the competition between nations, with implications for resources.

This means that the types of dilemmas faced by different states are changing too. For example, there are states that can seek security and defence in their size, access to resources and share of the market. But there is a growing number of states who sit outside these regulatory blocks, who seek and need access to resources and technologies that they do not possess or cannot produce themselves.

The multilateral system offers increasingly less assurance. Therefore, contemporary statecraft requires greater agility and deeper and broader partnerships that go beyond traditional defence and intelligence relationships. And statecraft must enter new frontiers such as artificial intelligence and biotechnology because they are sources of power.

9. A recognition that grand strategy is the highest form of statecraft

Statecraft needs grand strategy more than at any point since the Cold War. A statecraft that simply refines or adapts to the world around us is not enough for the era in which we live.

Grand strategy is a higher form of statecraft. It combines all the traditional components of statecraft – history, strategy, warfare, international relations and diplomacy – with the newer elements: economics, technology, research and science. And it tries to combine them with national purpose.

'The role of Grand Strategy – higher strategy – is to coordinate and direct all the resources of a nation, or band of nations, towards the attainment of the political object…the goal defined by fundamental policy,' wrote the British strategist Basil Liddell Hart. He went on to argue that this included the 'moral resources' of a nation, 'for to foster the people's willing spirit is often as important as to possess the more concrete forms of power'.

The return of inter-state war and the sharpening of geopolitical competition makes this broader and higher understanding of statecraft as important as it has been in generations. As Liddell Hart put it, in his book *Strategy*, 'The base from which victory will arise is built not only of material resources or of military and industrial techniques, but also of social organization, religious ideals, methods of education and so forth, all of which must be maintained in times of peace.'

10. Embracing the centrality of planning (as a precondition of good statecraft in the twenty-first century)

Finally, for grand strategy to work, one cannot leave oneself open entirely to the vagaries of fortune. An ability to adapt is vital; and a plodding fidelity to ends, ways and means is a recipe for sluggishness. But a merely adaptive approach is not good statecraft. It was Francis Bacon, the advisor to Queen Elizabeth I, who once complained that 'the wisdom of all these latter times, in princes' affairs, is rather fine deliveries, and shifting of dangers and mischiefs when they are near, than solid and grounded courses to keep them aloof'.

Planning is something that liberal democratic societies and free market economies feel somewhat uncomfortable about. But it is a necessary response to adversaries and challengers who make a virtue of best laid plans.

We must avoid grandiose projects to remake the world. But being passive respondents to the planning of others is a recipe for disaster. We need not mimic the acts of others as we have a rich heritage of our own. In Western foreign policy, the art of policy planning was born in the 1930s in response to epochal great power competition and carried the West through the Second World War and Cold War.

Our plans need not be the best laid plans. They may get cracked and sometimes even scrambled. But we must at least try to lay the egg.

Charles de Gaulle and Georges Bidault
in front of Arc de Triomphe, Paris, 1944.

DE GAULLE'S WORLD IN MOTION

Julian Jackson

In his recent book on leadership, published a year before he died, Henry Kissinger distinguishes between two ideal types of leaders: statesmen and prophets. Statesmen 'temper vision with wariness, entertaining a sense of limits'; prophets invoke a transcendent vision of the world to 'redefine what appears to be possible'. What light do these distinctions throw on the leadership of Charles de Gaulle?

What makes de Gaulle especially interesting is that, before emerging as a national leader in 1940, he wrote extensively about the nature of leadership. His highly cerebral *The Edge of the Sword* (1932) cites a plethora of authorities, including Goethe, Bergson, Bacon, Tolstoy, Heine, Rousseau, Racine and Cicero. De Gaulle's vision of leadership is bleak. A successful leader must cultivate aloofness, mystery and ruse. The solitude of leadership, he writes, 'lacerates the soul as the flint tears the feet of the penitent sinner'. It imposes 'unceasing self-discipline, the constant taking of risks, perpetual inner struggle'. The leader needs the strong nerves and iron self-control of a gambler whose 'elegance consists in reinforcing his outward appearance of sangfroid at the moment he takes the winnings'.

Profoundly influenced by the anti-positivist writings of Henri Bergson, de Gaulle argued that the leader must combine reflection and intuition, analytical intelligence and moral courage. He wrote many years later: 'Great men have both intellect and impulse. The brain serves as a brake upon pure emotional impulse. The brain surmounts impulse; but there must also be impulse and the capability for action in order not to be paralysed by the brake of the brain. I remember this from Bergson who has guided me through my entire life.' The impulse – the moral courage – required of a leader might require him radically to break with convention. De Gaulle quoted a judgement on the British admiral Lord Jellicoe after the Battle of Jutland: 'He has all the qualities of Nelson bar one: he does not know how to disobey!'

The leader must be attentive to contingency and constantly ready to adapt to circumstances. De Gaulle valued the statecraft of the *Ancien Régime*: 'Avoiding abstractions but holding on to realities, preferring the useful to the sublime, the opportune to the spectacular, seeking for each particular problem not the ideal solution but the practical one.' One of his books opened with a celebration of the restrained order (*mesure*) of the French classical garden. For the same reason he was critical of the hubris displayed by Napoleon: 'Once the balance between the ends and means is snapped, the manoeuvres of a genius are in vain.'

It is the role of the leader to analyse the situation and set goals but he must not become mired in details. He reflects, he consults, he decides, but then he leaves the details of execution to others: *'L'ordonnance suivra'* (the supply train will follow), as he famously remarked.

The leader has to be able to stir the imagination and excite the 'latent faith of the masses'. This vision of charismatic leadership was much influenced by Gustave Le Bon, whose writing on crowd psychology influenced figures as diverse as Theodore Roosevelt, Freud and Mussolini. In the spirit of Le Bon, de Gaulle says that the leader's authority is not susceptible to rational analysis ('love which is explicable only as the action of an inexpressible charm'). To this he adds, however, that the leader needs to take the people with him by explaining his actions: charismatic leadership had a didactic element.

Thus, de Gaulle's conception of leadership fits both of Kissinger's ideal types. It is a combination of reason and sentiment, eighteenth-century classicism and nineteenth-century romanticism, the statecraft of Cavour and the romantic nationalism of Mazzini.

The blend of willpower and analytical intelligence, impulse and reflection, was perfectly exemplified by the act through which de Gaulle entered history on 18 June 1940 with his short speech on the BBC calling on the French to reject the armistice with Germany and remain in the war. Leaving France for a country he hardly knew and openly defying the government of Marshal Pétain, France's most venerated military figure, was an act of extraordinary moral courage. As de Gaulle later wrote: 'I appeared to myself, alone and deprived of everything, like a man on the edge of an ocean that he was hoping to swim across.' De Gaulle's *'Appel du 18 juin'* was not only visionary and prophetic ('the flame of Resistance must not be extinguished') but it was also underpinned by a rational analysis of the future of the war. He argued that the lost battle of France was just the beginning of a world war in which the economic superiority of the British and Americans would prevail.

This speech was only the beginning. Although it had secured for de Gaulle the initial backing of Churchill, this did not imply any recognition of his claims to be the sole representative of French national interests. Over the next four years he would deploy an astonishing mixture of bluff, eloquence, adaptability, willpower and nerve to assert himself in the face of the scepticism, and even hostility, of Churchill and Roosevelt. As he later commented: 'People go on about the Appel of 18 June…What every-one seems to ignore is the incredible mixture of patience…of obstinate creativity…the dizzying succession of calculations, negotiations, con-flicts…that we had to undertake in order to accomplish our enterprise.' De Gaulle's often provocative and abrasive style of leadership between 1940 and 1944 probably came naturally to him, but it was also the result of a rational calculation. Since he had so few means at his disposal, his main weapon was intransigence. After the war he humorously summed up his strategy of negotiation to an aide: 'Always begin by saying "no"! Two things will follow: either your "no" is destined to remain a "no" and you have shown yourself to be someone of character. Or eventually you end up saying "yes". But then (a) you have given yourself time to reflect; (b) people will be all the more grateful for your final "yes".'

What de Gaulle achieved in those four years was remarkable. The man alone on the shores of the ocean in 1940 had succeeded in having France accepted among the victorious nations in 1945, with a zone of occupation in Germany and a permanent seat on the United Nations Security Council. In a speech at the Albert Hall in November 1942, he quoted the eighteenth-century moralist Chamfort: 'The reasonable have survived. The passionate have lived…During these two years we have lived a lot because we are passionate. But we have survived as well. Ah yes, how rea-sonable we are!' Reason and sentiment, calculation and intuition: all de Gaulle is there.

De Gaulle's ten years in power as president of France were less obvi-ously 'heroic' than his four years at the head of the Free French, although one could read the constitution of the Fifth Republic which de Gaulle introduced in 1958 as an institutionalisation of the style of charismatic leadership he had theorised before, and practised after, 1940. His star-tling provocations when president meant that foreign diplomats were often reduced to reading his pre-war writings on leadership to decode this unpredictable man. There could be no better example of mystery and ruse than the way he slowly extricated France from Algeria, starting with his speech on 4 June 1958 assuring a frenzied crowd in Algiers that 'I have understood you.' After this moment of supreme duplicity, his speeches over the next four years were a slow process of pedagogy explaining why sentiment had to bow to 'circumstances'. As he declared in 1960: 'It is entirely natural to feel nostalgia for the Empire, as one can regret the gentle light of oil lamps, the splendour of sailing ships...But there is no value in a policy that does not take account of realities.'

In conformity to his idea that the leader must not become mired in details, de Gaulle left much of the running of day-to-day politics to his prime minister. And, to a surprising extent for someone so seemingly authoritarian, he was remarkably open to advice and to listening to advisers. One civil servant, meeting him for the first time, commented: 'I found the General quite different from what I had imagined: very simple, very relaxed, almost respectful...After having listened to me, when he made his comments on what I had said, he took up exactly what I had said, word for word, almost to the last syllable! He had a fantastic memory... One cannot exaggerate his capacity to listen.' Another adviser had the impression, as de Gaulle peered at him intently at him through his thick glasses, 'of being listened to with greater attention than had ever happened to me anywhere before'.

Until the events of May 1968, the Fifth Republic did provide France with ten years of political stability, underpinned by strong economic growth. Nonetheless, in his foreign policy, de Gaulle's achievements fell far short of his ambitions. Perhaps one reason for this was that he failed to achieve the necessary balance of 'prophetic' vision and 'realistic' statecraft. His long-term ambition was to overcome the bipolarity of Cold War politics which, in his view, squeezed out any space for medium powers like France to assert their existence. Not only did de Gaulle believe that the end of the Cold War was desirable, he also believed that it was inevitable because the fundamental reality was not ideology but the nation-state. He only ever referred to Russia – often 'eternal' Russia – and never to the Soviet Union, claiming that Russia would eventually absorb Bolshevism as blotting paper absorbs ink. He enjoyed lecturing American leaders about the folly of their engagement in the Vietnam War, which he viewed not as a struggle of the values of the 'Free World' against communism but as a national struggle for liberation.

While working to overcome the Cold War by reaching out to the Eastern Bloc and distancing France from America, de Gaulle sought in the short term to secure for France a role in the governance of the Western Alliance equal to that of the United States and Great Britain, while simultaneously building up Europe politically so that it might be able to act as an independent force in world politics between the two hegemonic superpower blocs. The key to that policy was persuading Germany to distance itself from the United States. None of these aims were achieved.

His attempt to push for a tripartite directorate of NATO was simply ignored by the British and American governments. As for his initiatives to promote closer political union among the European powers, this failed partly because he underestimated that, if France resented the domination of America, Holland, Belgium or Italy might reasonably feel the same about France. De Gaulle had tried to play on two stages – the great power one and the European one – but France was not big enough for the first (not yet having nuclear weapons) and too big for the second.

Although de Gaulle did succeed in signing an historic Franco-German Treaty in 1963, it was eviscerated of real impact when the Bundestag added a clause reasserting German commitment to the Atlantic Alliance: the Germans were not ready to trade in American protection for the nebulous possibility of some future European protection under French leadership. So de Gaulle's foreign policy achievements were essentially negative. He twice blocked Britain's application to join the Common Market (1963, 1967), partly because he feared that the British would be a kind of Atlanticist Trojan horse, but he failed to achieve his ambition for a more cohesive European political bloc. He took France out of NATO but that was because he had failed in his attempt to be treated as an equal partner with Britain and America. As for his attempt to reach out to the Eastern Bloc with a long visit to Moscow in 1966 and another to Poland in 1967, this did not prevent the Soviet Union sending tanks into Prague in 1968.

In the last two years of his presidency there was a general sense that de Gaulle, in his late seventies, was losing his touch. He seemed more and more like an old man in a hurry, and his provocations became more outrageous. This was certainly the case of his famous '*Vive Québec libre*' speech of July 1967, or his characterisation in November that year of the Jews as an 'elite people, sure of themselves and domineering' when he tried to justify his criticism of Israel during the Six-Day War. (In this case his provocation had the unfortunate result that his wise and prophetic remarks on the long-term negative consequences for Israel of finding herself forced to administer occupied territories went unnoticed.)

Considered in broad terms, however, de Gaulle's foreign policy was not entirely unsuccessful. It had been conceived in the service of a vision to restore France's international prestige after the eclipse of the Fourth Republic – to make France once again a player in world politics. The aim was to have a 'great national ambition' and to 'sustain a great quarrel' (this was the prophetic de Gaulle speaking). When Kennedy visited Berlin in 1963 and made his speech declaring that '*Ich bin ein Berliner*', he was pitching himself as a rival to de Gaulle's triumphal tour of Germany a year before. On his return, one of Kennedy's advisers commented that a public opinion survey showed that 'you [JFK] beat de Gaulle in a close election in Germany'. This illustrated that the Americans took de Gaulle seriously as a rival. Had he known what one of President Kennedy's foreign policy advisers remarked at the end of 1962 – 'de Gaulle stands at the centre of all questions' – de Gaulle would surely have felt that he had not entirely failed.

In the end, however, de Gaulle was sceptical about drawing up balance sheets of success and failure. In his Bergsonian view of the world, nothing was ever fixed or stable. Asked once by a journalist what he believed to have been his greatest successes and his greatest failures, he replied: 'How do you define success and failure? Only history itself can define these terms. In reality, life and action are always made up of a series of successes and failures. Life is a combat and each one of its phases contains both successes and failures…Success contains within itself the germs of failure and the reverse is true.'

East Berliners arrive in West Berlin
on 9 November 1989.

OF WALKMANS AND SPY GEAR:
HOW EAST GERMANY LOST THE BATTLE
FOR TECHNOLOGY

Katja Hoyer

In July 1958, Walter Ulbricht, First Secretary of East Germany's ruling party, was feeling optimistic. The 65-year-old dictator had survived two world wars, the Nazi regime, Stalin's murderous purges and a mass uprising against his regime in East Germany in 1953. Now things appeared to be settling. Granted, well over 100,000 of his people had left the German Democratic Republic (GDR) every year since the state was founded; in the crisis year of 1953 the figures had risen above 300,000. But the easing of restrictions and improvements in living conditions had led to a record low in 1958.

The leader of the ruling Socialist Unity Party (SED) took the opportunity of its Fifth Congress to share his optimism with his comrades. Inspired by the motto of the event, 'Socialism Will Win!', he declared that he intended to develop the economy 'within just a few years so that it proves once and for all the superiority of the socialist system of the GDR as compared to the imperialist forces of the Bonn state [ie West Germany]'.

In hindsight that sounds at best a bold claim, at worst delusional. By the GDR authorities' own admission, the small state's economy lagged around 30% behind that of its much bigger and more prosperous Western counterpart. It had paid the lion's share of war reparations as the Soviet Union continued to take what it needed to nurse its own ravaged economy back to life while the Western allies held back, allowing Chancellor Konrad Adenauer to rebuild and rearm, supporting him in the process with $1.5 billion from the Marshall Plan.

In addition, the East German economy, such as it was, was strangled by a lack of trading opportunities caused by Bonn's policy of isolation. West Germany's Hallstein Doctrine, introduced in 1955, postulated that it would not establish diplomatic and economic relations with any country which chose to recognise the GDR as a sovereign state. Given the size of the West German economy compared to the East, few countries dared to pay the economic price for snubbing Bonn's express wish. A trade embargo in anything but name, it forced the GDR into economic and diplomatic isolation and complete reliance on Soviet goodwill for imports and exports. The Hallstein Doctrine would not be lifted until 1970. The result was that products such as coffee, soap or chocolate, and anything else that needed to be imported, were hard to come by.

Such troubles notwithstanding, Ulbricht was by no means the only one to feel optimistic in 1958. The last ration coupons were on their way out and would completely disappear the following year. The hard work many people had invested in removing the rubble from cities like Dresden, Magdeburg and Rostock was beginning to clear the way for a slow but visible rebuilding process. And it was the Soviets who had shot the first artificial satellite (Sputnik 1) into space in 1957, causing shock in the West and astonishment in the East.

If the economically weaker Soviet Union could push ahead of the prosperous United States in the space age, then perhaps East Germany could overtake West Germany, too? This thought process was quickly turned into a propaganda slogan and one of the GDR's early mantras: 'Overtaking Without Catching Up'.

So how could the GDR's isolated economy work? For all his faults, Walter Ulbricht understood that the answer wasn't to create a bigger economy but a better one. In other words: technology would be key. Or, as Ulbricht put it, 'We have little plaster, so we'll have to think faster.'

And so, the socialist state invested enormous resources in innovation, data processing and microelectronics. In some areas, there were remarkable, if punctuated, successes. Take the Trabant, perhaps East Germany's most emblematic product. In the West, the drab, outdated car symbolised the technological underachievement of the GDR as a whole. Its undersized engine produced only 23 bhp, while the smell and sound of its output were distinctly reminiscent of decades gone by when models that were practically unchanged since 1963 rolled across the open inner-German border in 1989.

By the 1980s, the Trabant had indeed become the dated and underpowered relic that the West so ridiculed. In the early 1960s, however, it helped to support Ulbricht's rebranding of the GDR economy and get the public on board. A special new edition had been developed for the Sixth

Congress of the SED in 1963: the 'Sachsenring Trabant 601'. Built in Zwickau, Saxony, it bore resemblance to the British Triumph Herald, following the same design techniques, which were indeed modern and considered fashionable at the time.

The zeitgeist spoke of technological progress. Many films, including those produced in East Germany, featured futuristic themes of technology and space exploration, which fascinated young people especially. With Yuri Gagarin, the Soviets had sent the first man into space in 1961, and in 1963 Valentina Tereshkova became the first woman, orbiting the earth 48 times in her three-day solo tour. When the pair visited the GDR in October 1963, many people were genuinely excited to see the famous cosmonauts.

Ulbricht's economic reforms were designed to match and encourage this spirit of technological optimism. The 'New Economic System' (NES) was introduced in 1963, which introduced some market-like conditions back into the socialist economy. Even the West German newspaper *Süddeutsche Zeitung* speculated that the GDR might be 'returning to a form of capitalism'. The politburo decided that the 'theory of the prevalence of politics over economics' must come to an end – 'economic tasks will have priority'.

So for a time state intervention and investment focused on technological progress, not just political control. More responsibility and freedom over development and production methods were handed back to the country's highly specialised companies with their long and proud traditions of research. They should get a comparatively free hand to do what they do best: develop world-class technology.

For example, Carl Zeiss Jena, a company that to this day produces lenses and other high-precision engineering in the field of optics, complained in January 1962 that the demands placed on it by centralised economic planning were stopping it from 'concentrating on the development of the data processing technology needed for the completion of Zeiss's own measuring devices'. That began to change. Ulbricht's NES enlisted experts such as Erich Apel, one of the rocket engineers who had worked on Nazi military projects in Peenemünde during the Second World War. Accordingly, East Germany's GDP and productivity rose. Even the West German Cologne Centre of Historical Social Science reckoned that the GDR was beginning to catch up.

In a planned economy, however, innovative zeal is dependent on political whim. Ulbricht was getting old in the late 1960s, his dream of a technology-based economy was interpreted by many of his comrades as the fantasies of an old man in search of a legacy to build. There was to be no more such supposedly futuristic nonsense for the 1971–75 plan.

Ulbricht's successor Erich Honecker initially wanted to tighten relations with Moscow and this also meant not pressing ahead with the development of new technology in the GDR single-handedly. Much later, one of the GDR's key economic policy makers, Günter Mittag, bitterly commented that when it came to a push in technological development, 'we still laboured under the illusion that it was possible for the GDR to do this in close cooperation with the Soviet Union'.

With the Soviet Union jealously guarding its own research and development while denying the GDR many of the resources it needed to continue with its own, Honecker eventually began to look to non-socialist countries for partnership and inspiration in the technological sector. There was one natural candidate: Japan. Throughout the 1970s, the two countries began to collaborate and trade chemicals, metals and electrical engineering. The last had been of particular interest, given that the GDR needed desirable new electronic devices that were becoming increasingly affordable and widespread in the West such as radios, TVs and stereos.

In May 1981, Erich Honecker travelled to Japan on a full state visit where the two countries concluded trade deals totalling $440 million. The general secretary was also deeply impressed by Japanese work culture and marvelled at the automation processes which used robots to make high-end products.

But the more the GDR managed to fulfil the desires of the population, the more they demanded. By 1980, there were 105 television sets per 100 households, but this also meant that more and more people were exposed to Western culture, including advertising.

Karl Nendel, State Secretary of the Ministry for Electrical Engineering and Electronics, found it impossible to keep up the pace. He tasked VEB Electronic Components in the city of Gera with the production of an affordable cassette recorder, but the company found this difficult. Nendel, frustrated with the lack of results, summoned the director of the state-owned works and snapped: 'You must understand that it is politically necessary to finally have our own recorders!' It was too much for the director, who now clutched his chest. He had suffered a heart attack.

In the end, the decision was made to import entire production lines. A deal was struck with Toshiba, for instance. The Japanese industrial giant already had a footing in the GDR, where it was helping to establish factories for the production of colour TV sets in Berlin and Ilmenau, with imports to the tune of 850 million West German marks. On 13 May 1982 it added a factory for audio technology, with the capacity to produce 750,000 cassette recorders and 30,000 hi-fi cassette decks. VEB Stern Radio Berlin, the state-owned radio production company, used Japanese systems and parts imported from the US.

Herbert Roloff, General Director of International Trade for the Import of Industrial Technology from 1980, remembered that the success of this huge undertaking was limited: 'Yes, we managed to put new types of entertainment electronics and household appliances on the market. Instead of one model, there were two or three. But on the shelves in the West – and that includes our Intershops [which sold Western goods for Western currency] – there were 20 models.' Focusing on microelectronics and rationalisation wasn't enough to heal the GDR's festering economic wounds, even if some in the politburo never stopped believing it would.

By 1989, Honecker was severely ill and frail. But the illusory belief that technology could fix everything remained. The dictator made a rare public appearance, visiting the VEB Kombinat Mikroelektronik Erfurt, where he was shown the prototype of a 32-bit processor. He seemed entirely detached from the protests that were now underway and would soon help bring down his regime. Enamoured with the technology he had just been shown, he proclaimed: 'Neither ox nor ass can stop socialism in its path.'

The unshakable belief that technology would render socialism victorious had been the problem all along. Yes, the GDR did manage to make remarkable technological advances given its size and the difficulties it faced. But these successes were all state-driven and therefore dependent on ideology.

For almost all of its existence between 1949 and 1990, the GDR saw the technological battle as 'a question of survival' and 'an intrinsic component of the entire system of economic warfare'. Money for technology was therefore not always spent on useful or economically viable projects. Indeed, a lot of it was funnelled into the coffers of the Ministry of State Security, better known as the Stasi.

Controlling and pedantic, its boss, Erich Mielke, demanded to 'know everything'. He established a firm grip over the members of the politburo themselves in order to get vast amounts of public funds for projects that stemmed from his own paranoia. A thoroughly ruthless man to begin with, this Moscow-trained terrorist was now allocated huge amounts of money to follow his pathological instincts to monitor and control.

The Stasi concentrated much of its efforts on what it called the OTS, its Operative-Technological Sector. This oversaw the development of highly specialised surveillance technology, such as separate camera systems for people, buildings and documents. Some of its equipment consisted of ordinary civilian technology imported from the West, such as Polaroid cameras, which were used during covert house searches to ensure items were placed back exactly where they had been.

Other areas of development produced elaborate technology that wouldn't be out of place in a James Bond film. There were tiny cameras disguised as lipsticks that activated when they were opened, so that a planted secretary might film documents on her desk. Hidden infra-red cameras could photograph through special leather briefcases.

Mass surveillance and data processing were also very important to the most effective state surveillance system that ever existed. The so-called Central Control System or Ceko became operational in 1973 at the cost of 150 million marks – the equivalent to the annual pay of around 10,000 engineers. This allowed the Stasi to tune in to 4,000 telephone conversations at the same time – in addition to local and mobile stations, for example in important factories. The Stasi even eavesdropped on its own employees, such as in the Cottbus branch where 20 control units had been installed.

The recording and processing of these conversations were labour-intensive and happened at district level. The conversations were recorded on cassettes and stored for around two weeks, depending on how important they were deemed to be. The cassettes were then blanked and reused. If what was on them was of long-term interest, they were transcribed by typists.

Given the limitations of the East German economy, the elaborate expenditure on technology that was used to suppress opposition and monitor the everyday lives of citizens highlights the fundamental issue: overall state control stifled innovation, made bad use of the significant human resources available and sought to repurpose much of what it gained for political ends.

The successes of the GDR compared with other states within the communist bloc show that it achieved a lot within the limitations it had.

There was a lot of potential. With its focus on hard sciences, and the possibility for targeted investment of vast sums of state money into specific areas for specific purposes, it might have worked miracles.

But it's exactly that 'purposeful' investment that stands in the way of fruitful tangents. The same ideological zeal that leads individuals or states to invest eye-watering sums in specific sectors of development, often those that seem remote, futuristic and utopian, also inevitably tempts them into misusing technological development for political purposes.

East Germany's impossible struggle to catch up with the West and eventually overtake it in the technological field was motivated by more than sheer economic necessity or vanity. The technological battle was no less than a question of survival, prompting targeted investment and strategic planning, which often led to remarkable successes. But it also surrendered much of the control over it to a security apparatus unique in world history for its compulsive mass surveillance.

There are clear parallels to countries like China and Russia today, where technology is highly political and entire sectors are controlled, supported, dropped or invested in according to the aims of the regime. But East Germany's obsession with technology poses even broader questions about the implications of state intervention globally in the sector – with outcomes that span from the good to the bad and the ugly.

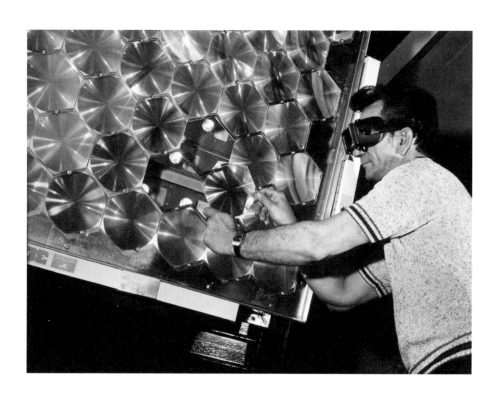

A technician at NASA's Lewis Research Center in
Cleveland, Ohio, assembles an artificial sun, 1974.

WILL MACHINES MAKE STRATEGY?

Kenneth Payne

On the streets of San Francisco recently, Waymo's ubiquitous autonomous cars hit a snag. By gently placing a traffic cone on a car's bonnet, protestors discovered a way to confuse Waymo's algorithm, stranding its cars mid-street.

It was a beautiful illustration of a more general problem. Intelligent machines, as we know them now, are brilliant in structured worlds, where there is a clearly defined problem to solve, like playing chess, or working out the shortest route on a satnav. And they are also increasingly adept at complex control problems, like those facing robotic surgeons, or machines that speedily handle packages in warehouses. Navigating unpredictable human minds, on the other hand, is much harder.

That is a problem in all sorts of fields where enthusiasts hope that AI might bring gains – like healthcare or education. Understanding minds matters here, too, just as it does in warfare. Today, AI drones can find targets and drop bombs as though a game of *Space Invaders* had been transposed onto the real world. These, though, are merely tactical control problems – ethically unsettling, certainly, but basically computable. The larger challenge in war is to think strategically about aims and ways – both our own and those of our adversaries. To date that has been much too difficult for AI.

But now? It's a challenge I took up recently with the help of a large language model, of the sort that's currently getting a lot of attention in AI circles and the wider public. We had a fascinating discussion about Russia's invasion of Ukraine – fascinating not least because its training data extended only until the summer of 2021, well ahead of the February 2022 invasion. The model knew nothing of what happened, but its insights were nonetheless remarkable. At my suggestion it adopted the probabilistic rubric used in UK intelligence assessments and assessed an invasion as 'likely' – that is, in the order of 60 to 79% probable. Language models are known to be somewhat inconsistent, but this one was resolute – sticking with that verdict on nine of the ten times I asked it.

Among other factors informing that assessment were aspects of President Putin's personality. That is, the machine explicitly engaged in reflections about another mind. Specifically, it highlighted Putin's defensiveness and sensitivity to slights, as well as his marked secrecy and tendency to manipulation. In this, it agreed with the leading American Russia analyst, Fiona Hill, in her deeply researched psychological portrait of Putin. But the model was not just parroting Hill's view back to me – it took issue with some of her analysis, arguing that she might be oversimplifying Putin's complex psychological make-up, and pointing to the inevitable distortions that come from our own biases and our partial evidence.

It was an eerie experience. What did it mean? Was the machine really thinking like a human, empathetically imagining Putin's intentions? How far did it really understand his mind? AI sceptics often point to machines' limited grasp of meaning. There is something to this. Success at board games and map-reading requires aspects of intelligence that play to computers' strengths – prodigious memory and enough processing power to search through vast amounts of data. Ultimately, machines excel at finding patterns, or correlations. That is 'meaning' of a sort, but it is qualitatively different from the human version. Humans are embodied thinkers. Meaning for us usually has some deeper relationship to our physical being, and it typically comes with an emotional hue. It is certainly a long way from crunching through possible chess moves. Can the gap be bridged? My encounter with the language model suggested it might.

Knowing me, knowing you
When we talk about meaning, we often mean *social* meaning. How to understand others is perhaps *the* essential cognitive challenge for humans. The legendary Chinese strategic theorist Sun Tzu outlined the benefits in warfare. 'Know yourself and know your enemy,' he counselled, 'and you will not be defeated in a hundred battles.'

We are an intensely social species whose success depends on our ability to cooperate and coordinate with allies, to exchange information and to learn, ratchet-like, from the behaviours of others. It is an ability grounded in our human evolution. There is an ongoing debate about the main driver for our distinctive 'mind-reading' ability. Perhaps it was to coordinate hunting of large-prey animals, perhaps it was to facilitate child rearing – intuiting empathically what our big-brained but essentially helpless babies want, or working out who to trust with childcare. Perhaps it was to collectively counter the threat of violent males – both inside our groups and outside. All these have been suggested by prominent theorists and, in truth, all are plausible reasons. The basic problem for each human individual is the same – who to trust. No man is an island, after all.

Human 'mind-reading' is typically a blend of instinctive empathy and conscious reflection. It is channelled inevitably by our emotions and influenced by our underlying motivations. This is no dry logical model, but a living, dynamic process of seeing others, refracted through our selves. It helps explain many of our distinctive cognitive heuristics – those mental shortcuts we use, often departing from abstract rationality. Hence our tendency to groupthink, or to value the opinions of similar others over a more rigorous, objective appraisal of evidence. That makes sense if what matters most for us to thrive is our group identity. *Our truth* is more important than any objective truth – an observation that in these 'fake news' times is uncontroversial. Hence also our instinctive but imperfect empathy. It is all an attempt to get under the skin of others. Human empathy is often fragile; it is easily undermined, by stress, by anger or, when it comes to empathy with strangers, simply by making our in-group identity more pronounced. Our 'mind-reading', in short, may be imperfect, but it is often good enough for useful action.

Machine mind-reading

Machines take a rather different approach to mind-reading. Their intelligence was not carved in deep evolutionary time down the same intensely social path we have followed. They do not share our embodied cognition either – with emotions helping us to prioritise, in the service of deep, underlying motivations. Until recently, in fact, most AI acted without any attempt at mind-reading at all. As Lee Sedol was trounced by AlphaGo in 2016, the world Go champion flicked an anguished look across the board at the human opposite – but he was just there to move the machine's pieces. There were no mind-reading insights to be had from gazing into his eyes. There was no other mind to be read at all. AlphaGo triumphed against Sedol, as AI had elsewhere, by formidable powers of memory and searching ahead for valuable moves.

That is now changing. Elements of mind are coming to AI, and in turn they're affording it insights into our own minds. As readers of Sun Tzu would anticipate, there are important strategic implications.

One obvious way to model other minds is to think like them. From the beginning, AI researchers aspired to create intelligence that was human-like. Their early efforts drew on formal logic – 'if this, then do that'. Conveniently, this approach resonated with cognitive psychologists, who were much taken with the metaphor of human minds as computers. So minds, artificial and human alike, could be modelled as symbolic proces-sors. You could even introduce uncertainty to the models, to approxi-mate the messy complexity of the real world, so that formal logic became 'fuzzy' and so perhaps more authentic.

But humans are more than naive logicians. How to explain phenom-ena like our systematic overconfidence in our own abilities, or our ten-dency to credit information that confirms existing beliefs rather than challenging them? As psychologists unearthed cognitive heuristic after heuristic, it became clear that we possessed a distinctive form of rational-ism, far removed from the abstract symbolism of those early AI systems.

How, then, to design AI that could better emulate the manifestly crooked timber of humanity? Handcrafting human knowledge for machines was the next attempt. It failed. 'Expert systems' were the focus of AI hype in the 1980s, and could, under favourable conditions, make use of knowledge in a particular domain. But they were brittle – easily flummoxed by novelty. Evidently, general-purpose cognition requires much more than laborious coding of specialist knowledge.

A more realistic alternative would imbue your AI with more general human heuristics – ideally many of them. But these heuristics evolved in a particular context. Handcrafting them one by one is a formidable chal-lenge. Anyway, the triumph of the human mind is to seamlessly integrate its multiple modes of thinking. It is hard to parse one heuristic from the whole; they all emerge somehow from the same vast, integrated network of embodied neurons and its trillions of connections. So: two very differ-ent sorts of intelligence, with sharply contrasting attributes. And there, until very recently, matters lay.

I speak, therefore I am

Coding human heuristics looks like a forlorn endeavour, but perhaps there is a shortcut: language. We can see language as a special sort of heuristic itself – one that models the world by categorising, abstracting, conceptualising, and establishing meaningful relationships.

There is more. If, as the anthropologist Robin Dunbar avers, language emerged in humans to gossip strategically about other minds, then mastery of language is, at least in some degree, synonymous with the acquisition of mind itself. Language allows me to present myself as a single, autobiographical whole, and to understand others in similar terms – even though in reality we are both complex networks of interacting cognitions, many of them unconscious. The 'ceaseless chatter in my skull', as Zen master Alan Watts put it, is only a part of what makes me myself, but a large part, nonetheless.

An example: scripts, or ingrained cognitive narratives, notably analogies, are much studied in international affairs. Leaders often draw, sometimes unwittingly, on the lessons of the past to guide them. In deliberating on the Cuban Missile Crisis, Robert Kennedy counselled his brother against a surprise American attack – it would be an unethical Pearl Harbor. Air Force chief Curtis LeMay, by contrast, urged Kennedy to attack – anything less, he argued, would be like appeasement at Munich. In truth, leaders are just doing what we all do – stripping out the noisy clutter of reality in search of understanding and guidance. Their use of language models the world and the various minds in it.

Could today's large language models, such as ChatGPT, do something similar?

Yes. It is early, and evidence is limited, but there are already some tantalising hints. Language models sometimes hallucinate crazy nonsensical answers, and struggle with causal reasoning. But, with careful nudging to break down tasks and explain their logic, they do better. More intriguing still: in using language, they appear to have absorbed some of our psychology.

So, if we prime a language model with emotional terms, can we affect its subsequent decision-making, as might happen with a human? Apparently so, according to one study, which found that anxious priming makes machines more biased in subsequent judgements – in this case, becoming racist and ageist. Another paper found that GPT-4 aced analogical reasoning tasks, surpassing human performance. 'Low shot' learning from a few historical examples is now possible for both leaders and machines.

What about mind-reading itself? In one striking study, GPT-4 passes 'theory of mind' tests of the sort that developmental psychologists give to youngsters. That is, it appreciates that others can have mistaken beliefs – an essential cornerstone of strategy. And in another dramatic illustration, language models outperformed humans in estimating the emotional response of characters in various fictitious scenarios. The field of AI psychology is just getting started – but these are striking findings, with more arriving weekly.

And in Meta's Cicero, we now have a practical demonstration of what is coming. This hybrid AI has demonstrated proficiency in the multiplayer wargame *Diplomacy*. The twist is that players communicate naturally about their intentions – introducing scope for deception. Cicero wins by combining a tactical, board game-type engine, of the sort used so productively in chess and Go, with a language model. Online players were apparently unaware that their adversary was a machine.

Clearly something interesting is afoot. The uncanny sense of a mind behind language models is more than the mere anthropomorphising, to which we are all susceptible. Machines do not feel, and did not evolve via natural selection, but they have imbided the models of our world that are inherent in our language. Language, unsurprisingly, does not float free from the rest of our cognition. It models the world and our experience of it. It captures, albeit imperfectly, something of our emotionally imbued connection to reality. In their linguistic facility, machines have acquired a window into human minds.

While they lack our rich, multimodal cognition, they have contrasting advantages. For one, they can master more languages than us and flick effortlessly between them, even developing their own. In their use of coding language, meanwhile, they have a powerful means of bringing rigour to their thinking. And they have tremendous potential: biology constrains human cognition in ways that do not apply to machines. If mind and self are emergent properties of networks, as it seems, what happens as language models continue to scale?

Reading Putin

The implications for strategy are profound. The board game *Diplomacy* is a pale simulacrum of real-life diplomacy. No one, I hope, is seriously proposing to outsource geopolitical decisions to machines. That still leaves plenty of scope for machines to contribute, however. My exchange with the large language model about Putin's personality and the prospects of Russia invading Ukraine suggests one possibility.

It is all too tempting to anthropomorphise AI. One Google engineer shared his suspicions that his language-model interlocutor had become sentient. Faced with a fluent, insightful, all-source intelligence analysis, one that offers plausible interpretations of other minds, it is tempting to agree. Perhaps more so if you think, as I do, that consciousness emerged specifically to track other minds. But these machines are not conscious, I'm sure of it. Language is only one, albeit important, facet of our subjective experience.

Still, my model was doing more than probabilistically matching words. Or, rather, that is precisely what it was doing, at a foundational level, but in doing that, some new property emerges. The model, with its vast corpus of training data, has captured an echo of human reasoning and insight. That allows it not just to regurgitate Fiona Hill's deeply researched and astute take on Putin, but to critique it and offer further analysis. All this mind-reading might not be sufficient for truly general AI – the flexible, all-purpose intelligence that many AI researchers aim at. There is more to human intelligence than mind-reading, and human intelligence itself occupies only a small space in the universe of possible intelligences.

While they give a passable impression of insight, the suspicion remains that language models are lacking something important. Sceptics argue that they are inconsistent – hit 'regenerate' and you might get a radically different response. Humans change their minds, too – sometimes on a sixpence, but at a minimum they should feel a twinge of cognitive dissonance, or shamefacedness about an abrupt volte-face. Another criticism is that models lack imagination – they are certainly plausible and fluent, but where is their creativity? There is not, or at least not yet, any landmark AI literature, music or artwork. Everything is a knock-off, at some level, of their ingested knowledge base. Perhaps creativity demands more than facility with language – a more *gestalt* cognition, maybe, than can be captured in words. That may come in time, alongside a deeper form of mind-reading, with the development of new AI philosophies and archi-tectures. Biocomputing looks like a promising, albeit long-range, candi-date technology.

In the meantime, we have language models that seem increasingly adept at human-like reflection. If there are gaps in their ability to reason – and there are – we'd do well to remember our own shortcomings. We are no longer the sole strategic intelligence in town. Decision-making, including in war, will henceforth involve non-human intelligence. It's an intelligence, moreover, that now manifestly possesses insights into other minds. We have created an artificial mind that 'knows itself and knows the enemy' in ways that seem both eerily familiar and oddly alien.

President Truman shakes hands with
Secretary of State George Marshall at
National Airport in Washington, DC, 1947.

CAN THE US MAKE THE WORLD
SAFE FOR DEMOCRACY?

Kori Schake

There is a tendency when debating issues of international consequence to prejudice against the present in favour of a more virtu-
ous past. We persuade ourselves that there was a time when our
leaders were far-sighted statesmen, people of stature and vision, rather
than grubby politicians driven by the same tawdry domestic and elec-
toral considerations that motivate our current crop of elected and
appointed government officials. I search in vain through our history for
those statesmen.

A case in point is George Marshall, the ascetic five-star general, Chief
of Staff of the Army during the Second World War, Secretary of Defense
and Secretary of State in the Truman administration, awarded the Nobel
Peace Prize for his development of a plan for post-war European recon-
struction. *Time* magazine named him Man of the Year in 1943, terming
him 'Civis Americanus'. Marshall is widely admired in civil-military circles for saying he had never cast a ballot. And yet, when President Truman
informed Marshall he intended to support the creation of the state of
Israel, Marshall expressed his objection saying he wouldn't ever vote for
Truman if he did. So not even that patron saint of statesmanship was
above politics and politicking.

Nor should political leaders in free societies soar above the surly bonds
of domestic attitudes. Leaders in free societies are rightly bound to public
support for their policies. It is the essential accountability of those who
govern in the name of the people. It also makes democratic societies more
reliable allies. There is no substitute for winning the political argument
for leaders in free societies, and it makes their commitments more dura-
ble when tested by adversity.

But there is another reason, a rationale of our own civic virtue, that
should motivate us to blow away the mists of untrammelled statesmanship from our predecessors. It has been best expressed by revolutionary era
historian Joseph Ellis, author of both *Founding Brothers* and *His Excellency*

George Washington. Ellis insists that by carving America's political founders out of marble rather than acknowledging their flaws and frailties, Americans exonerate themselves from doing the important work of our time. In averting our eyes from the tawdry politics, blatant self-dealing and moral failings of those great men, we risk excusing ourselves for not meeting political challenges with the necessary dedication and creativity and fortitude. That is, contemporary observers make themselves comfortable holding past figures to a higher standard than they hold themselves.

It is especially true of the United States that its history does not provide such statesmen. The very best of its political leaders considered themselves tightly constrained by public attitudes and expended considerable effort to bring the public along. Foremost, of course, is Abraham Lincoln, the Great Emancipator, who led the nation through its most trying crisis by initially denying that abolition of slavery was the basis for the Civil War and drawing the Union cause ever more committedly toward it. Lincoln began the war arguing 'we must not interfere with the institution of slavery in the states where it exists'. By 1865, his inauguration speech rang with condemnation of slavery as the cause of the war: 'If God wills that it continue until all the wealth piled by the bondsman's two hundred and fifty years of unrequited toil shall be sunk and until every drop of blood drawn with the lash shall be paid by another drawn with the sword as was said three thousand years ago so still it must be said "the judgments of the Lord are true and righteous altogether".'

America was astonishingly lucky to elect Lincoln to captain its national ship through the Civil War (it is practically a proof of Bismarck's quip that God has a special providence for drunks, babies and the United States of America). And while there have been other good, and even one or two great, American presidents, mostly it has been governed by mediocrities – and even a few dangerous renegades.

My favourite description of Americans comes from British historian Bertha Ann Reuter, who wrote: 'Americans are a people too radical either in religion or politics or both, to live peaceably in their original home.' Nor is early twentieth-century satirist H L Mencken far off the mark with his derisory description that 'Congress consists of one-third, more or less, scoundrels; two-thirds, more or less, idiots; and three-thirds, more or less, cowards.'

It is important to keep in mind that the American political system was designed by people who feared government. Power is distributed among three co-equal branches of government; the two houses of Congress have distinctive functions – even the responsibilities of leading the nation in war are divided between the executive and legislature. It was designed to do nothing without consensus. To jealously guard against use of governmental power without political consensus, and even with consensus if public attitudes traduced fundamental rights. So to an even greater degree than most other free societies, America's role in the world depends on winning public support.

In addition to the structural argument, there is another reason American internationalism depends on public support, which is that the United States won the geopolitical lottery: its territory is vast, bounded by oceans on two sides and friendly neighbours in Canada and Mexico. It merits mention that the US has not been a great neighbour to either Canada or Mexico, having wrung territory and sent extra-legal military expeditions into both. And that is before reckoning with our history toward Native American nations.

Having few and good neighbours means that the US has had the luxury of ignoring much of international relations. It also has a dynamic economy that relies less on international markets and inputs than most developed economies. The US simply has a wider margin for error in international relations, politically and economically, than most countries, and that means other states will be preyed upon or feel the effects of international disturbance sooner than it will. We are not natural internationalists, because we have the luxury of being provincial.

America's geopolitical circumstances also mean that in order to motivate Americans to care about the world, it is difficult to win the argument on strategic interests. Because no state can sustain policies that are fundamentally incongruent with what the nation is as a political culture – and that means confronting the fact that Americans are a people extreme in politics and religion, who are difficult to be persuaded to care about the world. What motivates Americans to care about the world is values: the truths we hold to be self-evident.

Americans want to defend religious and political liberty because it is who we are. We want to create an international order of states that believe people have inherent rights and loan them in limited ways to governments for agreed purposes. For geopolitical reasons, the US is a reluctant hegemon, but one strongly motivated to the creation of an international order that is a macrocosm of its domestic political order.

Thomas Wright has an interesting assessment in his book *All Measures Short of War* that there is no point in the US adopting a policy commitment not to pursue regime change in China, Russia or other authoritarian states. Wright considers the normative momentum of US policy to be so deeply ingrained that no authoritarian state should believe such a declaratory policy, because it cannot be true that a state constructed as the US is could insulate its policy from working toward the democratisation of repressive regimes.

International relations theory is mostly a parlour game that is neither descriptive nor predictive of what actually happens in the world. It is least persuasive when arguing that all nations behave similarly irrespective of their unique histories. The United States cannot sustain a policy for long that affronts its values – this is where realpolitik as both descriptor and predictor of US policy runs aground.

Values have become an increasingly central element of US foreign policy over time. It is endearing, actually, that as America has grown more powerful, it has also grown more idealistic. Historically, the arrow tends to go in the other direction: as states become more powerful they become more ruthless. The direction of travel of US foreign policy also validates that the country is capable of grand strategy (a subject often debated in strategic studies about a country so fissiparous and disputatious).

And that grand strategy, evident at least since 1918, is to make the world safe for democracy. The US feels most secure when surrounded by states similarly constituted. It is an ideological conceit, but there is data to back up the argument: democratic states fight a lot of wars, but they tend not to fight each other. It is difficult to think of examples beyond the Cod Wars between Britain and Iceland – and it is instructive of the norm that democracies compromise rather than fight each other that Britain capitulated to a much weaker power.

The political culture that motivates US power in shaping the order also restrains its use, particularly where allies are concerned. There is a wonderful example during the 1958 Berlin crisis: President Eisenhower sent his Secretary of State, John Foster Dulles, to Bonn to assure Chancellor Konrad Adenauer that the US would actually carry out its policy of quickly escalating any conventional conflict with the Warsaw Pact to a general nuclear war – a policy designed to spare Europe becoming a battlefield. Adenauer's response: 'Good God, no! Not for Berlin.'

The US is often more willing to fight than are its allies, even when their own security is at stake, a cultural characteristic likely resulting from a political and religious extremism, a frontier mentality that looms large in American self-conceptions, and having had little historical experience of surviving through occupation. Nor is the bellicosity of the US necessarily detrimental to allies: more Americans are willing to risk their children – the young men and women who fight their wars – to defend Germany than Germans are willing to defend Germany.

Where these proclivities lead the US – and its allies in the ideological West (which incorporates countries of the geographic east, such as Japan, Australia and South Korea) – is to a continuing grand strategy of democratic expansion: a strategy of taking opportunities to incentivise through assistance and attention and potential security guarantees, an international order that advances freedom. Because they cannot persuade people to shoulder risks and burdens, whether aid expenditures or wars or simple diversion from the work of improving our societies, unless there is a component which addresses values.

This does not mean that Western governments will not sometimes have to grit their teeth and accept unpleasant realities, like those Turkey has imposed on Sweden to gain support for NATO membership. But it does mean the surest guide to Western policy is to bet that when sacrifices are needed from free peoples, values are what motivates their voluntary action. The Free World has the means to protect and advance its interests. Its challenge is how to use the tools of free societies to advance our free societies in the face of repression and aggression by our adversaries. And, in the final analysis, that is what Joseph Ellis was arguing for when he advocated that America's founding fathers be removed from their pedestals – and for US policymakers to meet the demands of our own historical time with courage and creativity.

Dr Robert Oppenheimer (1904–67),
points to a picture of the atomic
bomb explosion over Nagasaki.

THE RISING NUCLEAR RISK

Kristin Ven Bruusgaard

'Thus far, the key objective of military strategy has been to win wars. From now on, the key objective of military strategy must be to avert wars. There can be no other objective.'

So wrote Bernard Brodie, one of the key strategists of the early nuclear age, whose writings still inspire and shape debates about how nuclear weapons affect international politics. The formulation epitomises what other scholars would later call 'the nuclear revolution': the transformational effect nuclear weapons would have on international statecraft, making war less, not more, likely.

This theory posited that the catastrophic effect of nuclear wars would be apparent to all, meaning many states would seek nuclear weapons and an ability to use them to deter aggression. Having achieved an ability to deter aggression with a promise of secure retaliation, however, such states would fall back and relax their inherent impulse for competition and expansion, leaving the world a more peaceful place.

This theory always remained just that: a mere theory that could not explain the way states with nuclear weapons behaved after they acquired them. In recent years, substantive new critiques of the nuclear revolution theory have emerged, substantiating claims that theory does not align with reality. And yet, the revolutionary and transformational effect of nuclear weapons continues to affect international relations and debates. Although the mere presence of nuclear weapons did not necessarily produce a more peaceful world, many still surmise that the lack of direct great power confrontation may be ascribed to their existence.

But 70 years after their ascendancy, the risk of their use in conflict seems larger than ever. Although the Russian invasion of Ukraine reignited such scenarios in the popular imagination, resurgent great power rivalry globally over the last decade has steadily elevated the risk of nuclear war. In Asia, the Taiwan scenario looms large, with questions on both sides regarding the adversary's nuclear intentions. In Europe, any direct confrontation between Russia and NATO or the United States could rapidly turn nuclear, as per Russian promises of nuclear first-use in any large-scale conflict. Scenarios for great power nuclear escalation look perilous in northern Europe, home region of Russia's secure second-strike force.

Are nuclear weapons not the ultimate bringers of peace, reducing the potential for great power confrontation? Does the nature of contemporary great power rivalry undermine the apparent deterrent, and thus peaceful, effects of nuclear weapons?

This essay elaborates three development that suggest that NWs are becoming more important to international politics in the future, but that this development may in fact prove less rather than more stabilizing.

The claim to universality does not align with empirical reality

Nuclear weapons are, for all practical purposes, the ultimate insurance and a guarantee of security for the states that possess them. But those states conceive of their deterrent effect in distinct ways; integrate them with their conventional military forces in distinct ways; and have distinct ideas about precisely how they can most effectively influence or shape adversary behaviour. A range of different factors impact such deliberations: geography, other military capabilities, perceptions, traditions and strategic culture.

Geography matters because the types of military threats states face are contingent on their geographic and strategic environment. A state with a large landmass encompassed by potential adversaries perceives graver and more pressing security threats than an isolated island. An ability to conceal military capabilities in the depths of the Siberian plains affects how Russia perceives of such external threats even states at a greater distance from Russia have to assess grave security issues.

Capabilities matter because states think differently about how nuclear and conventional weapons interact and will affect their adversary. Russian nuclear policy is the furthest developed theoretically, if not practically, in the contemporary era, while states such as Pakistan, and alliances such as NATO, have historically also capitalised on the link between conventional inferiority and nuclear compensation. China currently deliberates on this question in altogether distinct ways.

Perceptions matter because states formulate policy based on their understanding and interpretation of their potential adversary: their capabilities may seem frightful even if they believe their benign intentions are entirely clear. As nuclear deterrence remains an essentially psychological enterprise playing on cognitive dynamics such as fear, perceptions of nuclear capabilities and intentions matter more for international outcomes than perceptions of conventional military capabilities.

Traditions and culture matter because existing nuclear weapon states, including Russia, the US and China, all have decades of experience and large bureaucracies devoted to formulating nuclear policy and sustaining the nuclear enterprise. These complexes have their own idiosyncrasies and look different, and the strategic problems they face look different – which in turn produces differentiated solutions to the issues they face.

This variation in nuclear states' behaviour has been explored in contemporary writing, but this area of scholarship has not yet produced a body of work that explores what such variation may look like and how its dynamic produces separate international behaviours. One empirical case in point is the unfolding war in Ukraine, a nuclear-laden conflict that holds differentiated lessons for a range of the world's nuclear-armed and nuclear-aspiring states.

The differentiated nuclear lessons from Ukraine

The Russian nuclear rhetoric and signalling during the Ukraine war is unprecedented. Many fear that Russia is learning a key lesson: aggression under the threat of potential nuclear escalation brings fewer risks. The presence of the world's largest nuclear weapons arsenal is likely the key reason US forces are not currently deployed on a large scale in Kyiv. Russia's conventional performance has demonstrated that, in such an alternative reality, it would have been unlikely to take and hold any part of Ukrainian territory over a prolonged period.

Nevertheless, another lesson Russia may be drawing from this conflict is that nuclear threats and bluster only bring them so far. Repeated threats have not affected the Ukrainian will to fight and defend their country. Russian leadership may still be concerned about the military utility of nuclear weapons use and whether it would outnumber the political costs associated with crossing the nuclear threshold. Yet it seems prone to continuing to maximise the rhetorical utility of the largest nuclear arsenal in the world; not least in a period when its conventional military force is cut down to size, and when its immediate environment has turned ever more hostile.

Through its unprecedented nuclear bluster, Russia is also gaining novel experience in how its threats, combined with other coercive measures, affect adversaries. Russia is likely watching Western responses with great interest and taking notes. It openly conveys that in a war with NATO, and facing a threatening, conventionally superior force, it would consider nuclear use. Some question the credibility of nuclear threats to pursue aggressive goals in Ukraine. Fewer might question the credibility of threatening nuclear use to preserve state existence.

The United States, other Western nuclear-armed states and NATO as a collective are drawing other nuclear lessons from the conflict in Ukraine. To them, this war demonstrates once and for all the nuclear addiction of an adversary like Russia. It has demonstrated how any potential conflict would have a substantial nuclear component, on or before the first day of fighting. Nuclear weapons would constantly and consistently affect the course of such a war. The likelihood of nuclear use on European territory would increase dramatically. Although security circles have been primed to this reality for some time, the war has brought home this reality to Western policymakers in a distinct way.

NATO is renewing its nuclear competency, and trying to do so fast, because of this challenge. Security policy communities across the Atlantic are debating the most effective deterrence or influence on a nuclear-armed adversary. Most agree a modernised and reliable nuclear capability is a necessary component. Nuclear weapons will be a more important part of NATO's deterrent mix in the years to come. The NATO summit communiqué from Vilnius in July 2023 signalled as much through its rejuvenated nuclear language.

The Ukraine war has demonstrated to most of Europe the importance of, as well as the reliance on, a US security guarantee, including its nuclear umbrella. This point is one that American allies in the Asian-Pacific theatre have appreciated in a much more explicit way for some time. Japanese security and defence policy is transforming, with or without a nuclear component. South Korea has actively sought a more comprehensive conventional counterforce capability to influence North Korean nuclear calculations. Deterrence dynamics in the Asian-Pacific theatre are being revisited, both by novel developments such as the AUKUS collaboration and by observations and interpretation of the nuclear dynamic at play in the European theatre.

China may be drawing yet other nuclear lessons from the Ukraine war. Some fear that the country would draw similar conclusions to Russia regarding the potential for aggression under the shadow of nuclear escalation. The US, among others, has been doing its best to dissuade China that such aggression would go unpunished in the context of Taiwan. Chinese nuclear strategy thus far suggests hesitancy with regard to the compellent utility of nuclear weapons. Some argue China is betting more on other key military technologies in order to escalate and exert pressure on its adversaries. At the same time, China is also seeking to solidify its nuclear deterrent – in part perhaps in response to a perceived potential lower threshold on the part of the US to bring nuclear weapons into a direct confrontation.

These differentiated lessons all point in the same direction – that of an elevated role for nuclear weapons in a range of state military and political strategies. Furthermore, they point to an evolution where nuclear weapons may play a greater role in regional dynamics across the world. This includes Europe and its northernmost corner.

The new nuclear dynamic of northern Europe

It will take a lot to convince European states, at some point in the future, that Russia is not a force or threat to be reckoned with. It will take a lot to convince a future Russia, even with different leaders, that the type of force NATO is now generating across Europe and in its border regions harbours no aggressive intentions towards Russia. We are watching a new iron curtain dawn on Europe. The question is whether we are paying sufficient attention as to how it can be changed to something more constructive.

The greater relevance of nuclear weapons to both Russia and to NATO are likely to have direct implications for Europe's northern corner. This is already the case: Scandinavians live very close to a key area of Russian strategic retaliatory capability on the Kola Peninsula. In Norway and NATO, people have long been used to the strategic dilemma and confrontation this poses in the Barents and Norwegian Seas, as well as to Atlantic sea-lines of communication. In case of war between Russian and NATO, their interests will clash directly in Europe's northernmost corner: regardless of where the war starts.

An expanded NATO will change the strategic landscape in a part of Europe that traditionally has been characterized by low tension. It will likely be a question of time before this will affect Russian calculations and force dispositions. If no conventional forces are available, nuclear forces are the back-up that the Russians resort to, also for signalling purposes. The peacetime situation is likely to become more tense in the years to come. A crisis or war will have a substantive nuclear component right on Europe's doorstep, with potential implications for how countries fare in wartime.

Finally, differences in how Russia and NATO respectively think about the integration of nuclear and conventional forces will impact force dispositions in our region. As we have seen in the Asian-Pacific theatre, countries increasingly covet conventional counterforce or counterstrike capabilities. NATO may covet Russia's nuclear capabilities; but NATO's conventional capabilities are what Russia fears the most. New technologies impact how adversaries perceive their own critical vulnerabilities.

The new iron curtain in a transformed Europe is likely to produce novel dynamics and different hotspots of tension. Northern Europe will not be inoculated from this development. Striking the right deterrence balance to minimise the risk of nuclear confrontation will place greater demands on European security and policy leaders – greater than most have experienced in their lifetime. Heavily rests our common responsibility to ensure that future nuclear policies bring peace rather than war.

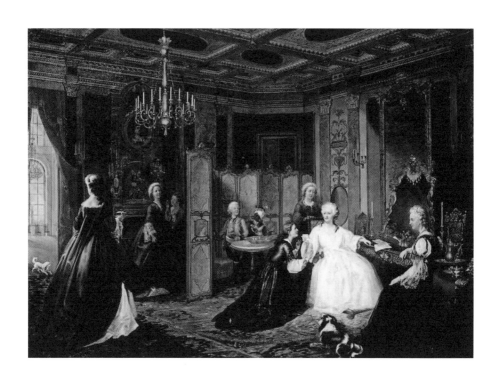

Empress Catherine the Great Receiving a Letter,
oil on canvas by Ivan Osipovich Miodushevsky
(1831–1906), 1861.

THE INVENTION OF CATHERINE THE GREAT

Lucy Ward

Less than a decade into her 34-year reign, Catherine II of Russia commissioned a commemorative medal from the engraver Timofey Ivanov of the St Petersburg Mint. On one side was a conventional image of herself in profile and on the other was something curious: a depiction of the empress holding the hand of her son Paul and reaching out to a grateful mother and her children. Behind her on the ground, below the classical façade of a temple, lay the slaughtered body of the multi-headed monster Hydra.

The scene was clearly allegorical, but what did it mean? To understand that we have to look at the date imprinted beneath: 12 October in the year 1768. On that day – six years after she overthrew her own husband to become empress of Russia – Catherine had herself secretly inoculated against smallpox, the most devastating disease of the eighteenth century, by an English Quaker doctor named Thomas Dimsdale. The procedure was the forerunner of vaccination and it involved deliberately infecting a healthy patient with a minute quantity of live virus. It was safer than it sounds (and far safer than most modern medics realise), but it still carried risk.

Catherine decided she and her son should undergo inoculation to protect their own lives in the midst of a devastating wave of smallpox in St Petersburg, but she also had a second motivation: she wanted to overcome the widespread superstition over inoculation in Russia and introduce the procedure across her empire. There was a benevolent element to this – smallpox was a hideous disease that at the time struck almost everyone, killed at least one in five sufferers and disfigured and often blinded those who survived – but there was also an economic purpose: every life saved increased the wealth of the state.

So, to return to the carefully curated image on the medal, we can see that the slaughtered Hydra represents not only smallpox, but prejudice itself. Supported by the power of the Orthodox Church – she had been careful to secure public praise from the metropolitan bishop of St Petersburg – Catherine has defied the monster and now receives the thanks of grateful Russia and her population. But there is a further resonance here, too; by casting herself in copper, Catherine is seeking to promote and immortalise not only this single political act but her leadership as a whole and Russia's status on the world stage. Above the image are the words 'she herself set an example'.

The phrase takes just three words in Russian – собою подала пример – but behind them lay a complex message. It is a very personal declaration: she *herself* has taken a risk, putting her own life on the line on behalf of her people, and now literally embodies an example of how to live. There is no dative object – the example is for everyone, all at once. Catherine is empress, but her leadership is personal – and it is specifically female: this test has been conducted on her own woman's body, with its weaknesses and frailties she willingly listed for her physician and told him to publish. Dimsdale dutifully obeyed: his *Tracts on Inoculation – Written and published at St Petersburg in the Year 1768, By Command of her Imperial Majesty, The Empress of all the Russias* included details not only of Catherine's symptoms while recovering from smallpox, but of her general health, including her headaches (from overwork), diet, drinking habits and bowel movements.

There were, it's worth noting, other prominent women who played significant roles in promoting smallpox inoculation in the eighteenth century – including Empress Maria Theresa of Austria, Caroline of Ansbach, wife of the future George II, and the British aristocrat Lady Mary Wortley Montagu – but they all used their inoculated children as examples. Only Catherine ran the risk herself, acting as a one-woman medical trial before having her son treated once her recovery was assured. Famously, her own body was, and remains, the target of lascivious gossip and ridicule, yet it was a feat of physical suffering that she promoted in a remarkable act both of self-creation as a leader and of statecraft. By projecting her actions through a battery of carefully managed weapons of influence, she helped stabilise her power at home and presented Russia, under her leadership, as a progressive, westward-looking European state. As we'll see, the confidence she gained from protection from smallpox also appears to have influenced an act of imperial expansion that has dramatic resonance today.

Having taken her risk and recovered from the very unpleasant side effects of inoculation – she claimed to have got through the accompanying dizziness and fever by having the works of her beloved correspondent Voltaire read aloud to her as a kind of literary pain relief – Catherine's first mission was to use her personal example to persuade her deeply sceptical subjects to follow suit. For that, she had to publicise the inoculation. Here, her brand of leadership began to emerge.

In a previously ignored sidenote in a treatise by Thomas Dimsdale on inoculation in Britain, the doctor describes a conversation with the empress during her convalescence at the palace of Tsarskoe Selo, near St Petersburg. Admitting that she had bribed local villagers to be inoculated (and even joking over the fact that the 'price' they exact from her has gone up), Catherine explained that although as an autocrat she could compel her subjects to be inoculated, she preferred to use 'persuasive means, rather than authority'. Coercion, she recognised, would not work when it comes to telling people what to do with their bodies – a familiar debate given new force during the Covid pandemic.

Instead, the empress opted to associate an undoubtedly alarming and counter-intuitive invasive procedure – a scratch on the arm with a lancet followed by a dab of infected pus and some three weeks of sometimes severe discomfort – with an atmosphere of celebration. She marked her son's and her own recovery with a huge national party: bells rang across the nation, buildings were lit up, fireworks cascaded skywards and cannons roared. Having brought the Church on side – an Orthodox Mass at the Winter Palace gave thanks for the whole episode and harnessed the full mystical might of Russian religious display – Catherine took a yet more popular step: declaring a national holiday each 21 November to mark her inoculation. The event had attained the same status as her birthday and coronation.

But the message was always more than 'get yourself inoculated' – which she underlined by building inoculation hospitals around her empire and by encouraging the practice for at least another two decades. Catherine's campaign was also about promoting herself and her own leadership. Her grip on power was stronger in 1768 than after the coup and subsequent violent death of her husband, but she remained a usurper, and a foreigner. Through the Orthodox service and political speeches of gratitude, the German-born empress had herself portrayed not only as 'Matushka', the 'little mother' of the Russian nation, but reached higher still for divine analogies. 'Now all ages and both sexes embrace your feet and praise you in the image of God the healer,' proclaimed Count Kirill Razumovsky on behalf of the Senate. In response, the empress likened herself explicitly to a Christ-like Good Shepherd, giving his body to protect his people. She had elevated her physical act to a spiritual one, turning inoculation under her leadership into a sacrament.

With religious and civil celebrations completed, Catherine turned to the arts. Here, as with the commemorative medal, she appropriated classical mythology, commissioning an allegorical ballet entitled *Prejudice Defeated*, in which she is represented as Minerva defeating the fire-breathing monster Chimera, freeing the Russian people from both smallpox and the grip of ignorance. The mythological theme continued with a five-act theatrical spectacular, *Triumphant Parnassus*, depicting Catherine as the Russian Pallas, Minerva's Greek counterpart, slaying the venomous dragon smallpox with her sword in one Herculean swipe. With the theatre symbolically illuminated, the play concluded with a lurch to contemporary politics and a stark warning to the Turks, now squaring up for war with Russia after a conflict in Poland had spilled over the border into Ottoman territory: 'The monarch here was able to quash evil, And Asia will know about those tempestuous days. When she ignites from Russia's spark...Turkey will know what it means to respect Russia.'

The connection between inoculation and war would bind ever tighter. But in the meantime, at the same time as building her image at home, Catherine turned abroad to maximise the promotional benefit of her inoculation. She fired off a storm of letters to influential correspondents whom she knew would immediately publish them, representing herself as a Western-orientated enlightened leader who trusted data and scientific facts, and as a hearty patient who had barely noticed her symptoms. She teased Frederick the Great, who had advised her not to risk the procedure, and boasted to Voltaire – an outspoken advocate of inoculation – that she had done it all as a tribute to him. With characteristically earthy wit, the philosopher wrote back admiringly, 'You have been inoculated as easily as a nun taking an enema.'

For Britain, whose place in her Anglophile heart had been reinforced by the medical triumph of her English doctor, Catherine had special thanks. She exchanged flattering letters with George III, another staunch supporter of inoculation, who had fretted over her fate throughout the secret treatment, while at an Orthodox service the metropolitan bishop noted that the Russians had 'borrowed assistance from Britain, that island of wisdom, courage and virtue'.

From this scratch of a lancet that took just a few seconds, Catherine fashioned a multi-faceted image of herself as leader: as loving mother, self-sacrificing spiritual healer and a rational philosopher-scientist leading an enlightened and progressive nation. Her process of deliberate self-creation was not only skilled but profoundly recognisable today. For women in particular, it is a case of moving fast before someone else does it for them.

The inoculation was not the first time Catherine had shaped her own story. From 1756, she had been writing an account of her life up to the coup that brought her to power, continuing to edit and re-craft the narrative right up to her death in 1796. The text concentrated on her childhood and her early and unhappy marriage to Peter, and its episodes were carefully selected and presented to portray her as intelligent, charming, energetic, ambitious and destined to rule. Often, she used personal physical anecdotes to help define her character: she describes enduring a corset and a black ribbon tied across her body to correct the curvature of her spine, or her love of riding horses astride, like a man, in order to gallop without restraint.

And here we can begin to see a pattern that prefigures Catherine's public presentation of her inoculation. She not only made the personal – the intimate, even – political, but deliberately took examples of female bodily weakness and vulnerability and demonstrated how she has subverted them.

Catherine acknowledged norms and expectations around power and leadership – their fundamental associations with masculinity – and played on the tension with her own identity as a rare female leader: not the first to rule Russia, but the last to date. In her memoirs, she wrote that she had 'a mind infinitely more male than female. But for all that, I was anything but mannish, and in me, others found, joined to the mind and character of a man, the charms of a very attractive woman.' She did not, in other words, simply ape masculine qualities. Rather, she celebrated and used her woman's body as part of her construction of her particular form of power. Frailty, or the perception of it, could be reversed to become strength.

My own book about this episode in Catherine's rule was written during the Covid pandemic. The parallels were obvious and startling: 250 years previously, she had recognised the power of personal example as a tool of influence in public health policy. As I researched her experiences, world leaders were rolling up their sleeves to be pictured receiving their Covid jabs, and debates were hotting up over vaccination compulsion – the course of action she had rejected in favour of encouragement, despite her autocratic powers. Those resonances were unexpectedly literal. But others are almost as familiar: the conscious image-making of political leaders through careful crafting of personal narratives and, for women in powerful public roles, the delicate balancing of authority according to a masculine script with nods to a performed femininity. In the archives of Churchill College, Cambridge, one of Margaret Thatcher's famous handbags – simultaneously a badge of womanliness and a symbolic weapon – is still one of the most popular exhibits.

Of course, women can never truly get this balance right. Catherine used inoculation to build her image as a female ruler, but by the last years of her reign – as Russia's empire expanded threateningly westward – political cartoonists were routinely employing sexist and salacious imagery to cut her down to size. The most famous example, captioned 'The Imperial Stride', portrays her rival leaders – all men – looking up her skirts and making lewd remarks as she steps purposefully across the map between St Petersburg and Constantinople.

That brutal satire was still a long way in the future, though; at the time, Catherine had the medal struck to mark her inoculation and cast herself, literally, as a benevolent protector of her nation – as both mother and Hydra-slaying warrior. Just days after her recovery, in November 1768, she took another step that would define her even more clearly as a strong leader: she declared war on Turkey, igniting the conflict that would see Russia take Crimea and other territory that today lies, pulverised by Putin's war, in southern Ukraine. In a letter to her new ambassador in London, Count Ivan Chernyshёv, she wrote gleefully that the pair had 'only two subjects to discuss – first the war, and second, inoculation'. Just as the theatrical spectacular had yoked the overcoming of disease with the prospective military threat to Turkey, so again the conquest of the virus (and of prejudice against inoculation) and the coming military campaign were inextricably bound together. Her victory in her inoculation against smallpox had made her feel invincible and drove her forcefully towards the war that would, ultimately, lead an ever more confident Russia to conquer Crimea and the Black Sea region that now lies in Ukraine.

Catherine, whose woman's frame had survived its struggle with smallpox, would not go to battle herself, but she sent her troops off in the depths of the Russian winter to sacrifice their own bodies in combat in the cause of imperial expansion. 'My soldiers go to war against the Turks as though they were going to a wedding,' she wrote to Voltaire. The next act of her self-creation was beginning.

The Olympic Games in ancient Greece.
Unknown artist.

GODS VERSUS MEN:
ANCIENT GREEK REFLECTIONS
ON HUMAN AND DIVINE LEADERSHIP
IN THE FOUNDATION OF CYRENE

Michael Scott

In or around 631 BC, the settlement of Cyrene, on the Mediterranean coast of modern Libya, was established by a community of Greeks from the Aegean islands. This was by no means unusual: between the eighth and sixth centuries BC, multiple settlements were founded around the wider Mediterranean, from Marseilles (ancient Massalia) in the west to Kerch (ancient Pantikapaion) on the northern coast of the Black Sea, as well as numerous settlements along the North African coast, particularly in Libya and Egypt, by communities based in mainland Greece and the Aegean islands.

The case of Cyrene is different, however. Here, we have multiple kinds of source material, from multiple points in time through the lifecycle of Cyrene as a settlement, which reflect on, and tell the story of, that foundation moment. What emerges is not only how important a settlement's foundation story could be – both to the new settlement and to its 'mother-city' back in mainland Greece – but also how malleable and changeable that story was. At stake in this changeability was not just the relative power and importance of both the new settlement and the original community, but also, crucially, the relative power and importance of different players – both human and divine – within the foundation narrative itself. In particular, the case of Cyrene, as we shall see, indicates a desire over time to minimalise, and indeed dispense with, human leadership as part of the foundation process, placing the emphasis instead on divine leadership.

In the 50 years following the foundation of Cyrene, a tomb was built in its agora – the main market square – at the heart of the new settlement. This tomb has been associated traditionally with the individual credited, in later literary narratives, with leading the foundation of the city: a man called Battus, who in turn became the first king of Cyrene and the progenitor of a line of monarchs through to the middle sixth century BC. That this tomb was part of the community's agora underlines its, and the person's, importance to the community. But it is curious to note that, both at the time and for the rest of the century, the tomb was not formally and architecturally incorporated within the boundary markers of the agora. Instead it is on one edge, tantalisingly left both inside and outside the space.

Just over a century and a half after the foundation of Cyrene, we encounter the first surviving literary sources relating to the foundation of the city. In 474 BC the poet Pindar, who wrote praise poetry for the victors in the great panhellenic athletic games of ancient Greece (which took place at the religious sanctuaries of Isthmia, Nemea, Olympia and Delphi), wrote a poem, 'Pythian 9', in honour of Telesicrates of Cyrene, who was victorious in the *hoplitodromos* – a running race in which people competed wearing parts of the armour of a *hoplite* soldier – at the Pythian Games, held at Delphi.

Pindar opens his ode to Telesicrates' triumph not by focusing on how he had been victorious, but instead on the origins of Cyrene itself – which extended far back in time before 631 BC, and which invokes new divine players rather than human ones. The god Apollo is said to have swept up the nymph Cyrene in his chariot and carried her 'to a place where he made her mistress of a land rich in flocks and most rich in fruits, to live and flourish on the root of the third continent' – that is to say, the settlement of Cyrene, which took its name from the nymph Apollo is said to have married there, with whom he had a child, Aristaeus, who would become another mythical hero of the city. Battus, on the other hand, is not mentioned.

In 462 BC, Pindar was commissioned to write again two odes of praise ('Pythian 4' and 'Pythian 5'), this time for the king of Cyrene, Arcesilaus, following his victory in chariot racing at the Pythian Games. Given that the victor being praised was the king, and a descendent of Battus, it is no surprise that Battus founded Cyrene, though Pindar makes it clear he only did so following the prompting of the Delphic oracle, in turn inspired by Apollo, which had been foretold many generations before Battus set sail for Libya by the mythical character Medea when speaking to Jason and his Argonauts.

By the mid-fifth century BC, therefore, there were multiple (overlapping, but perhaps not necessarily contradictory) ways in which to understand the foundation of Cyrene. These gave differing views of the balance of human and divine leadership, and also different timescales for the foundation, or at least its foretelling. These literary outpourings, which both promote and downgrade Battus, can be contrasted to what we know happened to his tomb in Cyrene's agora during the fifth century. In the course of the century's first half, it, and indeed the eastern side of the agora, was completely ignored in terms of construction, with all new monumental spaces for worship and gathering concentrated on the west side. In the second half of the fifth century, however, the eastern side of the agora was extended, the original tomb paved over and a new one built in a contemporary fashion, again on the very eastern edge of the agora.

While narratives of divine centrality and predetermination were being crafted and spoken at Delphi, at Cyrene itself there seems to have been greater indifference to the role of Battus, as evidenced by the attention paid to his tomb. This should perhaps be associated with political developments in the city, which saw the monarchy completely overthrown by the end of the fifth century and a more democratic political constitution set up in its place. This physical inattention and subsequent indiscriminate rebuilding of Battus's tomb is particularly notable when we recognise that in this period, a new shrine to Aristaeus, the offspring of the nymph Cyrene and Apollo, was constructed in the heart of the agora.

Things become more complex when we introduce the narratives of Cyrenean foundation told by the historian Herodotus, proclaiming his narrative for the first time, supposedly from the step of the temple of Zeus at the sanctuary of Olympia during the Olympic Games, in the last quarter of the fifth century BC. Herodotus records specifically in his *Histories* that there were simultaneous differing and competing versions of Cyrene's foundation and he recounts on the one hand what the Cyreneans said happened and, on the other, what the Therans said happened; the island of Thera, now Santorini, was where Battus came from.

In the Theran version, the king of Thera goes to the oracle at Delphi on 'other matters' but is told he is destined to found a city in Libya. The king says he is too old, and points to a man in his retinue, Battus, as the person who should be responsible. No Theran did anything about it – they did not know where Libya was, nor did they have the courage to set out to find it. For seven years, as a result, Thera was subject to drought. When its citizens returned to the oracle, they were reminded of the need to found a community in Libya. The Therans sent messages to Crete to find someone who knew something about Libya and, with their help, an initial reconnaissance mission set out. The Therans then left the Cretan on an island just off the coast of Libya and went home, eventually returning with a community of Therans and Battus to set up a permanent community, with Battus as its ruler.

In the Cyrenean version of events, Battus was the son of a Cretan mother and a Theran father. He, on account of a stutter, went to Delphi to ask about his speech impediment but was told by the oracle that Apollo commanded he go to Libya to found a colony. He protested, but the oracle kept repeating the command. He did not set out, and the Therans suffered badly until they returned to the oracle, who repeated they must send Battus with a Theran community to Libya. They eventually set off, but subsequently tried to return to Thera. At this point they were pelted with stones and refused permission to dock, so set off again for Libya, and founded a colony on an island off the coast. Two years later – given it was hard going – they returned to Delphi to complain and were told that they needed to settle on the Libyan mainland, not on an island. They did so. Six years later, the local Libyans showed them to a different site, where they finally settled and founded Cyrene.

While both narratives centre around the actions of humans, neither credits the human actors involved with much enthusiasm for founding the settlement at Cyrene, nor the general ability to do so. In both narratives, it is only thanks to the continuing pressure (and indeed harmful force) inflicted by the oracle at Delphi and by Apollo, that the settlement is finally founded. On top of this, Herodotus also recounts that some 60 years after the initial settlement, the oracle at Delphi once again demanded that Greeks from the mainland cross the sea and join with those already in Cyrene in creating more settlements in Libya.

In 375 BC, just 26 years after Cyrene overthrew its ruling monarchs, a document, 'The Stele of the Founders', was inscribed in stone in Cyrene, which survives to this day. It details the Cyreneans' agreement to a Theran request for civic rights, on the basis of the Therans' original role in its foundation. The 'original pact of the Theran founders' is quoted, which underlines the importance of the Delphic oracle who, 'of her own accord', encouraged Battus to found the community. Once again, in this contemporary document created by the Cyreneans and the Therans, the common ground is how the original motivation for the foundation of Cyrene lies with the oracle of Apollo at Delphi, and thus with Apollo himself. It is perhaps not a surprise that we can also date to this period the Cyrenean decision not only to contribute to the required rebuild of the temple of Apollo at Delphi following its destruction in an earthquake, but also to build a treasury within the sanctuary as an offering to the god. This was, by the fourth century BC, an unusual architectural choice of offering for Cyrene to make: treasuries – in effect mini temples, used to house other offerings dedicated to the god by that same community – had gone out of fashion at Delphi by the late fifth century BC. Cyrene's decision to construct a more archaic form of offering may thus be interpreted as a desire to underline their long association with the sanctuary and its oracle, and reflect the growing importance of the oracle and Apollo in their foundation narrative.

This desire, on the part of the Cyreneans, for an ever-closer association with Apollo, at the expense perhaps of equally close connections to their 'mother-city' communities, is also apparent in another inscribed document set in stone within the sanctuary of Apollo at Cyrene in the late fourth century BC. This contained a collection of sacred laws by which the Cyreneans lived, and it makes it very clear to whom the Cyreneans owe their laws. The first line of the text states 'Apollo issued an oracle: the Cyreneans shall inhabit Libya for ever'.

This desired continuity of connection with Apollo stands in contrast to Cyrene's political misfortunes in the last quarter of the fourth century. It suffered multiple revolts and changes of government as the Greek world was rocked by the death of Alexander the Great in 323 BC, finally being placed under the direct rule of a new king, Magas, as representative of Ptolemy the Great, the new ruler of Egypt. Magas initiated a massive restoration of Cyrene's agora, which included the rebuilding, once again, of Battus's tomb.

It was perhaps inevitable that the return of a king to Cyrene would bring with it a greater desire to re-emphasise the role of monarchs in Cyrene's past. But, in fact, the renewed architectural emphasis on Battus was short-lived. By the mid-third century BC, the ruler of Egypt, Ptolemy III, to celebrate his marriage to his new queen, Berenice, herself a Cyrenean princess, erected a piece of sculpture in Cyrene's agora. Carved in marble, it was a ship's prow, standing tall upon a high base, with a statue of Nike, the goddess of victory, leaping forth. The statue was breathtaking, and overshadowed nearly everything else in the agora, including Battus's new tomb. In fact, the effigy was placed right in front of the tomb, cutting it off from view to those moving through the agora.

In the same era, during the third century BC, the poet Callimachus, writing from Alexandria in Egypt, created his 'Hymn to Apollo'. Once again Apollo is praised, through his oracle at Delphi, as being the divine founder of cities, and is said to have personally led Battus to form Cyrene, after marrying the nymph Cyrene in the land of the future settlement of Cyrene.

From this point on, some alignment of narratives seems to have finally taken hold, in which the power and importance of divine leadership in the story of Cyrene's foundation is recognised at the expense of agency and leadership in the human sphere. Cyrene would survive as a community into the Roman era and beyond. Yet the tomb of Battus would not. Cut off from view in the third century BC, it was destroyed during a revolt in the town in the early second century AD, and never rebuilt. Its foundations were covered over by a colonnaded stoa – a type of covered public walkway – built in the mid-second century AD.

The tale of the changing foundation story of Cyrene underlines the gradual move away – within literary narratives, as well as within architectural and inscriptional constructions, and representations the community itself chose to make – from attributing agency and leadership to human individuals towards placing the motivation for, and leadership of, the foundation squarely within the divine sphere. At the same time, the literary, architectural and inscriptional evidence also points towards a desire to push the divine mandate of the community's foundation as far back in time as possible, before any human actors were involved at all. Cyrene, as a result, came to be able to claim for itself an eternal connection to Apollo, as well as an increasingly close link to Apollo's oracle at Delphi.

This link to the divine, rather than the human world, was beneficial to a community rocked by regular political upheaval, a community which also had to find its way and place within the ever-changing political and military tussles of the wider Greek (and Mediterranean) world. Cyrene, in moving from human to divine leadership, placed itself as a concern of the gods (rather than just humans), and, by putting its foundation and connection to the wider Mediterranean world above its constantly changing allegiances and political and military rivalries, ensured a sense of its unbreakable membership within it. The moral of the story is simple. Gods – and oracles – make better leaders in founding myths than humans ever can.

Moses and the Messengers from Canaan,
oil on canvas by Giovanni Lanfranco
(1582–1647), 1621–24.

STATECRAFT IN CRISIS: CULTIVATING ELITES IN MODERN BRITAIN

Munira Mirza

There is a paradox in public life in Britain today. The population is more highly educated than ever before, a larger proportion of young people attend university or further education today than in the past, the UK is among the highest-ranking countries for Nobel prize winners, and its cities are magnets for global talent in sectors such as finance, technology, arts, medicine and law.

Yet, despite nurturing an extraordinarily high stock of human capital over the last 50 years, Britain's political class feels more inadequate and ineffective than ever before. Logically, a rise in the general intelligence of the population should result in a larger, more diverse and more impressive talent pool for the political elite. The reverse seems to be the case in the UK. Has there ever been a time when the standard of the political class has felt so out of line with improvements in wider society?

None of this is to be glib – it is practically a national sport in Britain these days for armchair critics to lampoon politicians, but politics is a much tougher gig than most people realise. Theodore Roosevelt was surely right to say in his defence of those in public life: 'It is not the critic who counts; not the man who points out how the strong man stumbles, or where the doer of deeds could have done them better. The credit belongs to the man who is actually in the arena, whose face is marred by dust and sweat and blood.'

I write this essay as someone who has worked within the British political system and therefore has more sympathy than most for the people in it. For nearly three years I was the director of the prime minister's Policy Unit in 10 Downing Street and had the remarkable privilege of observing the inner workings of Whitehall. I watched ministers, MPs, senior civil servants and political advisors grapple with the turbulence of the EU referendum result, parliamentary deadlock, a general election and the Covid-19 pandemic. It was an unparalleled education in the way government operates and the nature of those who run it.

Many of them are talented people dedicated to public service, who go to work every day to make the country a better place. Yet, for all the good people I met, I came away convinced that our political system does not prepare leaders as well as it should, nor does it attract enough of the talent needed to deal with the challenges the UK faces.

The truth is that people within politics are themselves becoming aware that there is a *systemic* problem in how we as a country identify and train MPs, Cabinet ministers, senior civil servants and advisors. Many of the old pipelines of talent are losing their appeal, or no longer exist. And for those who do arrive in politics, they are unlikely to experience the sort of 'apprenticeship' journey their predecessors did. In the past, Cabinet ministers had built careers in other professions, then spent years acquiring knowledge and experience on the back benches and as junior ministers. Civil service mandarins were examined at entry – and frequently assessed – on their objective knowledge, not just their subjective qualities. All senior officials underwent rigorous training in thorough, structured courses at a national college. The political journey for many people running the country today is shorter, less demanding and more ad hoc.

The consequences of all this are that the quality of decision-making is often erratic, with government unable to think and act long term. Too often there is a lack of institutional memory and policy knowledge among legislators. Political parties struggle to generate new ideas and resort to familiar rhetoric invented for problems from decades ago. More than anything, a new generation of political leaders struggle to find a way to communicate their views at any length or articulate a vision with depth.

The quality of politicians (and public servants) is far from our only problem. Economic headwinds, global conflict, demographic change and other factors beyond individual control all play their part. But if politicians do not look like serious people, if they cannot develop credible answers or build support for their agenda, the result will be a declining faith in democracy. According to the Office for National Statistics, public trust in national government has now fallen below 40%. Whether it is chicken or egg, politicians themselves end up acting in ways that reinforce the problem. When they go on reality TV shows to try to engage an increasingly detached electorate, they are signalling that politics is more about 'personality' than purpose and ideas.

The problem is not unique to Britain either. Henry Kissinger – who in his liftime had probably met more significant world leaders than anyone else alive – wrote in 2022 about how the rise of social media has reduced the attention span of politicians and voters. Despite being more likely to have earned a degree than in the past, elites have lost access to the deep literacy that was a given for previous generations, and which is vital to understanding the situation of their country. The most impressive world leaders of the twentieth century, from Charles de Gaulle to Lee Kuan Yew, spent time learning about the global forces facing their countries, the diverse needs of their people and how to build a team that could pursue a vision. Today, the type of education and sense of duty that shaped the post-war generation is no longer present to the same extent. While we still have very good, talented individuals in society, we can no longer assume that the alchemy that attracts them into public life turns them into great leaders.

Why do we have this problem, and are there particular factors in the UK system that mean its political class is destined to fall short? There are structural reasons we can point to. First, what economists would call a classic 'misallocation of capital' problem: talented people are put off politics by the fact that it is poorly paid and increasingly low-status. The public dislike intensely the idea of paying politicians and civil servants more. A smart young person in their twenties would rather go into business or a profession where they can build high-status careers and gain esteem from their peers. If money is not a priority, they might be tempted into journalism or charity work. They are likely to live more comfortable lives and not endure the kind of hell-bent media scrutiny that is now a feature of political life.

With this talent drain, there is a doom-loop effect: the fewer good quality people become politicians, the lower status politics has and the less attractive it is to other good people. Britain's hair-shirt approach to paying politicians, but also civil servants, inevitably narrows down the range of people who apply. It also means that politicians find it increasingly difficult to stay on. Nearly 100 MPs have said they will step down before the election, including 61 Conservative MPs – the highest number since 100 Labour MPs stood down after the expenses scandal in 2010. Many face the near inevitable loss of their seat, but also the pressures of the job mean it is no longer as attractive to stick around.

This shrinking talent pool has been concealed for a long time by a growth in the number of politics courses in universities over the last 30 years. Young people are increasingly interested in politics for study.

However, the graduates of these courses tend to go on into the private sector – public affairs, corporate policy jobs in businesses, or non-government organisations. The Oxford PPE (Philosophy, Politics and Economics) course is no different, despite its infamous reputation as a pipeline for British politicians. And while the UK's most prestigious institutions offer a world-class political education, it is noticeable how few UK students they teach. The student body at the Blavatnik School of Government in Oxford, which was set up over a decade ago with the aim of becoming the UK equivalent of the prestigious Kennedy School at Harvard, is composed of 80 to 90% non-UK nationals. The London School of Economics' student body is 70% non-UK national. This attraction of global talent is tremendously important and lucrative, but to be clear, it is not resulting in better politicians at home. The UK is excellent at educating the world's leaders but this is not the same as educating its own.

These structural factors – low pay and low status – are real, but they are not inevitable. Why has society allowed public life to become so unattractive?

In the past, successful societies gave much thought to the question of what might be called 'elite formation'. Just as any family or business might do succession planning, different tribes, nations, city-states and empires have found ways to identify the people who will carry forward the legacy of one generation to the next. One of the most famous stories of succession planning in Western culture is Moses handing over the leadership of the Israelites to his apprentice, Joshua. Just before they reach the Promised Land of Canaan, after 40 years of wandering, Moses is told by God that he will die before entering their new home as punishment for an earlier transgression. Moses, concerned for the fate of his people, pleads to God for a replacement, 'so that the Lord's community may not be like a flock that has no shepherd'. God commands Moses to appoint Joshua, who has effectively been training as an apprentice with Moses in the art of leadership and statecraft. Moses lays his hands on Joshua in front of the community, reassuring them that his successor is 'full of the spirit of wisdom'.

As Adrian Wooldridge documents in his excellent 2021 book, *The Aristocracy of Talent*, different systems around the world throughout history have found ways of using meritocracy as a guiding principle, and creating institutions that would guide future leaders. In around AD 600, Imperial China introduced a national written exam, which was rigorous, fiercely competitive, open to anyone and acted as the gateway to a high-status career as a bureaucrat; by the seventeenth century, two and a half million people took the exam. Key elements still form part of the recruitment process for the Chinese civil service today.

In the modern era, European nations, and latterly the US, created a range of diverse institutions – grammar schools, public schools, universities – to teach the practical skills, as well as the moral character, that would be needed to cultivate future civic leaders. It is a well-worn cliché in Britain that the Battle of Waterloo was won on the playing fields of Eton, while in the US, the early Puritans founded the Ivy League universities (including Harvard and Yale) to train ministers. These went on to become the pipeline for future political leaders – Harvard alone counts eight presidents among its alumni.

So what has happened to this idea of elite formation in liberal societies? Arguably, something subtle has changed in the culture of these institutions and within the elite itself since the 1980s or 1990s. Modern institutions today emphasise their ethos of meritocracy (even though they continue to have a highly socially privileged and white intake), but Wooldridge argues they seem to have lost a vital characteristic of elite formation, which is the idea of '*noblesse oblige*'. Students are no longer trained to think of themselves as custodians of a nation who ought to 'give back' in return for their status, but as highly talented individuals who have earned their position through intellectual superiority and therefore deserve to pursue their own ambition first and foremost. As one disillusioned Harvard graduate, Saffron Huang, wrote recently of her alma mater: 'In place of elite formation is a production line of professional strivers – albeit ones with relative wealth and a valuable social network.'

In the UK, the business model of universities has underpinned this shift. In 1998 the government introduced tuition fees for students, which has shifted university funding from the state to individual 'consumers'. Universities have responded by increasing recruitment of international students who can be charged higher fees. In marketing literature today, universities are less likely to present themselves as educators of a national elite, but as powerhouses for global talent. Undeniably, this globalising of higher education has many positives, but it is surely one reason why it is less steeped in concern for the future governance of the country.

Another profound change is in the British political parties themselves, which have cut back on their own outreach and education. In the 1950s, almost one in ten people in Britain were members of political parties. It is hard to imagine now, but political life was ingrained in wider civic life and it was far more common to meet party members through church, working men's clubs, Rotary Club events and other local civic networks. Both the Labour and Conservative parties had their own adult education colleges, which produced mass pamphlets and where thousands of party members and activists heard varied lectures on politics, economics and philosophy. They would have the opportunity to meet each other, as well as senior politicians. This vast social network has largely disappeared – there are now only around 500,000 members of political parties and the colleges have gone.

As a result, many people coming into elected politics today receive little education in public policy, economics or how government works. They arrive in Westminster expected to work their ideas out in isolation. There is no way for them to learn about the big challenges facing the country – from AI to geopolitics – except by their own volition.

The UK civil service shut down its prestigious national college at Sunningdale in 2010 as part of a wider cost-cutting exercise, and there have been complaints ever since that civil servants lack expertise. Taken in the round, these are extraordinary losses to the professional development of those running the country.

When Singapore became an independent country in 1965, it was lacking in natural resources, an independent military and even direct access to water. Prime minister Lee Kuan Yew realised that excellence in public leadership would matter above anything else for his new country's success. He made an early and explicit decision to hire on merit rather than ethnic quotas and to pay junior civil servants well to ensure they could attract talent. He was very explicit with the public about why. Today, the modern Singaporean civil service website foregrounds the word 'excellence' as one of its values and applications are highly competitive. The seriousness with which Singapore takes elite formation is astonishing.

By contrast, all the changes I have described in the UK have taken place almost without comment or concern in the last 40 or so years. We have become relaxed, even complacent, about the idea of elite formation. Could the reason for this contrast between us and Singapore reflect an even more profound difference? In Singapore, the very survival of the state has been in question since its early years of independence. Its sense of vulnerability has forced the construction of new institutions, a ruthlessness in selecting leaders and a sense of duty imbued throughout its culture. The UK has not experienced this sense of existential crisis for many decades. In the 1990s, elites believed they were living through the End of History and the End of Boom and Bust. They had beaten the twin evils of communism and economic decline.

In a multipolar world, with a stagnant economy and the prospect of geopolitical conflict forcing us into ever tougher choices at home, we must think about leadership again with the kind of seriousness it deserves. Like Singapore, we should worry much more about who is going to take over and treat it as a crucial element in the future success of the country.

This means institutions that are responsible for elite formation thinking more consciously about how they can develop the discipline of statecraft and extend its spread to more people in politics and public life. It also means that those who care about this issue should – like social pioneers of previous eras – create new institutions that can take on this important work.

Turkish President Erdoğan and
Swedish prime minister Ulf Kristersson,
Ankara, 8 November 2022.

TRUST AGAINST MISTRUST:
SWEDISH AND TURKISH LEADERSHIP

Nathan Shachar

Vladimir Putin is a strong leader, but is he an example of good leadership? Some would say yes, because he plays a weak hand without losing. Most would say no, because the hand he now plays is much worse than the one he began with in February 2022.

Putin can kill his subjects or jail them if they don't obey. So they obey. But good leadership is the opposite. It is when you convince people to do something they are reluctant to do. I have seen that up close three times during my reporting career: first with the Egyptian president Anwar Sadat, who made peace with Israel in the face of extreme threats and protests from the entire Arab world; then with the Israeli prime minister Yitzhak Rabin, who carried on with the peace process with the Palestinians in spite of violence and incitement; and a third time with the Brazilian president Lula da Silva. When Lula was elected in 2003, both his enemies *and* his own leftist camp expected populism and big spending. Instead, Lula kept the currency stable and tariffs low, saved the economy and won several years of handsome growth which financed a successful anti-poverty programme.

Sadat and Rabin were murdered for what they did – by their own countrymen. Sadat's legacy, the Israeli-Egyptian peace deal, has long been a cornerstone of regional stability. Rabin's work, the Israel-Palestinian peace process, has been destroyed. Lula is now back in office, but with reduced power and a growing dependence on China.

Recently, we have been given a live experiment in leadership, during the past year's wrangling between Sweden, Turkey and NATO about Swedish accession to the Alliance. Rarely have two countries displayed such wildly different tactics during a diplomatic crisis – Turkey demanding, denouncing, preaching and insulting; Sweden hoping, pleading, grovelling and appealing to the Turks' good faith. The contrasting behaviour of the parties reflects something deep about both cultures.

The Russian attack against Ukraine shook up many countries, but none more than Sweden. There were three reasons:

1. We are next door to Russia and share the Baltic Sea.
2. We are almost defenceless. In the 1970s Sweden had impressive armed forces, including a huge air force. Only the US, the Soviet Union and Israel spent more on defence per capita. Today, the Palestinian Authority forces in Ramallah, not to mention Hezbollah in Lebanon, were they our neighbours, could overrun Sweden in days.
3. The events in Ukraine challenged a pillar of Swedish identity and self-regard: the neutrality policy, until recently almost a secular religion.

The first reaction of the Swedish Social Democrat government to the Russian attack was loud and shrill: 'We will never abandon neutrality, never join NATO!' Within weeks that same government declared: 'We must join NATO – at any cost!' This abrupt U-turn was not the result of any sober reflection. It was simply politicians realising that the public had changed its mind. It was leadership, but upside down, with the public leading and the leaders following. It became obvious that the people running the country had never reflected on strategic issues. They had grown up after 1989, under the impression that defence, danger and geopolitics were history. Between 2004 and 2009 the governing conservatives, unopposed by the Social Democrat opposition, all but abolished the national defence forces.

When Sweden and Finland applied to join NATO there were no Turkish objections. But before long someone in Ankara realised that this was a golden opportunity to squeeze concessions from Sweden and, more importantly, from the Americans.

The Turks published a long list of harsh conditions for accepting Sweden into the Alliance. After a summit in Madrid in June 2022 a memorandum was drawn up, where Sweden promised to get tougher on PKK activities in Sweden and to extradite terrorists. Immediately after the signing, Turkish president Recep Tayyip Erdoğan announced that Sweden had agreed to hand over 73 wanted Turks living in Sweden, many of them journalists, none of them terrorists in any objective sense. Sweden was shocked; it had not promised anything like that. But it was clever tactics: it put the Swedes on the defensive and sent them looking for other concessions to appease the Turks. The atmosphere of crisis and clashing values served Erdoğan well. It showed him as a principled defender of national interests and as a key player of NATO during his election campaign.

Soon afterwards, the Swedish Social Democrats lost the election and a liberal-conservative coalition took over. That changed nothing. The Swedish prime minister went to Turkey. The foreign minister went there. Others went, too. They went without anything having been settled in advance. They hoped to break the ice by showing their friendliness. Ahead of each visit there were hints from Swedish spokesmen to the press about an expected breakthrough and an end to the Turkish *nyet*. But the Swedes were given cool receptions, and more lectures, by their hosts and went home empty-handed. During all this the Swedes repeated how well they understood the Turkish position and how eager they were to curb PKK activities in Sweden.

The way Swedish politicians and spokesmen humiliated themselves before the Turks makes it hard not to think of the 'Stockholm syndrome' – captives identifying with their hijackers and kidnappers. It looked like masochism, but it was something else. There is in Swedish culture a natural inclination to look for common ground. Dramatic economic and political conflicts have been solved peacefully during the twentieth century. In 1931 five striking workers were shot dead by security forces, an event so unique in our history that it is still remembered by all. A Swedish politician, union negotiator or business executive is always eager to appear reasonable and trustworthy in the eyes of the public.

But Turkey is not Sweden. During its entire modern history Turkish regimes have murdered its citizens, Armenians, Kurds, Greeks, Alevites, leftists of all kinds. They have put Jews, Greeks and others in slave camps in order to destroy their businesses and 'Turkify' the economy. Sweden, entering modernity, was an extremely homogenous country; Turkey was extremely varied, ethnically, religiously, linguistically – but for a hundred years the official national culture of the Turkish republic has been one of ethnic unity. Turkey had a multicultural population but pretended it didn't. All Turks have non-Turkish ancestors, but until quite recently almost all of them kept quiet about it. Turkey was a multicultural society masquerading as a pure Turkish one. Sweden was homogenous but its elites yearned to become the opposite. In May 1975 the Swedish parliament declared the country multicultural – as if such matters were decided by majority decisions.

In international comparisons, Sweden rates very high both in interpersonal trust and in citizens' trust of the state. Turkey rates very low. Most Swedes trust most other Swedes until proven wrong, while most Turks mistrust most other Turks until proven wrong. Swedish governments also trust foreign leaders to a remarkable degree. Swedish leaders have believed that Fidel Castro, African tyrants, Vietnamese communist leaders and other authoritarians were, in some sense, their allies. They even believed Joseph Stalin's henchman Andrey Vyshinsky when he told them he had no idea what had become of the Swedish diplomat Raoul Wallenberg, who was disappeared by the Soviets in 1945.

So, while Sweden was eager to build confidence and profess partnership, the Turkish approach was purely transactional, although expressed in melodramatic terms. Friendly Swedish gestures did not soften the Turkish stance. Quite the reverse: Ankara interpreted Swedish affability as proof that its tactics worked.

At some stage the Swedish game became dysfunctional. It yielded no results and caused damage. But the government pushed on, further into the dead end of submission. The low-water mark was reached on 5 November 2022, when Sweden broke with Rojava, the de facto Kurdish state in northern Syria. The Syrian Kurds, who were leftists and feminists, had been a favourite Swedish foreign aid project, especially after the battles around Kobane in 2014–15, when their YPG militia helped NATO defeat Da'esh, the Islamic State. The natural candidate to fight IS was the Turkish army. Instead, Turkey discreetly assisted the jihadists, as revealed by the *Cumhuriyet* newspaper in a story which caused such fury in the government that the paper's editor had to flee the country.

So, for Sweden to turn its back on the Syrian Kurds was quite a step. Normally, in diplomacy, such a concession would be reciprocated. But Sweden got nothing in return. It was just one more friendly gesture – giving away the one strong card Sweden had. If given at all it should have been played at the very end of negotiations, when everything else had been wrapped up.

Thus, after giving up its cherished neutrality, Sweden had also violated its very first commandment: human rights. It had dropped a vulnerable ally in order to placate a bully. *And* it didn't work. Turkey became no friendlier. By then many Swedes began to be disgusted by the whole NATO ordeal. Swedish leaders had achieved the opposite of leadership; they had diminished broad public support for NATO accession.

Sweden used to be warlike and ruthless, just like Turkey was, and just like most powers used to be. In 1712, Altona, the second largest city in Denmark, was burned to the ground by the Swedes. They did that rather than plunder it, in order to project fear. Contemporary Europeans, less squeamish and more fatalistic about atrocities than we are today, still considered it a hideous crime.

But after Sweden lost its huge dominions around the Baltic and became a small insignificant country, it changed its image. After the loss of Finland in 1809, the national poet Tegnér called on Swedes to build great things at home, to invent and explore and expand in non-territorial ways. They did. Part of this reinvention was a new self-image: Sweden was proud to be peaceful, neutral and to show empathy with the weak. The law defining Sweden as 'multicultural' was an important step in this direction.

This tendency has gone a long way: for a Swedish leader, or political party, to speak openly of Sweden's greatness or past glory, or to appeal to national pride, would be impossible. The spectacle played out in Israel now, where the democratic forces have turned the national flag into a symbol of resistance and protest, could not take place in Sweden, where only right-wing extremists swing the flag. Even the populist-rightist SD party sounds kind and polite compared to its Turkish peers in the fire-breathing MHP party.

In Turkey it is the other way around. A leader who cannot radiate authority and give voice to national pride would be doomed. Sweden and Turkey are antipodes, in the way they imagine themselves, and in the roles they want to play in the world. Sweden wants to be liked; Turkey wants to be feared. It would be rare for a Swedish leader to speak the language of power, raise her voice and draw red lines – just as rare as it would be for a Turkish leader to be cooperative and accommodating. Both, it seems, are stuck in the mould of their national character.

Woodrow Wilson (1856–1924),
the 28th president of the United States
on his campaign trail, Virginia, 1912.

THE 'CRAFT' IN STATECRAFT

Philip Zelikow

Practical leadership has two dimensions. The first dimension is one we know well: choosing what to do. The second dimension is less well known. How to do it? If leaders provide guidance about what is to be done, and how to do it, the rest is management and execution.

The first part, the 'what to do' part, is an easy debate to follow. It is mostly about goals. People discuss problems and their values. Debating problems, they discuss what they read or hear about, since news is naturally devoted to spotlighting problems, and make a claim for attention. Debating values, they discuss which problems they care about, or their attitudes about the proper role of government.

The second part, the 'how to do it' part, is a good deal harder to understand, and the debates are far more obscure. People have to make judgements about practical action. That requires more specialised knowledge about the available instruments and relevant circumstances. The 'how' knowledge is the high card in the deck. When it is played, high-sounding goals often turn to dust. As the former American secretary of state Dean Rusk once put it, 'Ideas are not policies. Besides, ideas have a high infant mortality rate.'

The 'how' is the 'craft' in statecraft. It is the true source of practical leadership. Yet this dimension is not well understood, infrequently studied and rarely taught.

At the turning point of the First World War, in the second half of 1916 and the first weeks of 1917, the great secret was that the war was likely to wind down and come to an end. Leaders in Britain and France confided that they saw no plausible path to victory. Russia was tottering toward revolution. As I have detailed in my book, *The Road Less Traveled*, revealing the full details of this episode, the British and French leaders expected the American president, Woodrow Wilson, to convene a peace conference to end the war. Even those who wanted to fight to the finish knew – and this was an even greater secret – that the Allied side was running out of dollars to be able to purchase the food and munitions that sustained nearly half their war effort. The Americans cut off unsecured loans and the money would run out by the spring of 1917.

On the other side, not only had the Germans and their allies decided they had to end the war, the German leadership had made the first move. With his kaiser's approval, in August 1916 Germany's chancellor had reached out to Wilson and urged him to proceed with the peace conference. The Austro-Hungarian leaders secretly approved of this, and the large concessions the German chancellor confided he was prepared to make.

For Wilson, the 'what to do' part was clear. He was anxious to help end this awful war. He was ready and eager to move. The German ambassador to the United States, Johann von Bernstorff, rightly judged that, at least from May 1916 until 31 January 1917, Wilson was genuinely neutral and passionate about making peace.

Wilson was realistic. Informed by American military attachés and others watching the war, he was realistic about the prospects of either side in gaining a decisive victory. He was realistic in not trying to decide who was at fault for the war. One reason he was so eager to make peace as soon as possible was because he judged, realistically, that failure meant America might be forced into a war which he and the country fervently did not want.

Wilson was realistic in his modesty about trying to reorganise Europe. At that time, in 1916 and early 1917, one of the reasons he did not wish to engage on questions of territorial peace terms, one of the reasons he sought a 'peace without victory', was to encourage a reasonably conservative settlement, to avoid a series of annexations and humiliations that would only plant the seeds of future conflicts. In this respect, his fundamental outlook on Europe's evolution was similar to that of statesmen in both Britain and Germany.

Wilson was realistic when he accepted the British argument that the US had to take part in a post-war league of nations to reassure the Allies that a compromise peace could last. Wilson was not only realistic, he was also deeply perceptive when he explained – in his December 1916 peace note and his January 1917 speech – that a peace without victory was the best, and perhaps the only, way to secure a peace that might endure.

Having predicted, correctly, that a peace accompanying bloody victories and humiliating defeats would not last, Wilson was condemned, like some figure in mythology, to suffer the prolonged and painful validation of his own dark prophecy. Because America ended up entering the war, rather than ending it, the war widened and deepened. Thus, in 1919, Wilson found himself orating fruitlessly against the doom he had himself once predicted. Then, after his physical breakdown in September 1919, Wilson had to watch the ruin continue until death took him early in 1924.

In 1916–17, Wilson failed to make peace not because he was too encumbered by ideals. He failed because he simply did not know how to do it. He was the man who sits down at the poker game and, dealt a hand with three kings, throws back two of them in the hope of getting better cards.

By September 1916, all the stars were in alignment for Wilson's peace move. Leaders on both sides were pessimistic about their prospects in the war and worried about their ability to continue. The Germans had formally asked Wilson to act and had secretly volunteered the restoration of Belgium to show their readiness to reach a compromise peace.

The British and French were reluctant to make a peace based only on the mid-war status quo. It was a measure of their desperation that a significant faction was willing to contemplate even that. Others open to peace needed more.

They could have had more. Wilson could have brokered a peace conference conditioned on a plain German commitment to restore Belgium and withdraw from at least most of occupied France. He could have gone further and attempted to arrange armistice lines, while talks were underway, that accomplished much of those withdrawals in a civilised manner, perhaps accompanied by the relaxation of the sea blockades on both sides. The Belgium condition alone would have utterly transformed the politics surrounding peace, in Britain at least.

Instead, for two months, between September and November 1916, Wilson did nothing because of the happenstance that 1916 was a presidential election year and he could not move until he was re-elected. Then, for another month, a vital month from mid-November to mid-December, Wilson did nothing – even though he felt the urgency to act – because he was effectively delayed and deflected by his two relevant subordinates, and because his government had made no plans and offered no advice for what he should do.

After setting the stage with powerful added pressure on Britain at the end of November – he orchestrated the cut-off of unsecured loans and dictated a harsh letter to the British – Wilson then issued a peace note late in

December that was a misfire. The note, apparently inspired by newspaper editorials, took no practical action.

What followed was about six weeks of confused efforts to get a better peace move going. Bernstorff (and an influential British officer acting as the Washington representative of Britain's secret service) attempted to guide Wilson's key advisor, Edward House. Wilson, meanwhile, came up with another plan inspired by essays in the *New Republic*. Bernstorff followed through on the peace plan he thought he had. Wilson and House – startled, encouraged and further instructed, including by British parliamentarians and the American humanitarian envoy Herbert Hoover – then reset that plan so that finally, by the last week of January, Wilson was at last starting to construct the plan to set up peace talks that had actually been available to him for at least the previous five months.

When, on 31 January 1917, he discovered that his efforts had failed to ward off the expanded U-boat war, Wilson was stunned. Shocked and reeling, he then angrily brushed past the German chancellor's effort to keep the peace option alive.

Wilson still did not want to bring America into the war. Yet, having sent the German ambassador home, Wilson found that war was the only option he had left, his only remaining card.

Flash forward a hundred years. Pick a very different subject: the statecraft to cope with the global Covid pandemic. In the later stages of that crisis, a group of foundations asked me to lead a group of 34 experts to analyse what happened, from origins to vaccines, and what went wrong. Our report, 'Lessons from the Covid War', was published in 2023.

The most difficult issues in the crisis were not about 'what to do'. There was broad agreement on the need to warn of outbreaks, find out who was sick and develop effective medicines and vaccines available on a global scale. The hard problems arose in the 'how'.

Real strategy is not about what 'should' be done. It is about the 'how'. Many people have to be organised, funded, trained and equipped to play their part in a coordinated choreography, people who sometimes must do very difficult things.

America fought its Covid war without an army or a battle plan. It's not surprising we suffered many more casualties than any other affluent country, in a nation that also had the best access to vaccines. None of the fundamental problems have been fixed.

Americans spent more public money on the crisis than anyone. Our scientific knowledge was unsurpassed. Thousands of people and organisations made heart-rending, life-saving efforts. Yet the story of the Covid pandemic is the exact opposite of the story of the valorous but technologically feeble defence against the 1918–19 influenza pandemic. The Covid war showed how our wondrous scientific knowledge had run far, far ahead of the organised human ability to apply that knowledge in practice.

In a great emergency, as in wartime, the balance shifts away from the world of political posturing and posing, from the practice of politics as performance art to the world of producing results on the ground, through operations and action. Every big-city mayor who has to handle snowstorms knows this. When the weather forecaster predicts the blizzard, it's too late to start putting in orders to buy snowploughs.

To fight the Covid war the US needed to unify the three main cultures in governance, which don't necessarily talk to each other much. One is a culture of programmes and process. Programmes are created to dispense money and they do that, following the given process. Another is a culture of research and investigation, the dominant culture of high science and regulation. A third is a culture of operations, to produce results. It is a culture that can be resilient and adaptable, since the operators have to adjust to the real conditions they encounter. It is the dominant culture in most private firms, especially those that make products or deliver services.

The challenge in the Covid war, as in any great emergency, was to meld all these cultures in practice. What the Covid war exposed, what every recent crisis has exposed – even in Iraq and Afghanistan – is the erosion of operational capabilities in much of American civilian governance. Programmes, scientific knowledge and concrete operational responses were never well aligned.

A symptom of this failure was how often governments and agencies had to hire management consultancies – McKinsey, the Boston Consulting Group, Bain & Company, and a number of others – to perform basic operational tasks. That is the point when government starts outsourcing the know-how of governance.

In an early book about the pandemic, with the uplifting title *Doom: The Politics of Catastrophe*, the historian Niall Ferguson thoughtfully observed that 'pandemics, like world wars and global financial crises, are history's great interruptions…they are also moments of revelation'.

One reason the American response to the pandemic was discouraging was because, at least at times and to many, our governance seemed incompetent. If citizens do not believe their government can handle the largest emergencies, the republic is in trouble.

This image of relative incompetence was particularly distressing because it was the latest stumble in a series of tragic stumbles, including the catastrophes in Iraq and Afghanistan. And this was the performance of a country that once justifiably regarded itself, and was regarded by many non-Americans, as being best-in-world at handling large emergencies. America had been the exemplar of can-do, practically minded public accomplishment.

Fortunately, during the Covid war, a great many Americans ended up displaying that kind of will and know-how. But the positive lessons need to be noticed, studied and taught. Unfortunately, the policy agendas of both major American political parties appear almost entirely undisturbed by this pandemic. There is no momentum to recognise the failures or fix the system. Although several public health experts warned us about the usual cycle of 'panic and neglect', it still is astonishing to watch that cycle repeat once again.

Americans can reflect on a proud heritage, not far in the past, when they were known across the world for their skills in everything from fixing cars to designing European recovery to putting a man on the moon. Again and again, they tackled apparently insurmountable problems, public as well as private, in a relatively non-ideological get-it-done spirit. At one level the Covid crisis is another depressing story of how twenty-first-century Americans have fallen short.

Yet at another level, as we describe, many Americans rose to the challenge. The Covid crisis abounds with stories of desperate improvisations, in America and all over the world. Some succeeded; many failed; many were a mix of both. Any other great emergency might also exhibit all the problems of organised action manifest in the Covid crisis. We hope our country will reflect on this war to prepare, not just for another pandemic, but for the kind of global emergencies that already seem to mark the twenty-first-century, including the changes in energy use and climate.

There are obviously several ways to explain the decline in government performance and the collapse in public trust in the US government since the high-water marks of the late 1950s and early 1960s. Since the early 1960s, the government has tried to do much more – around the world and at home – and it is perceived to have usually fallen short, sometimes cata-strophically so.

It is not very useful to blame the anti-Washington discourse. Such scapegoating of Washington is not new. It is an old, old theme in American history. Nor should we blame incompetent delivery of basic services, which is still reasonably good in America.

Part of the story, repeated in the Covid war, is a record of policy fail-ures: the tendency to react to events rather than drive them, poorly spec-ified objectives, confusing guidance, reliance on weakly evidenced sup-positions, little grasp of organisational capacities, inability to adapt organisations to new problems, over-reliance on ill-managed contrac-tors. These are all symptoms. They are symptoms of policies that are badly designed.

Weak knowledge of the history of certain issues or even of the govern-ment's own policy record, a superficial grasp of other communities or institutions and a preoccupation with reactions to daily news: these, too, are symptoms. They are symptoms of a weakening capacity for in-depth professional assessment.

Of course, the marked tendency to militarise policy, to rely on military instruments and military policymakers, repeated again in the Covid war's Operation Warp Speed, is no cure. It is another symptom of the breakdown, as American policymaking is dumbed down and becomes praetorian.

Some of these problems can be blamed on bad structures and on polar-ised, dysfunctional politics. But that's not all of the story.

As China's immensely powerful Qing Empire began to decay in the early 1800s, a leading scholar began calling for reform of the Confucian system that selected and trained the country's administrative elite. He looked around and saw 'everything was falling apart…the administra-tion was contaminated and vile'. The scholar, Bao Shichen, 'found him-self drawn toward more practical kinds of scholarship that were not tested on the civil service exams', as Stephen Platt noted in his book *Imperial Twilight: The Opium War and the End of China's Last Golden Age.*

Bao would, in time, become one of the leading figures in a field known broadly as 'statecraft' scholarship, an informal movement of Confucians who were deeply concerned with real-world issues of administration and policy. Tragically for Bao and many of his allies, their efforts were not enough. They could not reverse the decline of their empire.

The United States government has plenty of problems, too. Fortunately, it is not yet at the point the Qing Dynasty reached. Americans' seemingly bygone skills for policymaking and tackling emergencies were not in their genes or in the air. They need not be consigned to wistful nostalgia. The skills were specific. They were fostered by the surrounding culture. And they can be re-learned.

Know-how relates ends and means. It guides and inspires confident performance. The study of statecraft would profit by spending less time on 'should' and more time on 'how'.

A nuclear-powered US Navy submarine
cruises into the Navy Port at Port Canaveral,
Florida, 8 March 2023.

THE SOUTHERN FRONT: THE AUSTRALIAN WAY IN A CONTESTED INDO-PACIFIC

Rory Medcalf

Russia's invasion of Ukraine has brought geopolitical struggle to Europe, but storm clouds are gathering across the Indo-Pacific as well, as the shadow of a global contest between authoritarianism and democracy becomes a reality. In this maritime super-region spanning the Pacific and Indian Oceans, the People's Republic of China is pursuing hegemony, an external manifestation of the nationalist authoritarian control that has hardened in recent years under Xi Jinping. This quasi-imperial push to dominate the region that is the world's economic centre of gravity is at least as much about subordinating the interests of a myriad of other nations and communities as it is about challenging the United States.

Understanding how these other powers are responding to this new era of strategic danger is thus crucial to helping Europe define its choices as the realities of confrontation and the risks of conflict involving China accumulate. In the multipolarity of the Indo-Pacific many such studies manifest: Japan's growing resolve, South Korea's self-assertion, the Philippines' maritime resistance, Vietnam's resilience, India's rise and Taiwan's special defiance. But for Europe, the Australian story may be most illuminating of all. Since 2016, Australia has dealt with influence and interference operations, economic coercion and strategic encroachments in its neighbourhood. Canberra's experience of weathering these challenges and preparation for future tension provides distinct lessons in statecraft, leadership and security, especially for the democratic middle and smaller powers of the world.

China's authoritarian assertiveness, pressure and expansive regional presence have given Australia a bracing reality check – so much so that an 'Australian way' of comprehensive national security is emerging. This journey is still at an early stage and no destination is permanent, but some features are already clear. The Australian way combines internal fortitude – including new safeguards for national infrastructure and democratic institutions – with external strengthening. The latter element involves alliance and partnership as much as national military modernisation. Indeed, given Australia's singular mismatch of extensive interests and limited capabilities, defence self-reliance is meaningful only in an alliance context.

Most historic among the country's defensive measures is the 2021 AUKUS arrangement to acquire nuclear-powered submarines and maintain an edge in critical technologies, in intimate cooperation with the United States and the United Kingdom. This is not only about ensuring Australia maintains a technological lead but has naval power-projection suited to the vast distances of its region: a kind of coming of age as a truly Indo-Pacific power. At the same time, there is a premium on statecraft: a strategic equilibrium in which the pursuit of deterrence is accompanied by diplomacy. Australia's tradition of aiding its neighbours in the Pacific Islands and South-East Asia has been modified with strategic purpose: to help them develop resilience and protect sovereignty, quietly proving the staying power of democratic partnership.

In Australia, it would be hard to imagine a bolder signal of strategic change than a left-wing stalwart of a Labor government preaching the virtues of AUKUS. But this is precisely what occurred when defence industry minister Pat Conroy confronted his own party faithful head-on about their anti-nuclear, anti-American and anti-British pieties, taking the stage at a 2023 party conference to insist: 'If you're pro-human rights, you need to be pro-AUKUS. If you're pro-peace, you need to be pro-AUKUS.' Just as the decisions by Sweden and Finland to pursue NATO membership have challenged old assumptions about neutrality and alignment, so, too, is Australia taking some profound departures to secure its future and a rules-based order in a contested Indo-Pacific.

At a superficial glace, Australia's strategic situation and policy choices would seem to have little meaning for Europe. So much is different. Australia is 'a nation for a continent and a continent for a nation', as described by its first prime minister Edmund Barton in the movement towards this federation of former British colonies in 1901. More than a century later, there remains an extraordinary dissonance between a modest-sized population (26.5 million people in 2023) and vast continental and maritime territory, which encompasses 5% of the Earth's surface. The confluence of geography, history, resources and population has bestowed the country singular circumstances. This is a developed democracy with Western political foundations. The country is located far from its traditional allies, and it has had a complex quest to find its place in an Asia-centric regional order. Its contemporary multiculturalism brings an advantage: far from the Anglo-Saxon bastion Chinese propaganda depicts, Australia is one of the most ethnically diverse nations in the world, with 29% of its population born abroad. At the same time, successive Australian governments have underscored a unifying sense of national values, marked not by race or religion but by political, economic and religious freedom, liberal democracy, equality and mutual respect.

Likewise, Australian statecraft has for many years now sought to define the nation's geographic place in the world as a source of strength and advantage. That is the story of the Indo-Pacific, which Australian diplomacy has pioneered for more than a decade – in a bipartisan fashion across two changes of government and five prime ministers – and which history will acknowledge as a significant legacy of its middle-power diplomatic activism. This reimagined the nation's home region as not Asia-only but Asia-plus. It reflected the connectedness of the Pacific and Indian Oceans as a strategic system and the enduring importance of global stakeholders in this vast maritime space. In 2013, an Australian defence white paper became the first official strategy by any nation to redefine its region of strategic interest as something called the Indo-Pacific. Not merely a new name for the late twentieth-century notion of the Asia-Pacific (which tended to exclude India and the Indian Ocean), this was a deliberate act of geopolitical imagination to define a region to which Australia automatically belonged, thus transcending debates about whether Australia could be narrowly defined as an Asian or Western country.

Admittedly, under the current Labor government of prime minister Anthony Albanese, Australia is being more selective in its deployment of the very Indo-Pacific terminology it has long championed. This is mostly to acknowledge the sensitivities of small Pacific Island nations, who read the language as embedding their region in a US-China power struggle they would prefer to avoid. Even so, Australia's most consequential policy actions remain unequivocally Indo-Pacific in character, from AUKUS (focused on a submarine base on the nation's west coast) to deep diplomatic investment in 'Quad' coordination with India, Japan and America, and an intensification of access and interoperability arrangements under the US military alliance – all in the context of balancing and deterring China.

The idea of the Indo-Pacific is not some cartographic fancy. For many nations, it is useful because it explains and encourages the balancing and dilution of Chinese power through an array of new partnerships across collapsed geographic boundaries. It undercuts China's insistence that its assertiveness in the vital sea lanes of the South China Sea is somehow not the rest of the world's business. It rejects Xi's conceit that international connectivity can be diminished to a Belt and Road that happen to begin and end in Beijing, with so many other capitals merely waystations. It provides a metaphor for collective action, code for a pivotal region where China can be prominent but not dominant. In a global discourse often dominated by Beijing's transgressions and triumphalism, or simplistic narratives of US-China bipolarity, the Indo-Pacific idea offers a useful alternative. It is about steadiness and solidarity among many nations.

Along with Japan, Australia quietly led an accelerating diplomatic campaign in the 2010s to promote the Indo-Pacific. This reframed an Asia-centric region to reflect growing economic connectivity and strategic contest across two oceans, driven in substantial part by China's expanding interests and influence, and the need for coordination in pushing back. Thus, starting as something of an intellectual insurgency, the term Indo-Pacific fast became a new orthodoxy. Australia's initiative in 2013 (reinforced in a foreign policy white paper in 2017) was succeeded decisively by Japan's Free and Open Indo-Pacific strategy in 2016, with the late Shinzo Abe proving the concept's most determined proponent – unsurprisingly, since it built on his 2007 idea of the 'confluence of the two seas'. Together, Abe and Australian conservative prime minister Malcolm Turnbull encouraged the United States to adopt an Indo-Pacific strategy, which it did initially (albeit with too narrow a military focus) under the Trump administration. Indo-Pacific strategy has been a vital pillar of continuity between the foreign and defence policies of Republican and Democratic administrations, with Joe Biden taking a more comprehensive approach that recognises economics, technology, development, information and public goods as integral elements alongside deterrence.

Success has many authors, and the Indo-Pacific idea has benefited from a diversity of champions. India was crafting its own inclusive vision, promoted by prime minister Narendra Modi in 2018. The initiative of Indonesia in pushing fellow South-East Asian nations towards the 2019 ASEAN Outlook on the Indo-Pacific was a crucial turning point in legitimising a much wider array of Indo-Pacific converts, especially in Europe.

In the past few years, the Indo-Pacific tide has spread to the EU, Germany, Britain, the Netherlands, Canada, New Zealand, Taiwan and South Korea. France, as a resident power with its Pacific and Indian Ocean territories, was an early mover towards the concept. It has maintained an Indo-Pacific vision, even though Australia's AUKUS deal – and sudden abandonment of a major French submarine contract – damaged trust between these democracies.

Although Chinese propaganda predictably seeks to accentuate the differences among the varied Indo-Pacific policies – and it is true that some recognise the need for deterrence more openly than others – the commonalities loom large, across Australian, Asian, American and European positions alike. These include respect for a rules-based order and peaceful status quo, the upholding of the sovereignty of nations large and small, and a recognition that the region's security challenges cannot be addressed in narrow, localised ways that enable coercion and aggression.

For Australia, the Indo-Pacific provides the conceptual framework for a broader strategy of national security, international engagement and coalition-building. This involves a recognition of darker currents of geopolitical competition and the end of a long era of hope – or naivety – in which security and prosperity were staked on the promise of globalisation. For a resource-rich nation, reliant on free if managed flows of trade, investment, people, technology and knowledge, this was of course an attractive proposition.

From at least the 1980s, Australia's economy became relentlessly open, diplomacy was underpinned by optimism and engagement, and security policy focused on non-state challenges, such as terrorism, disaster relief and – where necessary – the stabilisation of neighbouring weak states. Where larger geopolitics came into play, the United States came to the fore as Australia's ally and the sole superpower and underwriter of regional peace.

No single turning point explains the recent hardening of Australia's security outlook. It is a China story, but not about China alone. Australia has never been capable of providing for more than a portion of its own overall defence, but some steps towards greater security self-reliance came well before the contemporary China challenge. In the 1980s, a journey began towards self-reliant combat capabilities for the Australian continent, albeit against limited threats. This 'defence of Australia' concept was challenged amid the expeditionary demands of the global 'war on terror'. But echoes can be found today, as Canberra looks anew at the need for deterrence to keep a prospective adversary far from the nation's shores. The AUKUS nuclear submarine will take many years, indeed decades, to fully deliver, but other strike weapons such as missiles could be added to the Australian arsenal within years. Moreover, Australia is open about its possession of offensive cyber capabilities.

For the first decade of this century, a dominant narrative in Canberra's external policy thinking was that the rise of China was largely good news. Geopolitical rivalries from the twentieth century were diminishing through the logic of economic enmeshment. This story was consonant with Australian short-term economic interests. China was overtaking Japan as the nation's top trade partner, especially through its appetite for iron ore. The popular sense was that this relationship helped the nation weather the global financial crisis of 2008.

Yet the start of Australia's security wake-up was also around this time. America's economic pain gave China's strategic elite a jolt of confidence. The first ripples of Beijing's assertiveness were being felt in the South China Sea. And on Australian soil, the nationalist rallying of thousands of Chinese students – to suppress dissident voices during the 2008 Olympic torch relay – was a foretaste of the foreign interference controversy that would flare up some years later. Mandarin-speaking Labor prime minister Kevin Rudd was mistaken by some observers as being soft on China: in fact, his defence strategy of 2009 – calling for a modernised navy and expanded submarine fleet – was an early sign that Australia was worried about future major power aggression.

To be sure, the external policy settings in Canberra were still mixed. An 'Asian Century White Paper' in 2012 envisioned a cornucopian future. In 2014, the conservative (and otherwise hawkish) prime minister Tony Abbott welcomed Xi Jinping to parliament with words of a wide-ranging partnership of mutual benefit. But national security undercurrents were gathering force, driven by Xi's push for domestic control and regional dominance, and the growing clash of political systems and values. Many international observers were surprised when, from 2016, Australia began tightening its policy settings for self-protection; nominally in a country-agnostic fashion but in practice against China. This was very much a set of independent policy initiatives begun well before the Trump administration toughened America's own China stance;

indeed, Australia – along with Japan – led the way in this, as with wider Indo-Pacific strategy.

Under the conservative governments of Malcolm Turnbull and then Scott Morrison, a wide-ranging national security effort included laws to criminalise foreign interference, ban foreign political donations and invoke federal powers to restrict subnational governments from freelancing on external policy (such as a Chinese Belt and Road agreement by the government of the state of Victoria). Intelligence funding and powers increased, new security-related departments and agencies were established and security screening on foreign investment tightened. Most starkly, Australia in 2018 became the first nation in the world effectively to ban Chinese state-influenced vendors Huawei and ZTE from involvement in 5G networks, the nervous system of a wired economy. Defence modernisation was pursued with a stress on conventional capabilities for deterrence and warfighting in a maritime region. Internationally, Australia stepped up its involvement as a development and security partner in the South Pacific, pushed for the revival and rapid deepening of the Quad, strengthened alliance cooperation with the United States, and initiated AUKUS in 2021.

All these moves need to be understood in light of Australia's difficult choices as a middle power in a contested Indo-Pacific, where many nations now hold profound concerns about China's massive military expansion and its demonstrated willingness to coerce or compromise the sovereignty of smaller powers. But there is also an important global dimension, including Russia's aggression against Ukraine. Strikingly, the Albanese Labor government, elected in May 2022, has kept all the security building blocks put in place by conservative governments.

This is despite Labor's foreign policy settings and rhetoric placing more emphasis on engagement with South-East Asian and Pacific neighbours (including through a more ambitious stance on climate change). Notably, Australia has sustained outspoken bipartisan support for Ukraine, including in supply of military equipment, despite the ambivalence of many of the Asian nations that Canberra needs to work with in managing the China challenge.

In 2023, the Australian government is promoting a 'stabilisation' of relations with China, prompting some concern among partners and within conservative ranks that this could lead to the erosion of the national security achievements of recent years. The official rhetoric is cautious and disciplined. This is intended as a contrast to the Morrison government's willingness to get ahead of the global pack as one of China's most forthright critics, including in calling for an independent inquiry into the origins of the Covid-19 pandemic – the moment Beijing chose as the tipping point towards its campaign of economic coercion. But the policy settings seem little changed. Since 2020, Australia has weathered economic sanctions (especially against agriculture), and public opinion across the political spectrum has become deeply suspicious of Beijing.

No serious politician in Australia harbours the illusion that relations with China can be founded on trust. Foreign minister Penny Wong talks of the need for 'strategic equilibrium' in the Indo-Pacific. But in a region where China seeks hegemony, this does not mean equidistance between China and America. Rather, it is a polite way of talking about full-spectrum balancing involving diplomacy, economics and development as well as hard power – and working with a wide range of partners to ensure that what remains of regional order is preserved and temptations for aggression constrained.

None of this preparedness guarantees that Australia will be fully ready for the storms and shocks ahead. Like most democracies, this is a nation that remains less than the sum of its parts when it comes to being ready to mobilise for crisis. For instance, Australian politics, following the unpopular deployment of conscripts to the Vietnam War, has long been allergic to the idea of national service. The private sector and subnational levels of government remain only loosely connected to the national security effort. The nation's cybersecurity vulnerabilities have become plain, in embarrassing mass data breaches across the private and healthcare sectors. And above all, although the current Australian government has many of the building blocks of a whole-of-nation security strategy – especially in foreign and defence policy – it remains nervous about articulating the full challenge to the general public. There is yet to be a full and open acknowledgment that one day the nation may need to be ready for major conflict in its region; words like 'mobilisation' and 'war economy' are yet to enter polite discourse in Australia, but even that may prove a matter of time.

What has occurred in Europe today could erupt in the Indo-Pacific tomorrow, especially with China's regular threats to seize Taiwan. The Covid-19 pandemic, Putin's war, China's strategic tensions with other powers: all these factors have strained or jeopardised supply chains and

256

other global economic interactions in different ways. For Australians, they are raising awareness about economic dependence and a long complacency over national preparedness. Resilience, diversification and deterrence are becoming standard terminology in the policy debate. At the same time, parts of the business community would prefer to pretend away the woes of recent years (or the long-term brittleness of China's authoritarian model) and focus only on short-term profit. Moreover, the wider Australian community has plenty else to worry about – including cost of living, social cohesion and the impacts of climate change – and is not seeking conflict.

What happens next in Australia's strategic voyage is a matter of contingency, for sooner or later China's region-wide assertiveness is likely to present Canberra with hard choices. So many crises are plausible: confrontation in the East China Sea with Japan, in the South China Sea with the Philippines, across the disputed border with India, or with US forces anywhere across the Indo-Pacific. A Chinese effort to pressure or suborn a South Pacific government could compel a clash of wills with Australia, determined to remain partner of choice in its neighbourhood. Outright aggression against Taiwan remains a nightmare scenario, not only for US allies in the Indo-Pacific but for the whole world.

And any question of contingency is also a question of leadership. The several Australian prime ministers who have so far found themselves standing up to Beijing took on the mantle of national security with some reluctance. Australia's present leadership has the opportunity to consolidate their ragged but vital achievements, and with it the responsibility to prepare the nation for the Indo-Pacific tempest ahead.

ПУСТЬ ЖИВЁТ И КРЕПНЕТ
НЕРУШИМАЯ ДРУЖБА И СОТРУДНИЧЕСТВО
СОВЕТСКОГО И КИТАЙСКОГО НАРОДОВ!

Let our indestructible friendship live and strengthen!
Lithograph by Viktor Semyonovich Ivanov
(1909–68), 1951.

TWO TIGERS ON THE SAME MOUNTAIN?
REFLECTIONS ON THE TUMULTUOUS
HISTORY AND THE UNCERTAIN FUTURE
OF SINO-RUSSIAN RELATIONS

Sergey Radchenko

‘You [the Soviet Union] piss on my head and I should respect you?’ Mao observed gravely. He was speaking to a visiting communist leader, Romania's dictator Nicolae Ceaușescu, who was trying, in his usual self-promoting fashion, to mediate between Beijing and Moscow. Mao would have none of it. 'No matter who tries to persuade us [to mend fences], we won't move,' he said. 'The more they talk the worse relations will become.'

The two communist giants had been at one another's throats for more than a decade. What seemingly began as polemics over obscure doctrinal differences eventually evolved into a fully fledged confrontation, armies and all, with the Soviets dropping hints of nuclear obliteration and the Chinese digging tunnels under Beijing. In 1969 the two countries fought several border skirmishes; they later managed to at least begin a tentative conversation, but Mao wasn't willing to go beyond cold formalities. The Soviet Union was the enemy. The Soviets were 'pissing on his head'.

Mao had an outsize impact on China's relationship with the Soviet Union. He was the one who turned China towards an ideological alignment with Moscow. He, too, was the one who later quarrelled with his Soviet comrades. Now, given an opportunity to steer the relationship towards a rapprochement, he refused. China and the Soviet Union remained enemies for the rest of the decade, and even well into the early 1980s. It wasn't all Mao's fault, but if one were to look for reasons for the Sino-Soviet split, Mao Zedong's grievances and fears, his delusions and his ambitions would surely number among key factors that a historian would have to consider in reflecting on the ups and downs of the thorny relationship. Mao's role was in fact so profound that it offers a useful starting point for generalising about leadership and statesmanship in an authoritarian context, and for drawing lessons for the present state of Sino-Russian relations, which, too, are characterised by outsize roles played by individual personalities.

'Before I met with Stalin,' Mao recalled some years after the Soviet dictator's death, 'I did not have much good feeling about him…He was very different from Lenin: Lenin shared his heart with others as equals whereas Stalin liked to stand above everyone else and order others around.'

A guerilla, a philosopher, a survivor of the Long March and the trials of the Chinese Civil War, Mao emerged at the end of the 1940s as China's undisputed leader. But, by virtue of his ideological inclinations, Mao was from the start committed to a relationship with Moscow, and – much as he disliked the idea – was willing to subordinate himself to the centre, to Stalin himself. He understood that the wily dictator never fully trusted him.

Stalin had a particular resentment of self-made Communists like Mao. Just two years before the Communist revolution in China, Stalin broke with Josip Broz Tito of Yugoslavia (he was jealous of Tito's ambitions in the Balkans). Soviet relations with Yugoslavia nosedived and the two countries edged to the point of an outright war (while Stalin secretly planned to have Tito poisoned). Mao knew that Stalin regarded him as at least a potential Chinese Tito, and worked hard to reassure him. He proclaimed himself a loyal pupil of Stalin's and declared, in a famous newspaper editorial in June 1949, that China would 'lean to one side' – the Soviet side.

In December 1949 Mao travelled to Moscow. It was a trip that eventually resulted in the signing of the Sino-Soviet treaty of alliance. But it did not go particularly well. In fact, Stalin refused to sign the treaty at first, sending Mao to cool his heels at a dacha outside Moscow, where the latter nurtured his wounded pride and steamed in quiet fury. It was not very clear – neither then, to Mao, nor to historians who followed the documentary trail – why Stalin would do such a thing. The best explanation is that Stalin was worried – still very worried – about the prospect of American intervention in the Chinese Civil War. Only when these fears were allayed, or perhaps after he became worried that Mao's resentment would drive him towards the West, did Stalin change his mind and give Mao his treaty.

Even as he did, he attached multiple conditions and secret clauses, which Mao would later call 'bitter fruits'. Some of these – for instance the one about joint ownership of the trans-Manchurian railroad and joint enterprises in China – were blatantly neocolonial in character. Mao swallowed his pride. For him, allying with the Soviet Union was an exceptionally important foreign policy move that linked back to his revolutionary plans at home. He wanted to transform China. For this, he needed Stalin's help. And it came – in the form of advice, weapons, technologies, experts and, yes, an actual treaty of alliance.

'The Russian and the Chinese are brothers forever' ran a popular propaganda song in the early 1950s. 'The unity of the peoples and races is becoming stronger. The common man stands with his shoulders straight. The common man is marching with a song. Stalin and Mao are listening to you.' Yet for all the outwards signs of vitality – and at the time the alliance certainly projected internal strength and external menace – all was not well. Later Mao would grumble ceaselessly about his relationship with Stalin being like that between 'a cat and mice' or between 'a father and son'. He was willing to defer to Stalin while Stalin was alive. Mao considered the socialist bloc to be something like a family. But it was a family that lacked true love – only grudging respect. Mao respected Stalin the way a filial son would respect his distant father. The dictator's death in 1953 changed everything.

Stalin's eventual successor, Nikita Khrushchev, was, in Mao's considered view, an upstart. Unlike Stalin, a revolutionary leader and (however crude) a theorist of Marxism-Leninism, Khrushchev had not distinguished himself in any way that would impress the Chinese leader. Yet when Khrushchev reached the pinnacle of power in the mid-1950s, Mao offered his support. What he expected in return was a degree of deference to Mao's strategic outlook. Mao believed himself to be much better placed than Khrushchev to pass judgements on profound matters like war and peace, and the future of revolution.

Khrushchev did not see things this way. Although he initially sought Mao's approval – his very first foreign visit as a leader was to China (for the fifth anniversary of the establishment of the People's Republic of China in 1954) – he also grew to resent Mao, who he increasingly considered unbearably arrogant. Khrushchev did not consult with the Chinese leader when he decided, in February 1956, to speak out against Stalin at a closed session of the Twentieth Party Congress. That speech – and the broader 'de-Stalinisation' campaign – unsettled Mao. He cautioned the Soviets that Stalin had been a great Marxist-Leninist who, though he had committed a few mistakes (in Mao's estimation – mostly relating to his China policy), nevertheless remained a revolutionary leader, whose legacy underpinned the entire socialist project. When later that year unrest engulfed Poland and Hungary, Mao was confirmed in his worst fears.

Some Chinese historians today consider Khrushchev's de-Stalinisation the beginning of the Sino-Soviet split. In this reading, it was Mao's ideological disagreement with Khrushchev – over issues like Stalinism, or theoretical questions of war and peace – that laid the ground for the break-up of the alliance. Ideology was an important part of the relationship. One could interpret the ideological quarrel purely instrumentally – ie as a way to rationalise disagreements that developed for other reasons – but it seems that it played a more profound role, certainly in Mao's case. This was because Mao (who saw himself as something of a great philosopher though he despised intellectuals) internalised the arguments he was presently flinging at the USSR: that Khrushchev was a 'revisionist'; that he betrayed the revolution; and that China's own revolutionary future depended on its ability to stand up for true Marxism. In other words, Mao linked the Sino-Soviet relationship with the fate of the Chinese revolution.

This does not, however, tell the entire story, or even half the story. Mao clearly resented the relationship with the USSR because it was inherently unequal. It was a relationship where the Soviet Union was the 'older brother', whose dictates Beijing was expected to embrace with obedience and even enthusiasm. Mao, with his own unsatisfied ambitions of leading China to greatness, could not accept such a hierarchy.

During one infamous encounter with the Soviet ambassador (which followed a Soviet proposal to build a joint submarine fleet), Mao let out a stream of invective that betrayed the depth of his anger with Moscow: 'You never trust the Chinese!' he bellowed. 'You only trust the Russians! [To you] the Russians are the first-class [people] whereas the Chinese are among the inferior who are dumb and careless.' The ambassador, surprised by such an unexpected onslaught, anxiously reported it to Moscow and Khrushchev urgently flew to China to reassure Mao that he never meant to suggest anything so vaguely neocolonial as a joint submarine fleet.

But tensions did not dissipate. Khrushchev was angered by Mao's failure to consult when, in late August 1958, the Chinese launched an artillery barrage against the Taiwan-held islands just off the Chinese coast.

That action, which led to the so-called Second Taiwan Strait Crisis, risked entrapping the USSR in a superpower confrontation in spite of Khrushchev's best intentions.

For his part, Mao became furious when Khrushchev adopted a neutral attitude in the 1959 Sino-Indian border skirmish. For him, failing to side with China reeked of a betrayal of an ally in need. Khrushchev's flirtation with the United States annoyed Mao no end. In September 1959 Khrushchev made his maiden voyage to the United States for meetings with President Dwight D. Eisenhower, and then turned up in China and attempted to pressure Mao to release US citizens held in Chinese detention. The meeting between Mao and Khrushchev, and their lieutenants, at one point became so tense that the Soviet leader began shouting and even told the Chinese foreign minister Chen Yi to stop spitting at him: 'You do not have enough spit!'

Khrushchev left China in great agitation, never to return. The Sino-Soviet relationship rapidly went from bad to worse. Soon, Khrushchev, in a blatant attempt to put his ally under economic pressure, tore up all aid contracts and recalled Soviet experts working in China. Mao remained uncowed. He regarded Khrushchev as a fool and a bully, and was determined to push back.

Mao's deep personal dislike of Khrushchev and his resentment of the Soviet Union (which were fully reciprocated by the Soviets) led to a rapid unravelling of an alliance that was only recently deemed eternal and unbreakable. Beijing and Moscow increasingly perceived one another as rivals and began to compete fiercely for the hearts and minds of the revolutionary world. China made few gains, for, despite Mao's rhetoric, it had little to offer far-flung guerilla movements and struggling socialist regimes. It was desperately poor itself and, for a period in the early 1960s, found itself in the depths of the worst man-made famine in world history. Yet China's challenge in what was then called the Third World (the precursor to today's Global South) seriously worried Khrushchev.

Another worry of Khrushchev's was China's unexpected challenge to the Sino-Soviet border. Border tensions began to build up in the early 1960s. Beijing and Moscow agreed to border talks, which proceeded well until, in July 1964, Mao decided to torpedo them by declaring, in a meeting with Japanese socialists (who released this information to the public), that China was robbed of vast territories by the Russian tsars and that Beijing was yet to present a bill for the offence.

Khrushchev was outraged. 'Have you read the hideous document about the border?' he asked his colleagues. 'I read it yesterday and became indignant.' The Chinese, he continued, were 'evil, hypocritical, crafty and cunning', citing no less an authority than the nineteenth-century Russian explorer and spy Nikolay Przhevalsky, who had left many a racist reflection on China in his voluminous writings. 'It is completely evident that this is a person who has lost his mind,' Khrushchev commented disparagingly.

It is difficult to know – even today – why Mao raised the question of the lost territories. It is conceivable that he wanted to use the territorial non-issue (for it had not been an issue until then) to sabotage the improvement of Sino-Soviet relations, because any such improvement would be inconsistent with his plans for China's revolutionary transformation. This domestic-centred explanation has much to it. Indeed, within two years Mao unleashed his so-called Great Proletarian Cultural Revolution, which had a distinct anti-Soviet component. Or it could have been an unplanned jab at Khrushchev (whom Mao deeply despised).

Even Khrushchev's ouster in October 1964 failed to reverse the waning fortunes of the Sino-Soviet alliance. When the new Soviet prime minister Aleksei Kosygin turned up in Beijing to plead with Mao to forget old quarrels and start from a clean slate, the Chinese leader told him, mockingly, that Sino-Soviet disagreements would last for 10,000 years. When Kosygin called for shortening the time, Mao agreed to drop 1,000 years but no more.

Tensions between the two countries continued to increase until, in March 1969, border skirmishes broke out over a small disputed islet of Zhenbao on the Ussuri River, which separated the two countries in the far east. Worried about a fully fledged war with their neighbour, the Soviets made half-hearted moves towards rapprochement. Mao, though, remained adamantly opposed to mending fences. Instead, he reached out to the Americans. In 1970 he confided to a visiting US journalist, Edgar Snow, that he thought that President Richard Nixon was 'the No. 1 good fellow in the world'. The transcript of this conversation was forwarded to the party faithful across the country, and caused a great deal of confusion: how could the leader of American imperialism (hitherto daily vilified by Chinese propaganda) turn out to be 'the No. 1 good fellow in the world'?

But such was Mao's political power that he could overturn ideological taboos and turn around the ship of state in no time, and with hardly any need to consult his comrades, never mind the country. It was thus that he effected the Sino-American rapprochement and, for most intents and purposes, took China out of the Cold War. Revolution was out. Development was in.

Beijing and Moscow mended fences – eventually. Relations began to thaw in the early 1980s, with Mao already safely out of the picture (he died in 1976). There is a good reason why that had to be so. Mao's hatred of the Soviet Union was so profound that it was quite inconceivable that he could have put all that enmity aside and embraced his former comrades, now enemies. He became personally invested in the Sino-Soviet split, and he showed no interest in reversing course.

Sino-Soviet relations were fully normalised only in 1989, with Mikhail Gorbachev's trip to Beijing (a full 30 years after Nikita Khrushchev's last quarrelsome encounter with the Chinese leaders). Mao's heir and successor Deng Xiaoping (who, in his time, took a most direct and active part in splitting with the USSR) told Gorbachev that the time had come to 'close the past and open the future'.

That future turned out to be much more auspicious than the past. Although the collapse of the Soviet Union and the emergence of a new – and briefly democratic – Russia unsettled the Chinese leaders, they quickly recognised the new reality and embraced Russia as a partner. The relationship became ever tighter in the years that followed. There was, for once, an understanding across the policy-making elites in both Beijing and Moscow that they had to do everything to avoid a repetition of the disastrous confrontation that proved so costly, and that only benefited third parties (ie the United States).

China and Russia were, after all, natural partners – certainly economically (with Russia becoming a key supplier of energy), but also politically. It is that latter element in particular – political alignment – that became increasingly evident as Xi Jinping rose to power in China. Xi and Russian president Vladimir Putin shared a worldview: a similar set of grievances about their countries' positions in the world pecking order, and an ambition to change the global balance of power in a way that would favour their states. Unlike Mao and Stalin in their time, they were not themselves locked in a hierarchical relationship. This was an alignment, not an alliance. It was much more flexible, much more responsive to their needs. It was most certainly not ideological.

Yet there also appeared a continuity. As in the 1950s, Xi and Putin, presiding over two autocratic regimes, endowed with immense powers of coercion and seemingly unconstrained by institutional checks and balances, hold the fate of this relationship in their hands. China and Russia are vast countries that interact at multiple levels: political, economic and social, national and regional. But it is the personal relationship between Putin and Xi that defines the overall direction. Their grievances and hopes give state-to-state relations a meaning that they would not otherwise have. Understanding their personal interaction – still shrouded in secrecy – is important for deciphering the future trajectory of the Sino-Russian relationship.

Will the Russians and the Chinese become 'brothers forever' again, like in that song from the early 1950s? And how will the two dictators at the helm of great empires navigate their jealousies and their insecurities? The final verse of this song is still to be written.

The United State's President Biden
welcomes Ukrainian President Zelensky
to the White House, 21 September 2023.

UKRAINE AND THE FUTURE
OF US GLOBAL LEADERSHIP

Alina Polyakova

O n the eve of the first anniversary of Russia's full-scale invasion of Ukraine, President Joe Biden declared the US would support Ukraine for 'as long as it takes'. As the war enters its third year, the US maintains its support under this motto. American leadership has brought the Western alliance together in support of Ukraine's fight for freedom – Europe and the United States are more united on Ukraine than on any other issue, including China. Russia's brazen and brutal war has not only produced new-found Western solidarity, it has also forced European policymakers to prioritise security after years of neglect and divestment that left Europe's armies strained at best and completely inept at worst.

Russia's invasion was a wake-up call to Europe. In a historic speech three days after the event, German chancellor Olaf Scholz called this critical moment a *Zeitenwende*, or turning point, for German defence and security, committing €100 billion to Germany's defence budget. At the 2022 NATO Summit in Madrid, the Alliance committed to a significant reinvestment in its presence on its eastern flank, including a more than seven-fold increase to 300,000 troops on high alert. Finland and Sweden, two countries with a long history of neutrality, joined NATO, transforming the security dynamics in the Nordic-Baltic region. Countries that had sounded the alarm on Russia's imperial ambitions, most notably Poland and the Baltic states, have been shown to be justified in their views. Even France, where President Macron advocated for Russia's integration into Europe's security architecture, has made a U-turn, going as far as to support Ukraine's membership in NATO, and putting troops on the ground.

For its part, the US has led the way on military and security assistance, providing billions in military assistance to Ukraine, as well as weapons systems such as cluster munitions, Javelins, Abrams tanks and the Patriot air defence system. The US has also stepped in to authorise more than $110 billion of economic support, including direct assistance to Ukraine's government and economy. Even though military assistance is less than 6% of the overall US defence budget, when combined with economic assistance, its investment rivals its post-Second World War Marshall Plan outlay (of approximately $150 billion in today's prices).

When faced with criticism of slow response, delayed weapons deliveries and hand-wringing about whether one system or another would present an escalation, US government officials respond with the fact that this is the fastest release and supply of military equipment the Pentagon has carried out in decades. The hard truth, though, is that the best the US has been able to do is still not enough for Ukraine to win. Rather, as Ukraine fights to win – which, for Ukrainians, means a full restoration of all territorial integrity – the country only has enough resource to defend what territory it still controls. And US domestic politics have delayed much needed support even further.

Ukrainians feel they have no choice but to fight and to win, yet the Western alliance and the US in particular has no common vision on the outcome they want to see on the ground. In other words, the slow pace of weapon deliveries and political debates between allies send the signal that the West is not committed to victory. Simply put, the West made its choice to focus on avoiding escalation with Russia rather than fully supporting Ukraine to win.

Western leaders seem yet to realise that the consequences of failure in Ukraine will be profound and deeply damaging to US global leadership in the long term.

Russia's actions present a critical inflection point for the future of the US-led international order. When Russia invaded Ukraine in 2022, it unleashed the first conventional war in Europe since the Second World War, and replicated tactics used in Chechnya, Grozny and Syria against Ukrainian civilians. It challenged the underlying tenet of US grand strategy which, at least since the Obama administration, has seen China and the Indo-Pacific as the key area for competition and contestation. It heightened the risk of nuclear escalation, now once again a major concern for Western policymakers, and reopened discussion on NATO expansion. Russia's violent act has made it clear that Western security rests in the security of Europe. And Europe will never be secure unless Ukraine – Europe's second largest country by land mass – is secure.

As the history books are written, this moment will be seen as an inflection point. It will either lead to continued US global leadership rooted in a liberal democratic vision, or it will be the moment that marks the decline of the global liberal order. Any assessment of the US policy response to Ukraine must be looked at through this lens.

Presently, there are three potential ways to judge and understand US policy response to Ukraine and its implications: the US has done too much; done too little; or got it just right.

The level of support given to Ukraine has produced critics who believe in a binary choice between supporting Ukraine or focusing on other strategically important areas of the world. In this view, US support for Ukraine undermines its ability to take up the broader, long-term challenge: China. As the argument goes, the US cannot and should not take up the burden of confronting threats to its allies – European allies should bear the brunt of deterring Russia in their 'neighbourhood'. Proponents of the binary choice argue that the US must prioritise China as the most dangerous threat to American interests in the long run, and thus cannot continue to support Ukraine at the expense of Taiwan and the Indo-Pacific region.

This assessment is misguided, both from a strategic and tactical perspective. Strategically, the US cannot compete alone with China. Washington needs allies both in the Indo-Pacific and globally. America's strongest alliance, economically and militarily, is with Europe. As the wars of the twentieth century have taught us, US security is deeply intertwined with, and dependent upon, European security. A Europe that is not secure means a vulnerable US.

The US can and should tackle both threats by sequencing rather than choosing one or the other. Defeating the more immediate Russian threat in Ukraine weakens Russia militarily. It also deters the threat of an imminent maritime conflict in the Indo-Pacific, giving the US additional time to prepare, and protecting its international credibility. Tactically, Ukraine requires different military capabilities from those needed to defend Taiwan, Washington's greatest security concern when it comes to China. There is little overlap between the US capabilities needed in Ukraine and in Taiwan, due in large part to the fact that Ukraine is fighting a ground war, while defending Taiwan would require a maritime conflict. US security assistance is not a zero-sum calculus. The US can mitigate the need for prioritisation where capabilities do overlap.

Yet, instead of a full-throttled, values-based strategy to help Ukraine win the war, US policy has settled into incrementalism. A clear pattern has emerged in the past year: Ukrainians request a weapons system and Western governments refuse to provide it, only to change their minds a few months later after public debates and disagreements among allies. As a result, the Ukrainians are only partially equipped and Kyiv's full warfighting capabilities are still unknown. Incrementalism gives Moscow what it wants: a long drawn-out war that gives the Russian army time to adapt and Vladimir Putin time to expand the rhetorical wiggle room over his war aims. The incrementalist US approach increases the risk of locking the West into a forever war with Russia that makes the necessary decisive victory more difficult. Prolonging the war has allowed Moscow to mobilise nationalist sentiment, even as casualties mount and evidence of stress in Russia's ruling circles increases. Drawing out the conflict also allows Russia to invest in its war economy, mitigating economic effects by doubling down on war production. Its 2023 defence spending target was doubled to over $100 billion, and now accounts for one third of all public spending – the war is propping up Russia's entire economy.

If Russia is allowed to walk away with any of its ill-gotten gains in Ukraine, the deterrent power of the United States and the transatlantic alliance will be lost. Potential aggressors would no longer need to consider a Western response before invading or threatening a neighbour. It is vital the West is clear that anything short of the full restoration of Ukrainian sovereignty and territorial integrity will represent a catastrophic defeat for the United States and its European allies.

The bottom line is that the US has crafted its policy response through a prism of avoidance. Despite security concerns about the Indo-Pacific, the US has managed to avoid the extremes of either a nuclear confrontation with Russia or doing nothing, and has landed in the middle of the two. 'Just right', however, does not guarantee success in Ukraine or a good global outcome. Ukraine still lacks a strong security commitment from its allies and the transatlantic community. It continues to suffer from delays in the delivery of Western equipment for political and logistical reasons. There is growing scepticism about US investment in Ukraine, and a continuation of the status quo without an end in sight could result in losing domestic support for the war effort. The West has repeatedly declared that it will support Ukraine for 'as long as it takes', but that is a slogan, not a policy. It does not explain what the end goal is, and indeed signals to many Ukrainians that the allies expect the war to drag on for years, with Ukraine bearing the brunt of it. Getting it 'just right' will not hasten

Ukraine's victory if US policy remains vague and lacking in clear commitments. Basing policy on statements such as 'nothing is off the table' means that nothing is exactly on the table either. And after a year and a half of violence and bloodshed, continuing to get it 'just right' has not resulted in an end to the war.

Ukrania quae et Terra Cosaccorum cum vicinis
Walachiae, Moldoviae, by Johann Baptiste
Homann (1664–1724), 1720.

INSIDE RUSSIA'S FOREVER WAR
AGAINST UKRAINE

Gudrun Persson

An often-overlooked fact about the current Russo-Ukrainian War is that over the centuries Russia has waged several wars to try to conquer Crimea and the Donbas area. Bearing this in mind, it is necessary to put the conflict in context and explore the roots of Russia's strategic behaviour and its consequences for Russia and its neighbours.

In the 1890s, the then head of the Imperial General Staff Academy, Nikolai Sukhotin (1847–1918), conducted a study of Russia's wars since 1700. Crimea had finally been incorporated into the Russian Empire in 1783. It had taken Russia, according to Sukhotin, eight wars and 37 years to take the peninsula from the Ottomans.

In 1731, Voltaire, in his *History of Charles XII*, had already summed up the Ukrainian dilemma: 'Ukraine has always aspired to be free: but being surrounded by Moscovia, the Ottoman Empire and Poland, has had to look for a protector and master of either of these three.'

In addition, it is worth remembering the writings of Herman Gummerus (1877–1948), head of the Finnish Legation in Kyiv, between 1918 and 1919. He wrote about when Bolshevik fighters, including regular Russian armed forces, made incursions in north-east Ukraine, in the Kharkiv area. On 9 January 1919, the Ukrainian government sent a note to Moscow, asking for the war operations to be halted and the Russian troops withdrawn immediately. Moscow replied: 'No Russian troops are located in Ukraine. The Russian government has no responsibility what-soever if irregular formations have crossed.'

The Ukrainian efforts to gain independence then failed, but Gummerus was explicit: 'The world can no longer doubt the existence of a Ukrainian nation. The Ukrainian leaders are adamant: their goal is a complete divorce from Russia.'

The decision to launch a large-scale invasion of Ukraine in February 2022 was evidently taken within a small circle by President Vladimir

Putin and the security services. The General Staff, and thus the Russian armed forces, agreed to support the plan.

There are parallels to draw from the experience of the Soviet decision to invade Afghanistan in 1979. The decision was primarily taken by three people, Yuri Andropov (1914–84), KGB director; Andrei Gromyko (1909–89), foreign minister; and Dmitrii Ustinov (1908–84), defence minister. The other members of the Politburo, including Nikolai Ogarkov (1917–94), the then Chief of the General Staff, just had to go along with it. Ogarkov objected to the invasion in strong words, but in the end had no choice but to comply. This is not to exonerate Valerii Gerasimov, defence minister Sergei Shoigu or the Russian armed forces, but merely to point to the fact that the decision to go to war was taken in a small circle on both occasions, and that the security service had an influential role in taking it. Furthermore, it indicates that the Soviet decision-making process in 1979 was flawed. This is also the case in Russia today.

The blitzkrieg plan, aiming at taking Kyiv in a couple of weeks, toppling the Ukrainian leadership and eliminating Ukraine's independence, failed completely. The notion of blitzkrieg in Russian military thought has been discussed for years. This debate is particularly tied to the studies of the 2003 Iraq War. Both this war and the example of Kosovo have had a profound impact.

The Chief of the General Staff, Valerii Gerasimov, had been contemplating blitzkrieg for years. In a 2016 article on lessons from the Syrian operation, he used the term 'twenty-first century blitzkrieg'. His version of the new blitzkrieg focused on the combination of 'Colour Revolutions' and a concept titled 'Prompt Global Strike'. He wrote:

As you know, the United States has already developed and implemented the concept of Prompt Global Strike. The US military is calculated to achieve the ability to, in a few hours, deploy troops and defeat enemy targets at any point of the globe. It envisages the introduction of a promising form of warfare – of global integrated operations. It proposes the establishment as soon as possible, in any region, of mixed groups of forces capable of joint action to defeat the enemy in a variety of operating environments. According to the developers, this should be a kind of blitzkrieg of the twenty-first century.

He added 'in the era of globalisation, the weakening of state borders and development of means of communication are the most important factors changing the form of the resolution of interstate conflicts. In today's conflicts, the focus of the methods used in combat is shifting towards the integrated application of political, economic, informational, and other non-military measures, *implemented with the support of the military force* [emphasis added].'

In 2021, through the combination of several factors – Putin published an essay arguing that Ukraine has no right to exist; a revised National Security Strategy claimed that 'the importance of military force to achieve geopolitical aims is increasing'; and a military force assembled around Ukraine – the scene was set for an offensive military attack. And yet many European leaders seemed surprised when the full-scale invasion became a fact.

In a speech in Valdai, in 2022, Putin made clear that he saw the Chechen wars of the 1990s as the model to follow. The lessons learned by the Russian political and military leadership from that conflict and events in Kosovo in 1999 were summarised at the time by the Russian academic Aleksei Arbatov:

> The main lesson learned [in Russia] is that the goal justifies the means. The use of force is the most efficient problem solver, if applied decisively and massively. Negotiations are of dubious value and are to be used as a cover for military action. Legality of state actions, observation of laws and legal procedures, and humanitarian suffering are of secondary significance relative to achieving the goal. Limiting one's own troop casualties is worth imposing massive devastation and collateral fatalities on civilian populations. Foreign public opinion and the position of Western governments are to be discounted if Russian interests are at stake. A concentrated and controlled mass media campaign is the key to success.

In view of the current war in Ukraine, this article, written in 2000, seems uncannily prescient.

Throughout the large-scale war, the slogan from the Great Patriotic War (1941–45) has been echoed by the Russian leader and all the state media: 'All for the front, all for victory!' By doing so, the intention is to awaken Russians' collective memory of the Second World War, and appeal to people's willingness to sacrifice for the motherland.

War and conflict are seen in Russia as strategy at the highest level. They are politics by *other* means. Both the military and political leadership hold to Clausewitz, and the strategic political goals remain intact, regardless of the temporary setbacks on the battlefield. As for the goals, they have been articulated by the Russian leaders for more than 15 years: a new world order should be created; Russia has the right to dominate its neighbourhood; the authoritarian political system is right for Russia. Consequently, Russia is on a strategic offensive. Ultimately, this is about restoring the Russian Empire in some form or other.

All security policy begins at home and this is true of Russia. The drivers of the war against Ukraine emanate from within. Over the past ten years, Russia's security policy has been determined by the dynamic between inner repression and outer aggression. After the illegal annexation of Crimea in 2014, the intolerance of any kind of dissent started to make itself visible. Former Russian prime minister Boris Nemtsov, who had reacted strongly against the incorporation of Crimea and the military operations in Donbas, was gunned down in 2015, just a couple of hundred metres from the Kremlin walls.

In fact, in the 1990s, a more assertive Russian foreign policy was already beginning to take shape. 'Making Russia a great power again' was the theme of Yeltsin's presidential campaign in 1996. In addition, during Putin's long tenure, his foreign policy, including the illegal annexation of Crimea, has for many years scored the highest approval ratings.

Another factor may have influenced the decision. The military aggressions in Crimea in 2014 and Syria in 2015 could be interpreted as great successes. In that sense, the political and military leadership were perhaps 'dizzy with success', to use Stalin's phrase from a speech in 1930, and published in *Pravda*, where he criticised overzealous officials in the collectivisation process. During the eight years after 2014, Russia prepared for further aggression against Ukraine and against the West: financially, by building an alternative to SWIFT; in the information sphere, by meddling in Western elections; and by increasing propaganda at home. There were many signs that Russia had turned away from the West, and that the political and military leadership were preparing to move against Ukraine.

Currently, after well over a year and a half of fighting, the war has become intrinsic to the political system within Russia. Several draconian laws have been introduced to eradicate any form of dissent and opposition. People who have protested against the war have been sentenced to 25 years in prison. Such long prison sentences have not been seen since Stalinist times. Every opposition media outlet has been forced either to leave the country or to close. Russia is on a neo-Stalinist trajectory: censorship prevails, the denunciations are back and there is zero tolerance of any kind of opposition. The propaganda machine in state media is massive; it should not be underestimated. In the most recent illegally annexed areas in Ukraine – Donetsk, Luhansk, Kherson, Zaporizhzhia – deportations are back, and a state of war has been declared.

Furthermore, there is an ideological aspect to take into account, due to its long-term implications. In November 2022, the Russian president signed a decree listing 'traditional Russian spiritual and moral values'. The most important of these traditional values, according to the decree, are life, dignity, to serve the fatherland and take responsibility for its destiny, prioritise the spiritual before material matters, collectivism, the historical memory and the unity of the peoples of Russia.

At the same time, the so-called destructive ideology – that is, the West's – is defined. It is said to promote violence, egotism, permissiveness, immorality and non-patriotism; it therefore constitutes 'an objective threat to Russia's national interests'. It is described as 'alien to the Russian people'.

In schools, military training has become obligatory, just as it was in the Soviet Union. New history textbooks introduced for the start of school on 1 September 2023 describe the West in general and the US in particular as hostile and a threat to Russia. The withdrawal of Western companies, following the large-scale invasion, is framed in the following way: 'Many markets are open before you all. That means you have fantastic opportunities for careers in business and for your own start-ups. Don't miss this chance. Today's Russia truly is a land of opportunities.' In addition, a weekly ideological topic, 'Conversations about what matters', has already been introduced in schools. Most recently, a mandatory university course, 'Fundamentals of Russian Statehood', for all first-year students, has been created for the academic year starting in the autumn of 2023. The explicit purpose is to make 'the young understand ideology'.

Consequently, in the absence of Marxism-Leninism, the efforts to create an ideology are ongoing. This directly contradicts the Constitution, which stipulates that 'No ideology shall be proclaimed as State ideology or as obligatory' (Article 13.2).

In addition, the current war is a result of the prevailing Russian political leadership's view of the meaning of 'sovereignty'. According to this view, only a great power can be truly sovereign – others cannot. The world order should be built on several poles: Russia, China, US, Brazil, India. According to the Russian president, the Vienna Congress 1815 and Yalta 1945 are good examples to follow.

The essence of the efforts to create a Russian imperial ideology consists of three main building blocks: a strong centralised authority, mighty Armed Forces and a powerful Russian Orthodox Church. Led by Patriarch Kirill, the Church has become a vital ideological instrument of the regime. Russia is described by the Russian leadership as a 'civilisation', with a historic mission to fulfil as a great power, underlining its 'traditional moral and spiritual values'. The West is seen as an enemy. All of this echoes the thinking of the Slavophiles of the nineteenth century. In 2022, Putin cited one of their proponents, the philosopher Nikolai Danilevskii (1822–85), who in 1869, in explaining why the West was a threat, argued that Russia and the Slavic countries belonged to a special civilisation.

At the moment, this school of thought, which emphasises the imperial legacy, the need for buffer zones and the Eurasian character of Russia, dominates. But Russian history also holds another school of thought, one that advocates respect for human life, negotiations rather than bomb-dropping, respect for international agreements and the view that Russia is a European state.

By taking a longer-term perspective on Russia's strategic behaviour and its role as a geopolitical actor, a few observations can be made. Four variables, four structural conditions, stand out as influencing Russian strategy over time, with severe consequences for Russia's neighbours and the world. The four variables comprise:

1) The army's position as a founding – integrated – part of Russia as a state, the link between the military and the survivability of the ruler or regime. An unusually large part of the state's resources is allocated to the military and the defence of the country.
2) Territorial expansion driven, in part, by economic reasons, and to 'protect' the heartland, and preferably to wage wars away from the heartland. During a period of over 400 years, between 1500 and 1917, Russia expanded by 130 square kilometres per day. The Soviet

Union built up a whole chain of buffer states, through annexation and coercion. The uncertainty of the borders have played a critical role in the history of Russia, today especially so. From the Russian military's perspective, territories are crucial to the survival of Russia.

3) The demand for prestige and international great power status on the one hand, and an explicit feeling of insecurity on the other. In 1917, according to the American scholar William Fuller, this resulted in 'an avoidable overextension'.

4) The nationality question. Russia is not and never has been a nation-state. Today, there are over 90 ethnic minorities in Russia. Deploring the dissolution of the Soviet Union, Aleksandr Yakovlev, 'the father of perestroika', noted that he and the Soviet leadership under Gorbachev had ignored the nationalities.

For the future, these four variables are going to be handled, and balanced, by Russia's leaders, regardless of who is in power in the Kremlin. All of this touches on the question of Russian identity, once described by Putin as 'national sport'. Who are we? What kind of state will Russia be in the future and what kind of relationships should it have with Europe and the West? In turn, the West needs to relate to the four variables and consider its long-term relations with a future Russia.

To sum up, the consequences of the ongoing war are far-reaching and entail rapid changes in Europe, Ukraine and Russia. Russia's invasion of Ukraine, not for the first time in European history, poses pressing questions about the consequences of war. We are just at the beginning of trying to grasp the depth of what this means. The fate of Ukraine is dependent on what kind of future and security order there will be. This begs the question of when wars start, rather than the one more commonly asked these days: when does the war end?

It is clear that Russia's strategic, political goals remain intact, regardless of the different phases on the battlefield. President Putin has expressed several times that Russia has both time and history on its side.

Having said this, there is no need to become defeatist. The current Russo-Ukrainian war, and the severed relations with the West, are the result of political choices made by the Russian leadership. The increased repression in Russia has been going on for many years. There are plenty of instances over the years when Russian leaders could have made other choices but chose not to do so. It is important to keep this in mind for the future, regardless of who is in power in the Kremlin.

How will it all end? I do not know. I will just conclude with a quote from the Russian philosopher and writer Vasilii Rozanov (1856–1919), as a reminder that change, when it comes, can be sudden and is always unpredictable.

This is his very short drama, 'La Divina Commedia', published in 1918:

With a bang, a creak, and a squeal, an iron curtain descended over Russian history.

The performance was over. The audience stood up. It was time to put on the fur coats and go home. We turned around. But there were no fur coats nor any homes.

Heads of State attend G7 meeting in
Charlevoix, Canada, 9 June 2018.

GLOBAL JAPAN CHARTS A NEW COURSE

Kentaro Fujimoto

Since the establishment of the Abe government in 2012, Japan has been undergoing a quiet but significant change in its foreign and security policy. This trend has intensified under the Kishida government, which assumed power in 2021. This change has been triggered by a marked deterioration in the security environment around Japan. A consistent trend has been the rise of China and, more recently, Russia's aggression against Ukraine. These have dramatically changed the Japanese perception of international relations. The Japanese people believe that Japan has moved from the post-Cold War era to an era of more severe state-to-state competition. In this context, Japan has begun to respond to the changes in the security environment in a pragmatic manner, while maintaining its own identity of freedom and democracy.

In a deeper sense, Japan may be undergoing the process of reconstructing its 'statecraft'. 'Statecraft' is an unfamiliar concept for post-war Japan. Enjoying 78 years of peace after the Second World War, it was not as necessary to consider the role and actions of Japan as a traditional state. With the increasingly fraught security environment, however, Japan has needed to redefine its role as a state and its practice of 'statecraft'.

The late prime minister Shinzo Abe initiated this endeavour. He was a rare breed in Japanese politics and a true visionary. Perhaps 'statecraft' was part of his character, as the idea of a 'nation state' was so natural to him. He had no hesitation about the idea that states must strengthen their military capabilities to defend themselves in accordance with the changes in the international environment. Some of his critics called him a right-wing nationalist, but his character was multi-layered. He was fully committed to the alliance with the United States and basic values including freedom and democracy. More importantly, pragmatism was his key characteristic; he sought to change Japan's post-war security policy in a bold but flexible manner.

As prime minister, Abe established the National Security Secretariat (NSS) in 2014. Before that, the prime minister of Japan had only a handful of staff in his office to assist with his responsibilities in foreign and defence policies. The NSS was initially created with about 80 staff, which has now expanded to 120. One of its main purposes is to overcome stove-piping in the Japanese bureaucracy, especially between foreign and defence policies. The NSS has also played an effective role in formulating medium- to long-term strategies including the National Security Strategy in 2022.

In the Abe government, the legal structure of Japan's national security policy changed significantly. Due to the previous interpretation of Article Nine of Japan's Constitution, the exercise of the right to collective self-defence was prohibited. The Japan Self-Defence Forces (SDF) could not fight together when the forces of other countries such as the US were attacked. It was a long-held belief of Abe that Japan needed to change this interpretation. He took on the issue despite opposition and hesitation on the part of the public. The legislation to change this interpretation passed and Japan is now able to exercise the right to collective self-defence if the situation affects Japan's existential national interests. This is a major breakthrough in the history of post-war Japan.

Many other legal steps were also taken. For example, the SDF is now able to protect US and Australian military assets during joint drills and other activities. This legal measure will also be applied to the UK in the future. A decision was made to introduce the so-called stand-off missile capability. This is the origin of counterstrike capabilities introduced by the Kishida government. Previously, Japan did not even have medium- or long-range missiles that could strike targets 300 or 500 km away. However, Japan's neighbours, such as China, Russia, North Korea and South Korea, possess long-range missiles. The Japanese archipelago extends vastly from north to south. In particular, Japan is vulnerable in its defence of the Southwestern Islands, which span 1,000 kilometres in length. Therefore, in 2018, the Abe government introduced Norwegian-made JSM missiles (with a range of 500 km) to be loaded on F35 aircraft.

This direction did not change in the Kishida government. Prime minister Fumio Kishida is from a more centrist faction within the Liberal Democratic Party than Abe. However, as Kishida stated in an interview with the *Washington Post* in January 2023, 'The reality is that the leader of a country cannot choose the era in which the person takes that leadership position.' Kishida is also a pragmatist and has a clear direction for Japan at its historical turning point. Among his major policies is the 'drastic reinforcement of defence capabilities', a policy at least as bold as Abe's.

The Kishida government has placed economic security as one of the key issues in its national security policy. Given the existence of various threats through economic means, the government is taking necessary measures to improve Japan's self-reliance and resilience in technological areas. Specifically, the government passed comprehensive legislation in May 2022 to promote economic security, including supply chain resilience and protection of critical infrastructure sectors. Furthermore, discussions are underway in the government to strengthen Japan's information security, including security clearances.

Prime minister Kishida has made drastic reforms in defence policy, too. The size of Japan's defence budget was one of the main subjects that he tackled. Previously, Japan's defence spending was roughly 1% of its GDP. In the National Security Strategy published in December 2022, Japan decided to increase its defence spending to reach 2% of its GDP by 2027. In the strategy, the Kishida government opted to unequivocally recognise the possession of counterstrike capabilities. Japan possesses ballistic missile defence systems, but given the drastic development of the missile capabilities of countries surrounding Japan, there was a mounting need for Japan to possess capabilities to launch an effective counter-attack against an opponent to prevent further armed attacks from it. Japan plans to introduce Tomahawk missiles and develop its indigenous cruise missiles.

Kishida has said many times that it has become clear that globalisation and interdependence alone cannot guarantee peace and development in the international community. There has been a striking change in Japan's policy toward Russia, too. Russia's aggression against Ukraine has dramatically changed the Japanese view of security. For Japan, the Russian aggression against Ukraine represented the complete end of the post-Cold War world.

Japan is the only Asian country in the G7. Japan's participation in the measures against Russia has changed the nature of the fight from one confined to the Atlantic world to one of a global character. In this sense, it was a consequential decision for the entire international community. As a result of this decision, the relations between Japan and Europe have become even closer. The two sides must now think more seriously about how they can cooperate more strategically to deal with the geopolitical challenges in the Eurasian continent.

Even though the aggression took place in distant Europe, Japan considered how to respond to it as a matter of its security mainly for two reasons. First, Japan saw that the future of the free and open international order rests on the course of the war in Ukraine. Second, geopolitically, this war happened at the centre of the Eurasian landmass. This inevitably affected the security of Japan. One interesting parallel in history is Japan's response to the Nazi-Soviet pact in 1939. Having failed to grasp the dynamics of Nazi Germany – an anti-communist state that surprisingly made a deal with the Soviets – then prime minister Hiranuma stated: 'The situation in Europe was complex and bizarre.' Fast-forward to February 2022, and when faced with a major geopolitical event in Europe this time, Japan did not fail to take the right response. Japan decided to change its existing policy toward Russia and introduce severe sanctions. Kishida's geopolitical assessment is clear: if this unilateral change to the status quo by force is allowed, this would be followed in Asia and elsewhere in the world. As he has said: 'Ukraine today may be Asia tomorrow.'

The National Security Strategy describes China as an unprecedented strategic challenge to the peace and security of Japan and the stability of the international community. The Strategy cites such elements as China's national goal of 'the great restoration of the Chinese nation'; a broad and rapid build-up of its military power, especially nuclear and missile capabilities; and strengthened cooperation with Russia. Regarding Taiwan, China has not ruled out the possibility of using military force while adhering to its policy of peaceful unification. The strategy concludes that this is a challenge that should be met by Japan's comprehensive national power and cooperation with its allies and like-minded countries.

Based on this perception, prime minister Kishida iterated his clear views on the mid- to long-term goal of his policy toward China in his speech in Washington DC in January 2023. He said: 'We need China to make a strategic decision that it will abide by established international rules and that it cannot and will not change the international order in ways that are contrary to these rules. Efforts to do so will be long-lasting.'

The recognition of the long-term competition with China brings us to the next key question. What can we do to induce a strategic decision from China to coexist with the international community? It is difficult, however, to draw a sure path forward because China is a revisionist power that seeks to change the international order. An important element would be a sense of timeline. As an intermediate aim, Japan sets the goal of 'constructive and stable relations with China'. Japan will express its concerns directly to China and strongly urge it to adhere to responsible behaviour while seeking to cooperate where possible on common issues. This concept is almost equivalent to what the United States defines as a 'guard rail'.

Managing the relations in a constructive and stabilising manner will be impossible, however, if our side is weak and vulnerable. The National Security Strategy contains the phrase 'new equilibrium' to articulate the relations between deterrence and dialogue. This is an important concept, although it has not received much attention. What it meant was that we should restore the balance of power, enhance deterrence and reduce the likelihood of war. It is for this reason that Japan has decided to significantly strengthen its defence capabilities. At the same time, Japan will encourage serious dialogue with China. It is important to communicate concerns openly, and this must be done at the highest possible level. Communication at the leaders' level is particularly important.

The unity of the allies and like-minded countries is also crucial in conveying messages to China. For Japan, the alliance with the United States is vital, and in the Indo-Pacific region, cooperation between the two countries is being strengthened day by day. A uniform message on international peace and stability should be sent to show the seriousness of their position and to avoid misunderstandings and miscalculations by the Chinese.

Japan plays a unique role in strengthening the free and open international order. Order reflects the distribution of power, and power determines which order will prevail. But order is also a contest of ideas. Which ideas have the most appeal will also determine power shifts. As an alternative image to the post-Cold War international order, Russia is oriented toward a multipolar order; China was previously oriented toward the US-China bipolar order and, more recently, a multipolar order. In addition, between China, Russia and the West, some countries opt for the middle ground, the so-called Global South. The direction in which these countries move, and the degree to which they embrace any one vision, may also affect the future of international order and the balance of power.

In 2016, then prime minister Abe presented his vision of a 'Free and Open Indo-Pacific' (FOIP). The basic idea behind FOIP is to 'enhance the connectivity of the Indo-Pacific region and nurture and enrich it as a place that values freedom, the rule of law, and is free from force and coercion'. This was also put forward at the G7 Summit in 2023, under the presidency of Japan. This vision has resonated with many countries, including the United States, India, ASEAN, and Europe. FOIP is a watershed moment for Japan's foreign policy.

FOIP was advanced by prime ministers after Abe. In March 2023, Kishida developed FOIP in response to the international environment following the aggression against Ukraine. The backdrop to this was the divided response of the international community, particularly at the United Nations, to Russia's aggression against Ukraine. It came as a surprise to Japan that the reaction to the invasion was so divided. In response to the divided reactions of many countries to the aggression, the new FOIP reaffirms the minimum basic principles that the international community should uphold. These principles, which are stipulated in the UN Charter, like territorial integrity and refraining from using force, should be observed in all parts of the world.

For Japan, one of the most difficult aspects of the international order in the current international environment is the question of values. Japan is a member of the G7 and is fully committed to values such as freedom, democracy, and human rights. These values have become part of the identity of the Japanese people. However, the extent to which values are reflected in foreign policy is an increasingly difficult question. Especially as the influence of the countries of the Global South increases, this issue becomes even more important.

In an increasingly divided and chaotic international community, the G7 has proven itself worthy: it is a band based on common values, and it was the group that functioned most effectively during the Russian aggression against Ukraine. The G7 must first come together to maintain international peace and solve international economic crises, such as energy and food, and global issues, such as health and climate change. In particular, Japan, the United States and Europe must unite to manage relations with China.

At the same time, relations with countries outside the G7 and like-minded countries require a more pragmatic approach. In the speech in Washington, prime minister Kishida sought to articulate this. He said:

> Japan believes that the question of values in foreign policy needs to
> be considered in a historical and cultural context. The world that
> emerges after the current period of transition will not be one of

convergence on a single set of values, as was generally believed in the era of globalisation. We will not be able to force many of the countries of the Global South to accept our values as they are. We need to be more committed to our values, but when engaging with them, we need to be humble without preconceptions and have a good understanding of their historical and cultural backgrounds. It will then become increasingly important to share the vision of the FOIP, as I mentioned earlier, that is, the principle that the international community should be driven by rules, not by force, and not by the weak and powerful.

This approach was reflected in the discussions of the G7 in Hiroshima. The summit was challenging for Japan, as its host, since it needed to handle three critical international issues simultaneously: Ukraine; the Indo-Pacific including China; and the relationship with the Global South. Kishida invited the leaders from the Global South, such as India and Brazil, as well as President Zelensky of Ukraine. The leaders talked not only about Ukraine but also about the importance of resolving conflicts, violence and geopolitical tensions in other parts of the world. As chair, Kishida summarised the issues:

> We need to preserve the principles of the United Nations Charter like respect for sovereignty and territorial integrity.
> We support just and permanent peace, especially in Ukraine.
> We will not allow any unilateral attempts to change the status quo by force or coercion anywhere in the world.
> We need to protect the free and open international order based on the rule of law.

Japan's changing foreign policy was initiated out of necessity for its survival. That is, to defend its territory, to maintain its independence and a free and democratic system, and to reverse three decades of stagnation toward economic revival. Whether Japan succeeds or not is not a matter for Japan alone. It will greatly affect the future of the Japan-US alliance and the free and open international order of the entire world. Like it or not, Japan has become one of the most critical actors in contemporary international politics.

CONTRIBUTORS

ALI ANSARI is a professor of Modern History and founding director of the Institute of Iranian Studies at the University of St Andrews. His research interests include Iranian historiography, nationalism and British-Iranian relations. He is a fellow of the Royal Asiatic Society and the Royal Society of Edinburgh, a senior associate fellow at the Royal United Services Institute, and is honorary vice-president of the Governing Council of the British Institute of Persian Studies. He has written for the *Spectator* and the *New Statesman*, and his books include *Modern Iran Since 1921: the Pahlavis and After*; *Confronting Iran: the Failure of American Foreign Policy and the Roots of Mistrust*; and *The Politics of Nationalism in Modern Iran.*

BENEDETTA BERTI is head of policy planning in the Office of the Secretary General at NATO. She is also associate researcher at the Centre for Security, Diplomacy and Strategy at Vrije Universiteit Brussels, visiting professor at the College of Europe and a senior fellow at the Foreign Policy Research Institute. An Eisenhower global fellow and a TED senior fellow, in the past decade she has held research and teaching positions at West Point, the Institute for National Security Studies and Tel Aviv University, among others. Her research focuses on armed groups, internal wars, and protection of civilians.

JOHN BEW is a professor in History and Foreign Policy at the Department of War Studies, King's College London. He leads the department's Grand Strategy Programme, which aims to bring more historical and strategic expertise to statecraft, diplomacy and foreign policy. In 2019, Professor Bew joined the Number 10 Policy Unit and led the recent update to the Integrated Review of Security, Defence, Development and Foreign Policy. He has written for the *New Statesman*, the *Times Literary Supplement* and *New Republic*, and his books include *Citizen*

Clem: a Life of Attlee; *Realpolitik: a History*; and *Castlereagh: Enlightenment, War, and Tyranny.*

ELISABETH BRAW is a senior fellow at the American Enterprise Institute, where she focuses on defence against gray-zone threats. She is a member of the Krach Institute for Tech Diplomacy's advisory board, a member of GALLOS Technologies' advisory board, a member of the UK National Preparedness Commission and a member of the steering committee of the Aurora Forum (the UK-Nordic-Baltic leader conference). She is a columnist with *Foreign Policy* and *Politico Europe*, and regularly writes op-eds for the *Financial Times*, the *Wall Street Journal*, *The Times* and (writing in German) the *Frankfurter Allgemeine Zeitung*. She is the author of two books: *The Defender's Dilemma: Identifying and Deterring Grayzone Aggression*, and *God's Spies: the Stasi's Cold War Espionage Campaign Inside the Church.*

KRISTIN VEN BRUUSGAARD is director of the Norwegian Intelligence School, and an affiliate with the Oslo Nuclear Project at the University of Oslo. An expert in Soviet and Russian nuclear strategy, nuclear and non-nuclear deterrence, and crisis dynamics in Europe and the Arctic, she served as the deputy leader of the Norwegian Government Defence Commission 2022–2023. Her work has been published in *Foreign Affairs*, *Security Dialogue*, *Journal of Strategic Studies*, *Survival*, *War on the Rocks*, *Texas National Security Review*, *Parameters*, and the *Bulletin of the Atomic Scientists* and by the Cambridge University Press. She was awarded the 2020 Amos Perlmutter Prize from the *Journal of Strategic Studies* for her article 'Russian nuclear strategy and conventional inferiority'.

DAVID BUTTERFIELD is a senior lecturer in Classics at the University of Cambridge and a fellow and director of studies in Classics at Queens' College, Cambridge. His primary areas of research are Latin literature, textual criticism, and the history of scholarship. His publications include *Varro Varius: the Polymath of the Roman World*; *The Early Textual History of Lucretius' De Rerum Natura*; and *A E Housman: Classical Scholar*. He is editor of the Classics website Antigone, literary editor of *The Critic*, and is writing the new Oxford Classical Text of the philosopher-poet Lucretius.

J. C. D. CLARK is Emeritus Joyce C. and Elizabeth Ann Hall Distinguished Professor of British History at the University of Kansas. He was previously a fellow of All Souls College, Oxford and Peterhouse, Cambridge.

An expert on English history in the seventeenth and eighteenth centuries, Professor Clark has been highly influential in shaping the way in which historians categorise the chronology of 'the long-eighteenth century' (a concept he devised). His books include *Thomas Paine: Britain, America, and France in the Age of Enlightenment and Revolution*; and *Samuel Johnson: Literature, Religion, and English Cultural Politics from the Restoration to Romanticism*. His next book will be *The Enlightenment: a History*.

CLAIRE COUTINHO has been the Member of Parliament for East Surrey since 2019. Since her election to parliament, she has held the positions of Parliamentary Private Secretary at the Treasury and Minister for Disabled People, and is now the Minister for Children, Families and Wellbeing at the Department for Education. Before her election to parliament, Claire was appointed as a special advisor at HM Treasury, where she worked as an aide to the then Chief Secretary to the Treasury, Rishi Sunak. She is a visiting fellow of Nuffield College, Oxford and former senior fellow of the influential think tank Policy Exchange.

DAISY DUNN is an award-winning author and classicist who has published widely on a variety of biographical and classical themes. She was the recipient of the 2022 Classical Association Prize, in recognition of her efforts to bring classics to the public attention. She is now editor of *ARGO*, a journal published through the Hellenic Society. She writes regularly for the *Spectator*, the *Daily Telegraph* and *Literary Review*, among other publications, and her books include *Catullus' Bedspread*; *In the Shadow of Vesuvius: a Life of Pliny*; and *Not Far From Brideshead: Oxford Between the Wars*.

KENTARO FUJIMOTO is the director and deputy assistant minister of the Policy Coordination Division, Ministry of Foreign Affairs of Japan. He previously served in senior roles, including cabinet counsellor of the National Security Secretariat, counsellor in the Japanese Embassy in Washington, DC, and other offices within the Ministry of Foreign Affairs, which he joined in 1994. During his career, he was involved in major initiatives to transform Japan's national security policy. He earned his MA from Johns Hopkins University SAIS in 1997 and graduated from the Law Faculty at the University of Tokyo in 1994.

FRANCIS J. GAVIN is the Giovanni Agnelli Distinguished Professor and the inaugural director of the Henry A. Kissinger Center for Global Affairs at Johns Hopkins SAIS. Previously, he was the first Frank Stanton Chair in Nuclear Security Policy Studies at MIT and the director of the Robert S Strauss Center for International Security and Law at the University of Texas. He directs the Nuclear Studies Research Initiative, is a senior advisor to the Nuclear Proliferation International History Project at the Woodrow Wilson Center, and is a life-member of the Council on Foreign Relations. Professor Gavin's writings include *Nuclear Statecraft: History and Strategy in America's Atomic Age*; and *Nuclear Weapons and American Grand Strategy*. His book, *Thinking Historically: a Guide to Statecraft and Strategy*, is forthcoming.

KATJA HOYER is a historian and journalist. She is a visiting research fellow at King's College London and a fellow of the Royal Historical Society. Hoyer's expertise lies in German and European current affairs, which she comments on as a Global Opinions columnist for the *Washington Post*. She is a contributing writer for the *Spectator*, the *Daily Telegraph*, *Die Welt* and other newspaper. She co-hosts the podcast 'The New Germany'. Her books include *Blood and Iron: the Rise and Fall of the German Empire 1871–1918* and *Beyond the Wall*.

JULIAN JACKSON is Emeritus Professor of Modern French History at Queen Mary University of London. He is a fellow of the British Academy and of the Royal Historical Society and has been honoured as both a Commandeur dans l'Ordre des Palmes Académiques and as an Officier dans l'Ordre des Arts et des Lettres by the French government. He is a leading authority on twentieth century France, and his acclaimed works on the subject, include *France: The Dark Years*; *The Fall of France*, which won the Wolfson History Prize, and *A Certain Idea of France*, which won multiple awards and was longlisted for the 2019 Orwell Prize.

ALEXANDER LEE is an honorary research fellow in the Centre for the Study of the Renaissance at the University of Warwick, where he specialises in the cultural and political history of Italy between the fourteenth and sixteenth centuries. He has previously held positions at the universities of

Oxford, Luxembourg, and Bergamo. He is a fellow of the Royal Historical Society, a regular columnist for *History Today* and has written for the *Sunday Telegraph*, the *Wall Street Journal*, *The Atlantic*, and the *New Statesman*. His books include *Machiavelli: His Life and Times*; *Humanism and Empire: the Imperial Ideal in Fourteenth-Century Italy*; and *The Ugly Renaissance*.

FREDRIK LOGEVALL is the Laurence D. Belfer Professor of International Affairs at Harvard University. A native of Stockholm, Sweden, Professor Logevall earned his PhD in US foreign relations history from Yale University. He is a former president of the Society for Historians for American Foreign Relations. His book *Embers of War: the Fall of an Empire and the Making of America's Vietnam* won the Pulitzer Prize for History, among other prizes. His most recent book is *JFK: Coming of Age in the American Century, 1917–1956*, which received the Elizabeth Longford Prize and was *The Times* Biography of the Year as well as a *New York Times* Notable Book of the Year.

JAMES MARRIOTT is a columnist at *The Times* covering society, literature and the arts. Previously he worked as an assistant on *The Times*'s books desk as well as in the rare book trade, specialising in seventeenth-century poetry.

RORY MEDCALF is head of the National Security College at the Australian National University. He was a senior strategic analyst with Australia's peak intelligence agency, and a diplomat with service in India, Japan and Papua New Guinea. In 2022 Professor Medcalf was appointed a Member of the Order of Australia for service to international relations and tertiary education. He is a member of the ASEAN Regional Forum Register of Experts and Eminent Persons and the Scientific Advisory Council of the Finnish Institute for International Affairs. He is a specialist in the history of sport, military history, and post-war political history and his publications include the book *Indo-Pacific Empire*.

HENRIK MEINANDER is a professor of History at the University of Helsinki, formerly curator of the Mannerheim Museum in Helsinki and head of the Finnish Institute in Stockholm. He is a fellow of the Finnish Science

Society, the Royal Swedish Academy of Sciences and the Royal Swedish Academy of Letters. In 2017 he was appointed as a Commander in the Royal Order of the Polar Star. He is a specialist in the history of sport, military history, and post-war political history and his publications include *A History of Finland* and *Mannerheim, Marshal of Finland: a Life in Geopolitics.*

MUNIRA MIRZA is the chief executive of Civic Future, a non-partisan organisation. Previously, she was the director of the Number 10 Policy Unit between 2019–2022, where she chiefly advised the prime minister on UK domestic policy and before that served as deputy mayor for Education and Culture in London. She has worked in the cultural sector, academia and business, and served on the boards of the Royal Opera House, Institute of Contemporary Arts and Royal College of Music. She is the author of *Politics and Culture: the Case for Universalism.*

CHARLES MOORE, Lord Moore of Etchingham, is a journalist and biographer. He was editor of the *Daily Telegraph*, its sister publication the *Sunday Telegraph* and the *Spectator.* He still writes regularly for all three, and frequently makes appearances in other print and television media. In 2020, he was elevated to a life peerage. He sits in the House of Lords as a non-affiliated peer. He was personally selected by Margaret Thatcher to be her authorised biographer, a task he would duly accomplish in three volumes: *Margaret Thatcher: the Authorised Biography, Volume One: Not for Turning*; *Volume Two: Everything She Wants*; and *Volume Three: Herself Alone.*

KENNETH PAYNE is a professor of Strategy at King's College London. His research focuses on political psychology and strategic studies. He has consulted for the governments of the United Kingdom and the United States and appeared before parliamentary inquiries in the United Kingdom and the Netherlands. His works include *I Warbot: The Dawn of Artificially Intelligent Conflict*; *The Psychology of Strategy: Exploring Rationality in the Vietnam War*; and *The Psychology of Modern Conflict: Evolutionary Theory, Human Nature and a Liberal Approach to War.*

GUDRUN PERSSON is deputy research director at the Swedish Defence Research Agency and associate professor at the Department of Slavic

Studies, Stockholm University. She is an expert in Russian foreign policy and Russian military strategic thought, and is a member of the Royal Swedish Academy of War Sciences and the Royal Swedish Society of Naval Sciences. In 2023 she received HM The King's Medal (8th size) 'for outstanding research in the field of security policy'. She has published numerous monographs and articles, including *Learning from Foreign Wars: Russian Military Thinking 1859–73*.

ALINA POLYAKOVA is president and CEO of the Center for European Policy Analysis (CEPA) as well as an adjunct professor of European studies at Johns Hopkins SAIS. She is a recognised expert on transatlantic relations, European security, Russian foreign policy, digital authoritarianism, and populism in democracies. She was the founding director for Global Democracy and Emerging Technology at the Brookings Institution and prior to that served as director of research for Europe and Eurasia at the Atlantic Council She is the author of the book, *The Dark Side of European Integration*, as well as dozens of major reports and articles.

SERGEY RADCHENKO is the Wilson E. Schmidt Distinguished Professor at the Henry A. Kissinger Center for Global Affairs, Johns Hopkins SAIS. His expertise lies in the Cold War, nuclear history, and Russian and Chinese foreign and security policies. He has served as a consultant for the UK Foreign and Commonwealth Office. He is a frequent contributor to the *Spectator*, *Foreign Affairs*, *Engelsberg Ideas*, and the *New York Times*. His publications include *Two Suns in the Heavens: the Sino-Soviet Struggle for Supremacy*; *Unwanted Visionaries: the Soviet Failure in Asia*; and *To Run the World: the Kremlin's Cold War Bid for Global Power*.

ISKANDER REHMAN is an Ax:son Johnson fellow at the Kissinger Center, John Hopkins SAIS and senior fellow for Strategic Studies at the American Foreign Policy Council. His expertise lies in history, grand strategy, and US defence strategy in Asia. He has published a number of think-tank monographs, book chapters, and articles in journals such as *Survival*, and the *Washington Quarterly*. He is a contributing editor to *War on the Rocks*, and his work has also featured in the *Guardian*, *Engelsberg Ideas*, the *Financial Times* and the *Economist*, among others. He is the author of

Planning for Protraction: a Historically Informed Approach to Great Power War and *Sino-US Competition.*

ANDREAS RÖDDER holds the chair for Modern and Contemporary History at the Johannes Gutenberg University Mainz and is the Helmut Schmidt distinguished visiting professor at Johns Hopkins SAIS. He has been a member of the board of the Konrad Adenauer Foundation since 2006, and has been appointed to the Commission on Integration established by the German Federal Government in 2019. He has published six major books, including a history of the Federal Republic of Germany, a history of German Reunification and a history of the 'German problem' in Europe since the nineteenth century.

KORI SCHAKE is a senior fellow and the director of Foreign and Defence Policy Studies at the American Enterprise Institute (AEI). She has worked at the US State Department, the US Department of Defense, and the National Security Council at the White House. She has also taught at Stanford, West Point, Johns Hopkins University's School of Advanced International Studies, the National Defense University, and the University of Maryland. In addition to being a contributing writer at *The Atlantic* and *War on the Rocks*, Dr Schake is the author of five books, among them *America vs the West: Can the Liberal World Order Be Preserved?*; and *Safe Passage: the Transition from British to American Hegemony.*

MICHAEL SCOTT is a professor in Classics and Ancient History at the University of Warwick and director of the Warwick Institute of Engagement. He is a National Teaching fellow and principal fellow of the Higher Education Academy; fellow of the Royal Historical Society; trustee and director of Classics For All and an Honorary Citizen of Delphi. He was the recipient of the 2021 Classical Association Prize, in recognition of his efforts to bring classics to public attention. His publications include *From Democrats to Kings: the Downfall of Athens to the Epic Rise of Alexander the Great* and *Ancient Worlds: an Epic History of East and West.*

NATHAN SHACHAR studied Arabic, philosophy and Spanish history at the Hebrew University of Jerusalem. He is a foreign correspondent covering Israel-Palestine, Turkey and Spain. His books and essays have received some of the most prestigious Swedish literary awards, including the Övralid Prize in 2014. His works in English include *The Gaza Strip: its History and Politics from the Pharaohs to the Israeli Invasion of 2009*; *The Lost World of Rhodes: Greeks, Italians, Jews and Turks between Tradition and Modernity*; and *The Johnson Line and Latin America*.

EDWARD STRINGER is a former air marshal in the Royal Air Force who served as the director-general of the Defence Academy and Joint Force Development (DG JFD) until 2021. He has served and held operational commands in the Gulf War, the Balkans, Operation Northern Watch, Iraq, Afghanistan, and Libya. In 2015, he was appointed as the assistant chief of the Defence Staff (Operations), where he had responsibility for everything from flood-relief to the Nuclear Deterrent. He contributes regularly to publications including the *Financial Times*, *The Atlantic* and the *Daily Telegraph*.

LUCY WARD is an author and journalist. She initially worked as an education correspondent for the *Independent*, before spending more than five years as a Lobby correspondent in the UK's Houses of Parliament for the *Guardian* during Tony Blair's premiership. After a stint living in Moscow reignited her passion for Russian history, she published her debut book *The Empress and the English Doctor*, about Catherine the Great. The book was shortlisted for the Pushkin House Book Prize 2022.

ANNA WIESLANDER is the director for Northern Europe at the Atlantic Council and concurrently serves as secretary general of the Swedish Defence Association. She also chairs the Institute for Security and Development Policy, a Stockholm-based think-tank with a focus on Central and South-East Asia. She was previously deputy director at the Swedish Institute of International Affairs, and before that served as head of Speaker's Office at the Swedish Parliament. In 2019 she was elected as a member of the Royal Swedish Academy of War Sciences as well as the Swedish Society for International Affairs. She is frequently invited to speak on her areas of expertise by media outlets such as BBC, Reuters, Politico and *The Atlantic*.

PHILIP ZELIKOW is a professor of history at the University of Virginia and a distinguished visiting fellow at Stanford University's Hoover Institution. An attorney and former career diplomat, he served on the National Security Council staff in the George H W Bush White House, then taught at Harvard. He has served in six administrations. His last full-time service was as the counselor of the Department of State, a deputy to Secretary Condi Rice. He directed the 9/11 Commission and led the Covid Crisis Group that produced 'Lessons from the Covid War: an Investigative Report'. His most recent book is *The Road Less Travelled: the Secret Turning Point of the Great War.*

IMAGE RIGHTS

LEADERSHIP AND STATECRAFT
Studies in power

Published by Bokförlaget Stolpe, Stockholm, Sweden, 2024

The essays are based on the Leadership and Statecraft seminar held at
Engelsberg Ironworks in Västmanland, Sweden in June 2023.

Edited by
Kurt Almqvist, president, Axel and Margaret Ax:son Johnson Foundation
Alastair Benn, deputy editor, Engelsberg Ideas
Mattias Hessérus, director of the Ax:son Johnson Institute for Statecraft and Diplomacy

Text editor: Andrew Mackenzie
Design: Patric Leo
Layout: Petra Ahston Inkapööl
Cover image: *The Trojan War. The Destruction of Troy*,
Master of Coetivy, ca 1470. © Maeyaert/AIC/Bridgeman Images
Prepress and print coordinator: Italgraf Media AB, Sweden
Print: Printon, Estonia, via Italgraf Media, 2024
First edition, first printing

ISBN: 978-91-89696-98-3

Bokförlaget Stolpe is a part of Axel and Margaret Ax:son Johnson Foundation for Public Benefit.

BOKFÖRLAGET STOLPE

AXEL AND MARGARET AX:SON JOHNSON
FOUNDATION FOR PUBLIC BENEFIT